DATE DUE

Learnip

With deep admiration, respect for, and gratitude
to practicing and aspiring school leaders everywhere—and especially
those who courageously opened their hearts and minds to help us all to learn.

Learning for Leadership

Developmental Strategies for Building Capacity in Our Schools

Eleanor Drago-Severson

Jessica Blum-DeStefano

Anila Asghar

CORWIN
A SAGE Company

RWIN
GE Company

INFORMATION:

Corwin

A SAGE Company

2455 Teller Road

Thousand Oaks, California 91320

(800) 233-9936

www.corwin.com

SAGE Publications Ltd.

1 Oliver's Yard

55 City Road

London EC1Y 1SP

United Kingdom

SAGE Publications India Pvt. Ltd.

B 1/I 1 Mohan Cooperative Industrial Area

Mathura Road, New Delhi 110 044

India

SAGE Publications Asia-Pacific Pte. Ltd.

3 Church Street

#10-04 Samsung Hub

Singapore 049483

Printed in the United States of America

Library of Congress Cataloging-in-Publication Data

Drago-Severson, Eleanor.

Learning for leadership : developmental strategies for building capacity in our schools / Eleanor Drago-Severson, Jessica Blum-DeStefano, Anila Asghar.

pages cm.
ISBN 978-1-4129-9440-8 (pbk.)

1. Teachers—In-service training. 2. School administrators—In-service training. 3. Educational leadership. 4. Adult learning. I. Title.

LB1731.D72 2013
370.71'1—dc23   2013014233

This book is printed on acid-free paper.

Acquisitions Editor: Dan Alpert

Associate Editor: Kimberly Greenberg

Editorial Assistant: Heidi Arndt

Production Editor: Melanie Birdsall

Copy Editor: Lana Todorovic-Arndt

Typesetter: C&M Digitals (P) Ltd.

Proofreader: Caryne Brown

Indexer: Wendy Allex

Cover Designer: Bryan Fishman

Contents

Acknowledgments

What we are able to share in pages that follow is, like most gifts, the result of the support and help of others. Many generous, inspiring, beautiful, thoughtful people—family members, leaders of all sorts, friends, colleagues, students, mentors, and partners in thought—have contributed to and supported this work in meaningful and important ways. We will acknowledge them here. We also hope that they have known and felt our tremendous gratitude long before reading about these expressions.

First and foremost, we express our deep gratitude to all of the leaders who shared their experiences and practices of supporting adult development in their work contexts, including the triumphs and challenges of their work. While the lessons and wisdom presented in this book are gifts from the twenty leaders who participated in the interview phase of this research, there are some fifty leaders who participated in the survey phases of this work over the past ten years. An additional sixty leaders shared with us their experiences and leadership practices during interviews that we conducted and surveys that we administered in 2003, 2004, and 2005. We thank each and every one of you for your courageous sharing and for all that you have taught us. We thank you for the heroic work you are doing every day toward making schools better places for children and adolescents, as well as adults. While unable to name all of you here, we hope that you know and feel our heartfelt, tremendous gratitude. Your wisdom and insight infuse all that we are able to offer.

We also express deep appreciation for the many contributions from additional students who have allowed us to learn from them, from their practices, and from their experiences and wisdom. In particular, we thank the students whom we have been privileged to teach and from whom we have been privileged to learn at Teachers College, Columbia University, Harvard University's Graduate School of

Education, and McGill University. We also feel very grateful to have benefited for more than twenty years from the gift of learning from and with practicing and aspiring leaders in schools and districts. Thank you for welcoming us into your schools, onto your teams, and into your professional learning communities, your districts, your coaching practices, and your experiences. Thank you for sharing with us your inspiring teachings, insights, questions, and curiosities.

Both Teachers College at Columbia University and Harvard University's Graduate School of Education have supported the longitudinal research from which the lessons in this book are drawn. We express deep appreciation for each institution and for the leaders within them for all of the many ways that they have supported this work. They created the conditions within which we were able to work with and learn from practicing and aspiring leaders.

Collectively, we express our deep gratitude to Professor Robert Kegan of Harvard's Graduate School of Education for creating his constructive-developmental theory and for all of the ways in which it informs what and how we teach, and the learning-oriented model that we discuss throughout this work. Thank you for sharing your generous insights with us.

As authors, we also thank Professor Howard Gardner of Harvard's Graduate School of Education for sharing his generous insights about this work. We appreciate very much the important ways in which Howard's theories of learning and leadership inform our work and our teachings, as they also inform the work of educators everywhere. We are most grateful to you.

In addition, we voice special gratitude to Professor Pat Maslin-Ostrowski, Dr. Anne Jones, and Dr. Kara Popiel for thinking with us and for sharing with us their expertise about the implications of this work for policymakers and for policy development. We cherish your great company and mindful care.

We have enjoyed the blessing of collaborating with Dan Alpert, Senior Acquisitions Editor of Corwin/SAGE. Thank you, Dan, for sharing with us your wisdom and for helping us to learn from and with insightful you. Thank you for your *caring* attention, careful listening, and for your enduring, sensitive support. This work is indebted to your belief in the importance of this project, to your patience throughout the contours of this journey, and to the many sage contributions you have made along the way to this book and to each of us. We are deeply grateful for the blessing of you, Dan.

We also offer special thanks to all members of the Corwin team, and especially to Heidi Arndt, Melanie Birdsall, Lana Arndt,

Kimberly Greenberg, Bryan Fishman, and Karen Ehrmann. Thank you for your thoughtful communications, for your reliable attention to detail, and especially for your support during final stages of producing this book. We are grateful for this chance to learn from you and from your generosity in sharing your expertise so that readers can benefit.

We are also very grateful to and for the individuals who made time in their incredibly busy schedules to read and offer wise and generous feedback on an early draft of this work. Your ideas, suggestions, and insights have strengthened this work.

I, Anila, would like to thank my teacher, Professor Drago-Severson, and my cherished colleague, Jessica Blum-DeStefano, for taking me along on this incredible learning journey. I don't have the words to thank you both for teaching me so much in this process. I also thank my family for their love and support, always.

In addition to the sincere appreciations expressed above, I, Jessica, would also like to thank Ellie Drago-Severson for the incredible opportunity to be a part of this research and writing team. It has been an absolutely invaluable experience—and your genuine passion for supporting leaders and learners of all ages continues to amaze and inspire. Tremendous gratitude, as well, is offered to Anila Asghar for her insightful and poetic contributions throughout this collaboration. What a gift it has been to learn "with and from" both of you, as Ellie would say.

I hope, too, that Linda and George DeStefano know how much I appreciate their time, generosity, and unfailing support. Please know that your care has strengthened this work in innumerable ways.

Of course, I would also like to thank my parents, Deborah and Richard Blum, and my sister, Allison Blum-Kamalakaran, for being my first and best teachers, and for being constant pillars of strength, confidence, and love throughout my life. There are no words.

Finally, with special love and gratitude, I would like to thank George, Orin, and Perry DeStefano for their smiles, patience, hugs, and support throughout this project . . . and every day. You fill my heart in new and beautiful ways.

I, Ellie, would like to first express my tremendous admiration and deep appreciation for the gift of learning with and from you, Anila and Jessica, in general, and specifically for the many years during which we have collaborated on this learning project. Your wisdom, care, love, and insights continue to inspire and renew me. I feel incredibly grateful for the blessings of you in my life. This book is testament to the power of learning from and with each other. My heartfelt gratitude extends to each and to *both* of you.

I also offer special and deep gratitude for two of my many teachers and mentors. I thank you, Bob Kegan, dear teacher, colleague, and cherished friend, for developing your theory, for the ways it has altered the course of my life, and for teaching and modeling how to support adult development. You help me to understand better how to hold others, how to help them grow, and how to create conditions that support growth. I thank you for sharing your light, commitments, and ways with me. I hope you feel my deepest gratitude as I work to share light with others.

I offer heartfelt and sincere gratitude to you, Howard Gardner, for the gift of your special friendship and for your teaching, modeling, generosity, and theories, which continue to ever inspire my life, my teaching, and my commitments. You model goodness, and you inspire all who are blessed to know you. I am very grateful for your friendship, for your presence, for your brilliance, and for the gift that is you.

I express my heartfelt appreciation for my family, friends, colleagues, and partners in thought for their care and support that have strengthened me, the contributions I can make, and this work in powerful and inspiring ways. While I could offer pages or even chapters about the influence of your different forms of love and care, I trust you know why I mention you here: Richard Ackerman, Dan Alpert, Mary Anton-Oldenburg, Anila Asghar, Janet Aravena, Jessica Blum-DeStefano, Ira Bogotch, Robb Clousse, Caroline Chauncey, Betty Drago, John Drago, Bud Drago, Joe Drago, Paul Drago, Carl Drago, Mariann Drago, Jane Ellison, Howard Gardner, Anne Jones, Robert Kegan, India Koopman, Neville Marks, Pat Moran, Victoria Marsick, Pat Maslin-Ostrowski, David McCallum, Peter Neaman, Aliki Nicolaides, Kara Popiel, Steve Silverman, and David Severson.

In closing, I, Ellie, express my deepest gratitude for the many and different kinds of love those in my own family have and do give to me, love that has most shaped my life and what I am able to offer with care and in loving support to others. I thank my father, the late Dr. Rosario Drago, and my mother, the late Mrs. Betty Brisgal Drago, who have been my steadfast Guides and finest teachers. The memories of these two most wonderful human beings and teachers as well as their love carry, inspire, and lift me every day. Through their extraordinary love, wisdom, joy, exemplary hard work, and care, they modeled a love, a learning, a giving, a caring, and a leading that continues to lift, inspire, and hold me. I thank my siblings and their families for their love, care, support, and presence over many years and for all that you teach me.

I express my deepest gratitude—the soul-felt kind—for and to my husband, David Severson. No words can capture the depths of my love and the breadth of my gratitude to you. Thank you for being my teacher, my soul mate, my treasured Friend. Thank you for the impossible-to-describe ways in which you, your strength, your love, your goodness, your modeling, your courage, and your generosity inspire, fill, and renew my soul and heart. Thank you for the gift of you, every step, every day. Thank you for your enduring and precious love, for helping me to grow, and for your Light.

Publisher's Acknowledgments

Corwin gratefully acknowledges the contributions of the following reviewers:

Deanna Burney
Executive Director, Leading by Learning, LLC
Haddonfield, NJ

Jane Ellison
Educational Consultant
Highlands Ranch, CO

Kara Popiel
Teacher, Yonkers Public Schools
Yonkers, NY

William A. Sommers
Retired High School Principal
Austin, TX

Claudia Thompson
Academic Officer, Learning and Teaching, Peninsula School District
Gig Harbor, WA

About the Authors

**Eleanor Drago-Severson** is a professor of education leadership and adult learning and leadership at Teachers College, Columbia University. As a developmental psychologist, she is inspired in her work by the idea that schools must be places where adults and children can grow. She is dedicated to creating the conditions to achieve this and to helping leaders and educators of all kinds to do the same on behalf of supporting adults and youth. Ellie's work builds bridges between research and practice by supporting teachers, principals, assistant principals, superintendents, and other school and district leaders in their professional and personal learning and growth. Ellie is author of four recent books: *Becoming Adult Learners: Principles and Practices for Effective Development* (Teachers College Press, 2004); *Helping Teachers Learn: Principal Leadership for Adult Growth and Development* (Corwin, 2004); *Leading Adult Learning: Supporting Adult Development in Our Schools* (Corwin/The National Staff Development Council, 2009); and *Helping Educators Grow: Practices and Strategies for Supporting Leadership Development* (Harvard Education Press, 2012). Learning Forward (formerly The National Staff Development Council, NSDC) awarded the Outstanding Staff Development Book of the Year in 2004 to *Helping Teachers Learn* and selected *Leading Adult Learning* as their book for the Fall 2009. Ellie teaches, conducts research, and consults to leaders and organizations on professional and personal growth and learning, leadership that supports principal, faculty, and school development, capacity building, leadership development, coaching, qualitative research, and mentoring in K–12 schools, university contexts, Adult Basic Education (ABE), and English as a Second Language (ESOL) contexts. She is also an internationally certified developmental coach who works with principals, assistant principals,

district leaders, and teachers to build internal capacity and achieve goals. She served as lead researcher on the Adult Development Team of the National Center for the Study of Adult Learning and Literacy (NCSALL) at Harvard University and as teacher, program designer, program director, and professional developer in a variety of educational contexts, including K–12 schools, higher education, adult education centers, and ABE/ESOL programs (domestically and internationally). Her work explores the promise of practices that support adult development, leadership development, and capacity building within schools, districts, and organizations. Ellie's work has been recognized by and supported with awards from the Spencer Foundation, the Klingenstein Foundation, and Harvard Graduate School of Education (HGSE) where she served as lecturer on education for eight years. While serving at Harvard, Ellie was awarded the 2005 Morningstar Award for Excellence in Teaching. Most recently, she received three outstanding teaching awards from Teachers College. She has earned degrees from Long Island University (BA) and Harvard University (EdM, EdD, and Post-Doctoral Fellowship). Ellie grew up in the Bronx, New York, and lives in New York City.

Jessica Blum-DeStefano is an advanced doctoral student in education leadership at Teachers College, Columbia University, who is exploring how at-risk high school students in alternative education settings understand and describe good teaching. Jessica was awarded a research fellowship by the Teachers College Office of Policy and Research to support her work, and she has worked closely with Ellie over the past five years as a research assistant, teaching fellow, and coinstructor.

Anila Asghar is an associate professor in the Department of Integrated Studies in Education at McGill University. Her research and teaching encompass a number of interconnected areas: cognitive and emotional development; curriculum development; science pedagogy; teacher education; and educational leadership in a variety of international settings. She earned her doctorate from Harvard's Graduate School of Education and carried out her postdoctoral research at McGill University. She also received an EdM from Harvard University and an MA in science education from Teachers College, Columbia University.

PART I

Foundations

1

New Imperatives for Change in Support of Building Teaching and Leading

The Promise of Supporting Adult Development—Capacity Building—in Today's Complex Educational World

Orientation

> *Learning is a treasure that will follow its owner everywhere.*
>
> —Chinese Proverb

Today, educators' work is more complex and demanding than ever before. While the rewarding work of teaching and leading has *never* been simple or easy, mounting accountability pressures, increased public scrutiny, the rollout of new initiatives such as the Common Core State Standards, and evolving approaches to teacher and administrator evaluation add to educators' already challenging mission to serve all students well. Indeed, for adults throughout the system—teachers, teacher leaders, assistant principals, principals, district leaders, professional developers, and professors of education—there exists a palpable call to do more, to do better. Yet no clear consensus guides us through these murky imperatives. Many agree, for instance, that effective and accurate measurement is essential for forward progress, but it is less clear *what*, exactly, we should measure, and *how*. And what of those essential intangibles that are harder to see, let alone quantify? For that matter, how can we better prepare our teachers and leaders to face challenges that are yet unforeseen—challenges like those that, today, will likely have no "right" or "wrong" answers?

With these burning questions in mind, we emphasize and illustrate in this book a promising approach to school improvement: caring for—and teaching others to care for—*adult development* in our schools and districts. How can we improve professional development (PD) programs and professional learning opportunities in our schools, districts, and leadership programs in districts and universities to help educators and leaders support adult growth and increase the internal capacities needed, given today's challenges?

While the spotlight of public opinion shines brightly on *students'* educational experiences and outcomes, it is a significant and often overlooked fact that intentionally supporting the learning and growth of *adults* throughout the system has a direct and positive influence on student achievement (Donaldson, 2008; Guskey, 1999, 2000). Put another way, it is becoming increasingly clear that coprioritizing and supporting *adult* development in schools and districts (as well as students') can help educators of all kinds grow the internal capacities needed to more effectively teach and lead in our current—and future—educational milieus.

In response, in this book we offer a *developmental model* that can help you better support adult learning, growth, and capacity building in your school, district, coaching, professional learning, or university classroom. You will, for instance, learn about adult developmental theory, the qualitatively different ways adults make sense of their teaching, learning, leadership, participation in professional learning communities (PLCs), and all other experiences, and why understanding this kind of **developmental diversity** is essential for effective leadership and generative collaboration. In line with this, you will also learn about research-based practices that support the learning and **development** of adults—practices that, in turn, also enhance the experiences and performance of students. In addition, you will learn about how a group of practicing leaders (we define leaders broadly to include teachers, assistant principals, principals, district leaders, coaches, department chairs, university teachers, and others) who took a university course in 2003, 2004, or 2005 about adult developmental theory and related practices that support adult growth now employ their learning to support adult growth and capacity building in their own schools, districts, and workplaces.

The idea here is twofold. First, by laying bare the developmental design and theory behind a graduate course that focused on helping educators understand how to support adult learning and capacity building, called **Leadership for Transformational Learning (LTL)**, we offer promising strategies and practices *that you can use today* to enhance your own learning, teaching, and leadership, as well as to enhance the professional learning opportunities you offer to adults in your contexts.

While we zoom in closely and focus specifically on key components of the LTL course, it is important to note that these elements are *also* representative of a larger developmental approach to educational improvement that has been utilized and refined in schools, districts, and university programs for more than twenty-five years (Drago-Severson, 2004b, 2009, 2012)—and that we still use today.

Simultaneously, this book offers a detailed look at how leaders of all kinds are *currently using the developmental practices and ideas that they learned about in LTL in their actual on-the-ground leadership work—* as well as the obstacles they face and the supports they feel would help them do this work even better. In other words, in the chapters that follow, we present a model for developmental professional learning and leadership preparation *as well as close-up portraits of how these ideas and practices are working for educational leaders in diverse contexts*. Ultimately, we hope that each aspect of the book offers important ideas and takeaways that you can employ in your own practice to even more effectively build capacity, manage complexity, support leadership development, and care for the learning and growth of adults—both colleagues' and your own. In fact, in Figure 1.1, we offer an overview of how this book might be useful to you, regardless of your role or position.

Connecting This Book to Hopes and Urgent Needs in the Field

Recently, it was our honor to facilitate a full-day professional learning workshop that, like LTL, focused on adult developmental theories and practices that increase adults' internal capacities, build teacher

Figure 1.1   Potential Applications of This Book by Role

For Teachers

- Working collaboratively with colleagues and supervisors
- Building, facilitating, and/or participating in meaningful and safe reflective groups
- Mentoring or comentoring other teachers
- Developing goals, supports, and challenges to enhance your practice
- Leading professional learning opportunities in teams, departments, and beyond

For School Administrators

- Collaborating effectively with other administrators and supervisors
- Growing teacher leadership and capacity
- Providing more effective feedback-for-growth to teachers and colleagues
- Mentoring/coaching teachers and other professionals
- Leading staff meetings and feedback sessions
- Offering supports and challenges to teachers with different orientations to learning and teaching

For District Leaders

- Supporting principal and assistant principal leadership
- Creating and sustaining the conditions within schools and districts to support adult development—and student achievement
- Providing more effective feedback to school administrators and district level colleagues
- Working collaboratively with school leaders, school board members, and community partners

For University Professors/Teacher Educators

- Scaffolding learning opportunities for aspiring and practicing educators in university classes, workshops, and seminars
- Infusing traditional instruction with developmental intentions
- Structuring questions, discussions, protocols, and assignments to support learning and growth

For Everyone

- Growing oneself
- Working more effectively with colleagues and other adults
- Considering—and remembering—the importance of renewal

leadership, enhance PLCs, decrease isolation, and improve instruction and instructional leadership. At the start of the day, we invited the workshop participants—who held many different positions in schools and districts—to share their hopes for learning and help us understand why they enrolled in the session. While all of the leaders worked in different roles and settings, what was powerful for them (and for us) was how much they had in common in terms of their work and the challenges they were facing. Many workshop participants, for instance, commented about the "intense pressure" they were managing in their workplaces and about how they and their colleagues often felt overwhelmed and overtaxed in what they described as an "initiative heavy" environment. Given the daunting demands of new evaluation systems, standards, and other pressures, most of them explained that they enrolled in our workshop because they were searching for more effective practices that they could take back to their schools and implement "right away." They were hungry for "practical ideas and takeaways" that could help them and the adults in their care grow and improve instruction, and they were hopeful that learning about a developmental approach could help.

> **Reflective Moment:** What do you see as some of the greatest challenges you face in your work? What kinds of professional learning opportunities exist for you in your workplace? How do they help you to better manage the complexity of your work and your greatest challenges?

Toward the end of the day, the leaders offered some reflections on what they had learned, why it was important to them, and the implications they felt it had for their work in schools, districts, and university classrooms. While there were, of course, unique features as to *how* they said they would go about employing the developmental model and practices for supporting adult growth and capacity building, common themes emerged despite the leaders' diverse perspectives and roles—teachers, assistant principals, principals, coaches, professional learning specialists, and district leaders. (We've found this to be true in other workshops and PD opportunities as well.)

They realized, for instance, that they naturally differentiate when working to support *student* growth and learning, but "rarely" consider the "different needs and orientations of adults when offering professional supports and challenges to colleagues," in general and more specifically in PD offerings. In their post-workshop evaluations, they emphasized how understanding adult developmental theory and related practices "will enable them to better

> **Reflective Moment:** What are two practices you employ to support adult growth and learning? How do you think the practices are working? In what ways, if any, would you like to improve professional learning practices in your work context? What, if anything, do you wish could occur?

help the adults in their schools as they work together to meet the pressing demands of the Common Core State Standards, newer evaluation procedures, and rising accountability expectations." Similarly, many expressed that they could now be "better and more effective" leaders because of their new understandings about how and why it's vital to support adult capacity building—for its own sake and especially because of its link to student achievement.

Beyond Plans and Aspirations: How Are Leaders Actually Using These Ideas and Practices?

I hope you truly understand the impact your course has had on my life and my leadership. I see things from an entirely different lens.

—Safiyah, Practicing School Principal
and Founder of a Charter High School,
Aspiring Superintendent, December 2012

For many years, we (the three authors of this book) have had the honor of facilitating and learning from similar kinds of workshops and professional learning opportunities offered to educators and leaders in K–12 schools, districts, and PD initiatives, as well as in university leadership preparation and teacher education programs. As we described above, educators and leaders of all kinds share common challenges and needs in their different contexts—and, after learning about developmental theories and practices, many express powerful hopes for employing this new approach in their leadership and work.

When we began to reflect on and share these commonalities with leaders in subsequent workshops, seminars, and courses, educators were intrigued and found the connections meaningful. Earnestly wondering, many asked questions that went something like, "It's great that these learners found the content meaningful immediately after workshops and courses—*but what are they doing with what they learned? How is it impacting their practice, their efforts to support adult growth, the practices they currently use in their schools, districts, and workplaces to support adult development today? How are they transferring course ideas and practices? What difference is the course making to their actual work as leaders?*"

We thought, "Wow—those are really meaningful and *very* important questions!" We wondered, "How, if at all, *are* leaders who learned about these ideas using them in their current roles? In what ways—if any—are they transferring their learnings about theory and practice to their current work?"

After carefully considering how best to explore these questions, we thought back to a course that was designed and taught by the first author at Harvard's Graduate School of Education (HGSE)—LTL. The first and third authors cotaught a number of LTL offerings at HGSE, and the first and second authors still teach a version of this course— in its evolved form based on subsequent research and learning—at Teachers College, Columbia University, in New York City.

To begin our shared learning journey, we contacted LTL graduates from 2003, 2004, and 2005—who were aspiring and practicing leaders at the time of the course and who went on to work as educational leaders in the field. We surveyed those who responded (and volunteered) and then subsequently interviewed many of them about these very questions. The first author, though, who was lead instructor in the classes, did not conduct interviews so as not to bias leaders' responses. For more information about the research methodology guiding our investigation, please see Resource A, the Research Appendix.

Throughout this book, we present what these LTL graduates generously shared with us about how, if at all, they transferred LTL learnings to their real-life practices in support of adult development—as well as the challenges and creative strategies they have developed to overcome obstacles and do this work even better. This book is a tribute to *them,* their *courage,* and their *dedication*—as well as to others who engage in similar work. While we are the ones sharing their leadership experiences, it is truly a gift from them to you.

We think this book and the wisdom from these leaders will be helpful—a treasure chest of *practical learnings* and *takeaways* about how to build capacity and support adult growth—for anyone who is interested in supporting adult development in schools, districts, leadership preparation programs, or other contexts. We share their stories about how the concepts discussed and the practices employed in LTL made a difference to how they think about and practice building capacity in today's world. We offer their experience of what's going well for them, what's hard, and what different kinds of school, district, and systemic supports would enable them to do their work on behalf of supporting adult growth even more effectively. We offer all of this to be of help to you in your noble practice.

In addition, and importantly, this book highlights the promise of learning from practitioners' experiences and expertise in two ways. First, Drago-Severson's learning-oriented model (2004b, 2009, 2012)— which informed and infused the content and pedagogy of LTL—was derived from research with school leaders working to support adult development in a variety of different contexts. Second, this book extends earlier work by exploring how leaders who learned about this developmental model went on to use and adapt learning-oriented practices to enhance professional learning for adults in the field. By bridging theory and practice and illuminating—in an iterative and exploratory way—the deep wisdom, insight, and promise dedicated educators bring to their work every day, this book presents a body of knowledge and practices that can be used to improve schools and districts by supporting capacity building.

Ultimately, the goals of this book are to (1) raise understanding of the kinds of promising practices that support adult growth and capacity (and why this is important), (2) describe how a group of school leaders translate and implement learning from one university course to their practice, and (3) illuminate the developmental underpinnings of these efforts. In doing so, we offer practicing and aspiring leaders in schools and districts, as well as education leadership faculty and other teacher/leader educators and coaches, practical, effective takeaways for improving professional learning initiatives, supporting teacher and leadership development, and infusing teams, PLCs, and other PD opportunities with developmental supports and challenges.

We have the deepest respect for the hard and essential work you do every day and hope with all our hearts that you find the ideas in this book and these leaders' practices and experiences helpful and useful in your noble practice.

More About the Leadership for Transformational Learning (LTL) Course: A Preview

As we have explained, this book offers a close-up look at how leaders are employing theory and practice to improve their on-the-ground leadership to support adult growth in schools, districts, and university classrooms. You will see what they are doing to build capacity in individuals, schools, and organizations. Also, as we noted earlier, the LTL course that these leaders took many years ago is representative of *a developmental model that can be used to enhance professional learning initiatives, build more effective learning communities, and support adult development and capacity building in your own context.*

In the following chapters, you will learn more about the content, theory, and practices discussed in the course (LTL). For now though, it might be helpful to know that in 2003, 2004, and 2005, LTL was a fifteen-week spring semester course offered to graduate students—most of whom were practicing and aspiring leaders and educators from Harvard's Graduate School of Education—although every semester we welcomed graduate students from other professional schools (e.g., Divinity, Government, and Business) who were interested in learning about supporting adult growth and leading with a developmental approach in their work contexts.

LTL focused, in many ways, on addressing the kinds of questions and challenges we've noted above—in particular, how an understanding of adult development and practices proven to support it—might help us to better support growth in our schools, districts, teams, and practice. In case helpful, when we use the term "growth" we mean increases in our cognitive, affective (emotional), intrapersonal (self-to-self), and interpersonal (self-to-other) capacities that enable us to better manage the complexities of leading, learning, teaching, and living (Drago-Severson, 2004b, 2009, 2012). (We use the terms *growth*, *internal capacity building*, and *transformational learning* interchangeably, and we have also included a glossary of terms at the end of this book to be of support as you read. We hope this is helpful.)

In terms of specific content, LTL introduced the first author's learning-oriented model for school leadership (Drago-Severson, 2004b, 2009), which is derived from her research with practitioners (Drago-Severson, 1994, 1996, 2000, 2004a, 2004b, 2012) and informed by Harvard psychologist Robert Kegan's (1982, 1994, 2000) **constructive-developmental theory**. The model, composed of four pillar practices—that is, **teaming, providing leadership roles,** engaging in **collegial inquiry (CI)**, and **mentoring**—helped leaders learn about and experience the kinds of practices that actually support adult growth, and *why*.

The course, and other professional learning opportunities offered to school and district leaders domestically and around the globe since then, invited learners to explore important questions such as: How can leaders support adults' transformational learning (other people's and their own)? What practices support adult learning and development? What developmental principles inform these practices? More specifically, through lectures, readings, group discussions, case analyses, and interactive exercises, all participants learned about developmentally oriented leadership. In particular, we explored the following:

1. Conceptions of leadership in support of adult learning and development

2. Constructive-developmental theory (Kegan, 1982, 1994, 2000)

3. Essential elements for enhancing schools, systems, and work-places to be even healthier learning environments for adults

4. Practices that support adults' transformational learning (e.g., teaming, assuming leadership roles, collegial inquiry, and mentoring), as well as the developmental principles informing them

5. The importance of caring for one's own development and learning while caring for the learning of others

It is important to note that in addition to *teaching* about developmental theory and practices that can be employed to support adult growth, we sought in LTL to *establish and model* the conditions for supporting adult learning and development so that the learners could *experience the practices that support growth while they were learning about them.*

We invite learners to do this in any learning context or PD initiative we are privileged to facilitate because we have found that when leaders experience the practices that support growth, two big things happen. One, they can make an informed decision about whether or not they find the practices and big ideas effective and useful, and—two—they can walk away with firsthand knowledge of the practices and theory—an experience that we've discovered enables them to better implement the practices in their schools, districts, PLCs, coaching practices, teams, PD initiatives, and university contexts to support adult learning, growth, and capacity building. In this way, LTL activities and structures encouraged practicing and aspiring leaders to explore an expanded notion of leadership that included supporting adult development—and also provided learners with the building blocks of a developmentally oriented leadership preparation model that was developed, implemented, tested, and refined by the first author with educators of all kinds since 1996.

One of the promises of this book, we hope, is that it will offer you the tools to improve learning opportunities for adults in your context. As you'll see, we share many specific applications/takeaways for enhancing PD and implementing effective professional learning initiatives in schools and districts (e.g., workshops, PLCs, mentoring, and/or coaching) and for enhancing university leadership preparation courses. Ultimately, this model and all of the strategies contained in this book are developmentally oriented leadership initiatives that you and others can employ to support adult learning and growth in your own contexts.

Situating This Book in the Context of Education Today

When living in and surveying the current educational landscape, we know a few things for sure. We know, for instance, that supporting adult development makes schools better places of learning for both children and adults (Donaldson, 2008; Fullan, 2005; Kegan & Lahey, 2009). In fact, research indicates that students benefit *and that their academic achievement increases* when adults learn and grow in schools (Donaldson, 2008; Guskey, 1999; Mizell, 2007). Moreover, we know that effective school leadership is one key to school improvement (Barth, 1990; Howe, 1993; Moller & Pankake, 2006), and that teachers as well as principals, assistant principals, and district leaders play key roles (Ackerman & Mackenzie, 2007; Drago-Severson, 2009, 2012; Wagner et al., 2006).

Yet as leaders and educators, we encounter many implicit and explicit challenges every day as we dedicate ourselves to serving children and youth. As we have learned and as we discuss throughout this book, these challenges demand that we—as both people and professionals—demonstrate *new* kinds of internal capacities to help us navigate the complex terrain of contemporary education. And this has implications systemwide. *We need each other to lead and teach most effectively, and we need each other to grow.* Employing a collaborative, developmental approach to school and district leadership—as well as leadership development, preparation, and PD—is one promising way to help improve experiences and outcomes for *all* school participants and is, as we will discuss further, an approach that can be adopted and adapted by leaders of all kinds in schools, districts, universities, and beyond.

Given these truths, we thought it might be useful to even more explicitly situate this work and its importance within the current, complex context of education today. In the sections that follow we do just that. We hope you find it helpful.

Current Challenges: Technical and Adaptive

As we've emphasized above, today's educational challenges place new, multifaceted demands on practicing and aspiring leaders within schools and districts who dedicate themselves to educating children and youth (Bogotch, 2002a; 2002b; Childress, Elmore, Grossman, & Johnson, 2007; Elmore, 2004; Kegan & Lahey, 2009; Richardson, 2008; Wagner, 2007). This calls for changes in how we work and learn together—and it calls for more effective ways to support adult growth and development in our schools, districts, and university classrooms.

Indeed, the challenges that teachers and educational leaders encounter today require more than the managerial approaches we've had in hand (Kegan & Lahey, 2009; Olson, 2007). Scholars and practitioners agree, for instance, that twenty-first-century educational leaders must be well prepared to support adult development in schools, school systems, and other educational organizations (Ackerman & Maslin-Ostrowski, 2004; City, Elmore, Fairman, & Teitel, 2009; Donaldson, 2008; Elmore, 2004; Kegan & Lahey, 2009; Mizell, 2006, 2007; Murphy, 2002, 2006; Peterson, 2002; Wagner et al., 2006). Similarly, all educators will need the **developmental capacities** to manage more than what leadership scholar Ronald Heifetz (1994) describes as **technical challenges**—or those challenges and problems of practice that we can identify and those for which *someone* (if not us) has a solution.

Indeed, leaders must tackle many pressing challenges in education that are emergent, evolving, and undefined. Undeniably, we are facing profound **adaptive challenges,** which Heifetz (1994) defines as problems that are murky and hard to identify, and for which no one has a solution—not even experts. To meet these challenges, he and others maintain that new approaches, new internal capacities, and new tools are needed. We must have the internal capacities to manage tremendous amounts of complexity and ambiguity and be able to solve problems *in the act of working on them* (Wagner et al., 2006). In other words, educators of all experience levels need the developmental capacities to live and learn their way through the ambiguity and complexity these kinds of challenges create.

As we've learned from practicing and aspiring leaders in schools, districts, and university education leadership preparation programs, building growth-enhancing cultures and implementing practices that support adult growth to help leaders and all adults develop, build human capacity, and increase student achievement is of utmost concern, every single day—especially in light of these mounting challenges. Indeed, *all of us*—regardless of our positions—can play a direct and essential role in improving school conditions and student outcomes by helping each other grow to best serve our students and each other. We all want to—and must—increase student achievement, make a difference as we care for the growthand development of youth and adults, and help leaders grow. Doing this will help us to better manage the mounting explicit and implicit demands of leading, teaching, learning, and living—each and every day.

A Call for Change in Educational Leadership and Leadership Preparation

As you know, there are urgent calls in K–12 schools and districts and in university education leadership preparation programs that emphasize the importance of better supporting adult growth in schools, school systems, and leadership development programs (Donaldson, 2008; Fullan, 2005; Hoff, Yoder, & Hoff, 2006; Kegan & Lahey, 2009; Silverberg & Kottkamp, 2006; Young, Mountford, & Skrla, 2006). Across contexts, educators share a deep commitment to strengthening education for *all* and for making contributions that will make the world a better place.

While new approaches to PD and to leadership development are emerging (Byrne-Jiménez & Orr, 2007, Donaldson, 2008; Stoll & Seashore-Louis, 2007), the field currently recognizes the need to teach aspiring and practicing leaders about relational learning, collaborative leadership, and reflective practice (Donaldson, 2008; Moller & Pankake, 2006; Osterman & Kottkamp, 2004). In addition, programs are learning that it is essential to help leaders understand how to support their own and others' adult growth and leadership development (Boyatzis & McKee, 2005; Donaldson, 2008; Kegan & Lahey, 2009; Mizell, 2006; Lugg & Shoho, 2006; Wagner et al., 2006). In other words, education leadership programs have become acutely aware of the long-standing knowledge gap and lack of preparation when it comes to how school leaders support adult learning and growth in schools (Capper, Theoharis, & Sebastian, 2006; Hargreaves & Fink, 2006; Silverberg & Kottkamp, 2006). While we know that deep learning depends on good teaching in a safe space that enables risk taking, it is unclear how to achieve such learning among skilled professionals in university classrooms (Browne-Ferrigno, 2007; Pallas, 2001). It is also unclear how the study of adult learning and development might cultivate the leadership capacities of aspiring leaders. The model informing the LTL course is one promising pathway to addressing some of these important questions. And we hope that this book, which focuses on how leaders who successfully completed this course are actually using their learnings to support adult growth, is helpful to educators in the field as well as teachers in universities.

For example, throughout this book, we detail specific applications for implementing effective professional learning initiatives in schools and districts (e.g., workshops, PLCs, and/or coaching) and for enhancing university leadership preparation courses. In particular, we describe how writing, dialogue, shared reflection, pair work, triad work, teaming, mentoring (developmental coaching), leadership roles, and case-based discussion can support adult development and offer examples of protocols so that leaders can implement these ideas immediately. In addition, we outline strategies for applying theoretical concepts to real-life experiences (i.e., personal leadership cases) and how to help adults with different developmental orientations reflect on practice. Moreover, we describe how to purposefully and frequently invite adults to engage in private and collaborative reflection as a way of identifying, assessing, challenging, and altering the fundamental beliefs and **assumptions** that influence behaviors.

Ultimately, all of the strategies contained in this book invite educators across experience levels to consider developmentally oriented leadership practices that can translate to their own work contexts. We know that within and across the system we need to embrace new ways of leading *together* to improve conditions in schools and to support adult growth. This, as we all know, is not easy—and we also know that it is a critical challenge we must tackle together.

A Note About the Cover

We would like to share a little bit about why we selected the images we did for the cover of this book. We hope that this brief sharing is useful and that it resonates with you in some way.

First, in our experience, we have found that very few people describe their intentions in aligning their book cover designs with the messages of their books. In our case, after thinking long and hard about the kinds of images that might best symbolize the gifts of trust, care, and hope offered by the leaders who participated in this research, we decided that the Pōhutukawa tree would be a meaningful choice. Why, you might wonder?

Well, we find it such a fitting representation of this work. More commonly known as "New Zealand Christmas trees," Pōhutukawa trees—like those growing so magnificently on the cover—are *evergreen* trees that, much like leaders today, can grow and thrive in the most precarious situations. We learned, for instance, that the Pōhutukawa can flourish on the sides of steep cliffs or even lava plains. Perhaps most striking, however, were the trees' vibrant blooms. These flowering bursts of red suggested to us the promise of a growth-oriented approach to learning and leadership. And they reminded us of the great beauty and power of being cared for and nurtured in ways that support our development.

As for the particular Pōhutukawa on the cover, we couldn't help but notice how the intricacy of their multiple trunks paralleled the complex and multifaceted roots of effective contemporary leadership, and how the majestic network of the two trees' intertwined branches spoke to the important truth that leadership, today, cannot be accomplished alone. Even the picnic table, we thought, was a vivid reminder that—from our view—leadership is not a "throne." Rather, it is something like a picnic—with the meal better served and better tasted when trusted others are invited to the table.

Of course, and in addition to all of this, you may have noticed the birds. Like the leaders we learned from in this study, these many different birds have taken flight from a common perch, and are heading—in different directions and at different altitudes—to find their own paths and destinations. It is our hope that you, too, can find something of value in this book to incorporate into your own noble practice, and that you—like the Pōhutukawa—will continue with strength, courage, and heart to share your gifts with the world.

Research Informing This Book

The research informing this book stems from earlier research conducted by the first author (Drago-Severson, 1994, 1996, 2000, 2004a, 2004b, 2009, 2012), which we describe briefly in the opening of the Research Appendix (i.e., Resource A). This research, which began in 1991, has been refined, expanded, and tested in the field ever since, and it undergirds the learning-oriented model for school leadership at the center of this book and the LTL course.

This book is also largely informed by longitudinal research that focused on how learners who successfully completed LTL experienced the course in terms of its content and pedagogy and how, if at all, learners transferred learnings, practices, and theory to their actual work as leaders. More specifically, the research questions that guided our study investigated (1) the LTL structures, practices, and content that supported leaders' leadership development; (2) the ways LTL content and modeling shaped their work as practicing leaders in support of adult development; (3) the challenges they face in their leadership practice, including the structures and conditions they need to do this work even more effectively; and (4) the leaders' strategies for personal growth and renewal. This research was conducted in multiple phases, which included iterative rounds of surveys and interviews. In the final phase, we conducted qualitative interviews with twenty diverse educational leaders from the 2003, 2004, and 2005 cohorts years after they completed the course (interviews ranged from 90 to 150 minutes), for a total of approximately forty hours of in-depth interviews. Many of the stories and examples that we share throughout this book are drawn from this phase of the study. Additional methodological details are included in the Research Appendix (Resource A).

Organization of This Book

We divide this book into three main sections: (1) Part I, Foundations; (2) Part II, Lessons and Examples From Leaders in the Field; and (3) Part III, Implications for Practice and Policy. In the first section, which includes Chapters 1, 2, and 3, we focus on the underlying purposes, theory, and developmental practices that serve as the foundation for the learnings and strategies that follow. We hope that outlining the intentional design and theoretical underpinnings of the learning-oriented model employed in LTL will help make clear and transparent the applicability of these ideas and practices for your own work and leadership.

For example, in this first chapter, we emphasized the need to better support adult growth and leadership in schools, districts, and universities as educators of all kinds strive to meet the mounting demands of our current high-stakes climate. We also described the urgent need for leadership preparation programs of all kinds to adjust content and pedagogy in order to equip practicing and aspiring leaders to better meet and manage the *adaptive* challenges they encounter in their work. In other words, we discuss why teachers, school and district leaders, as well as professional development leaders and university professors need to focus on more than managerial skills, since these—while important and essential—will not adequately help leaders meet the complex demands they face (such as increasing accountability requirements, the introduction of the Common Core State Standards, and new approaches to teacher and principal evaluation).

In Chapter 2, Leadership for Transformational Learning: A Developmental Model for Building Human Capacity in Diverse Contexts, we provide a detailed overview of the LTL course content, as well as key structures, practices, and assignments that were employed to support students' learning during the course. In particular, we discuss the four pillar practices for growth (i.e., teaming, providing leadership roles, mentoring, and collegial inquiry) that comprise the first author's learning-oriented model of school leadership (Drago-Severson, 2004b, 2009), since these practices were both discussed and modeled in LTL. This chapter is intended to offer rich descriptions that situate LTL leaders' stories in the chapters that follow and also illuminate concrete strategies and applications that you can employ right away in your own context with developmental intentions.

In Chapter 3, A Close-Up on Constructive-Developmental Theory: Using Theory to Guide Adult Learning in Schools, Districts, and University Preparation Programs, we outline essential principles from Robert Kegan's constructive-developmental theory (1982, 1994, 2000), since it informed the design of LTL (and related professional learning opportunities) and because it helps shed light on the qualitatively different ways adults make meaning of learning, teaching, leadership, and life. As we will share, deliberately and transparently infusing principles of adult learning (Mezirow, 2000) and constructive-developmental theory (e.g., Kegan, 1982, 1994, 2000; Kegan & Lahey, 2001, 2009; Drago-Severson, 2004b, 2009, 2012) into the course design, teaching practices, feedback (written and verbal), and interactions with individual learners helped make visible the principles and conditions for supporting adult growth so LTL participants could experience these practices as they were learning about them.

The second big section of the book, Part II, Lessons and Examples From Leaders in the Field, which is composed of Chapters 4 through 7, focuses on the learnings, practices, challenges, and supports that the LTL graduates in our research described as most important years after completing the course.

In Chapter 4, for instance, Learning About Leadership for Adult Development: LTL Ideas and Practices That Made a Difference for Leaders, we present educational leaders' thinking about the LTL learnings and practices that informed their understanding of leadership during, immediately after, and years after enrolling in and successfully completing the course. First, we share leaders' descriptions of the changes in their thinking about leadership and supporting adult development both immediately following the course and years afterward, including the importance of their new ideas about how to help adults grow. We next highlight key LTL learnings and ideas that these leaders reported as helpful to their leadership development and understanding. We then raise up educational leaders' descriptions of practices employed in the context of LTL that made a difference for their understandings of leadership for supporting adult development. Finally, we offer key takeaways and an opportunity for you to apply these ideas to your own practice.

In Chapter 5, Transferring Powerful Learnings: Supporting Professional Growth From University Classrooms to Real-Life Practice, we describe the innovative ways these leaders are transferring their insightful learnings about developmentally oriented leadership practice from LTL to their actual leadership practice. We begin by sharing the hopes and ideas for developmentally oriented leadership that LTL graduates expressed immediately after completing the course years ago and then focus on how they are actually using and adapting the growth-enhancing practices and strategies that they learned about and experienced in LTL. Finally, we conclude this chapter by sharing larger takeaways—ideas and strategies for practice—and questions for reflection.

Chapter 6, Integrated Lessons From the Field: Three In-Depth Cases of Developmentally Oriented Leadership Practice, offers three holistic portraits of LTL-graduates' efforts to support adult development in their current school settings to help illustrate how the ideas and structures of learning-oriented leadership *actually work together in practice* to shape schools as true **learning centers** (also **mentoring communities**) that support the learning and growth of all educators. These real-life, case-based accounts show how school leaders are currently employing and intertwining practices that support adult growth and internal capacity building in their schools. We again offer important and practical takeaways for leaders of all kinds.

Chapter 7, Growing From, Through, and Beyond Obstacles: Leaders' Big Challenges and Their Strategies for Overcoming Them, presents the obstacles and challenges most frequently named by these leaders (e.g., changing and challenging norms in their schools and organizations, understanding and managing the resistance of colleagues, "managing up," or working with supervisors who are reluctant to adopt or appreciate developmental ideas, the hectic pace of and limited time in a busy school day, professional isolation and the need to renew and grow oneself as a leader) and their creative, on-the-ground strategies for overcoming them. This chapter offers additional tips and takeaways for addressing these important issues in your school and school systems.

The third and final section of this book, Part III, Implications for Practice and Policy, focuses on the implications of LTL leaders' sharings at both the micro and macro levels. Consisting entirely of Chapter 8, In the Spirit of Closing Well: Implications for Leaders, Schools, Districts, and Systems, this concluding section considers the kinds of supports LTL leaders feel would help them support adult growth in their unique contexts even better, and it offers implications for educational leaders, university faculty, schools, districts, and other educational organizations that can help educators of all kinds support adult development and build capacity across the system. From policy decisions to personal practice, we hope that the ideas and suggestions offered in this chapter help pave the way toward schools that support the learning and development of *all* participants—and an even brighter future for all of us.

Our Hopes for *You*: Enhancing Your Learning and Noble Practice

What all transformations have in common is that they begin in the imagination, in hope.

—Rebecca Solnit

As Rebecca Solnit wisely notes above, transformations—and real change—so often begin with sparks of imagination and with enduring hopes for something different, something better. It is our great hope that the practices and insights that the LTL leaders in this study generously shared with us and you prove helpful to your own important work and transformational journeys. We also hope that this book serves as a practical, field-tested portrait of promising practices for building human capacity in K–12 schools, professional learning initiatives, and university leadership preparation programs and classrooms.

In the chapters that follow, we will dive deeply into the ways leaders translated their LTL learnings to on-the-ground practices for supporting internal capacity building in their unique work contexts. This book also draws on other learnings to be of support to educational leaders of all kinds. More specifically, in this book we offer (1) practices and evidenced-based strategies that school leaders employ to support adult development in their schools and districts; (2) a close-up view of the challenges and obstacles practicing leaders encounter when devoting themselves to supporting adult growth in schools and the structures and conditions still needed to better help them in this work; (3) leaders' strategies for personal growth and renewal; and (4) a wealth of immediately applicable, evidence-based strategies from the course, employed by LTL leaders and implemented by the authors in university classrooms and many professional learning initiatives in schools, districts, universities, and professional and personal learning initiatives over the past twenty-five years.

In essence, you will learn how our learnings from leaders recognize, address, and help us to tackle the urgent call in schools, school systems, and university leadership preparation programs. This book offers practicing and aspiring leaders in schools and districts, as well as education leadership faculty and other teacher/leader educators, practical, effective strategies for foregrounding a developmental orientation and supporting the growth of adults in our schools. Ultimately, the goals of this book are to raise understanding of the kinds of promising practices that support leaders' growth, to describe how school leaders translate and implement this learning in their practice and to illuminate the developmental underpinnings of these efforts. This work and this book—we hope—will be of help to all of us as we work with care and conviction to create learning contexts that truly support authentic growth for all school participants—both children and adults—and as we find our way together through current challenges and those still on the horizon.

Reflective Questions

We offer these questions as an opportunity for you to reflect on learnings from reading this chapter, to connect them with your practice, and to offer a cherished space for reflection. Please take a moment to consider these prompts. You might want to respond to them privately first and then engage in collegial inquiry with a partner or group of colleagues.

1. What are two challenges that you currently face in your practice of helping adults grow? Do you think and feel that these are technical or adaptive? How so? What kinds of supports would be helpful to you in terms of better managing these?

2. In your view, what do you think and feel are the ingredients needed to help adults grow? And what would help *you* to grow in ways that would be useful to you, as leader?

3. Before reading Chapter 2, please take a moment to consider what your largest challenges are in offering meaningful PD. What do you consider to be the vital features of engaging educators in learning from PD? Why? What challenges have you experienced?

4. In what ways, if any, does this chapter help you think about the challenges you face as an educator caring for adult growth? What, if anything, resonates with your own experience?

5. What is one practice you engage in on a regular basis by yourself or with colleagues to support your growth? How is it working?

6. What is one practice you employ to support other people's growth? How well do you think this practice is working?

2

Leadership for Transformational Learning

A Developmental Model for Building Human Capacity in Diverse Contexts

Learning is not attained by chance; it must be sought for with ardor and attended to with diligence.

—Abigail Adams

[O]ne of the most important key learnings that I take with me from this course [a 2012 version of Leadership for Transformational Learning] is the importance of maintaining reflective practice. Very often, day-to-day needs prevent leaders from sitting down intentionally and reflecting. This course has taught me the power of this practice, and moving forward I have already built time for

reflection into faculty meetings and group gatherings to ensure intentionality about this work.

—Safiyah, Practicing School Principal and
Founder of a Charter High School,
Aspiring Superintendent, December 2012

Introduction and Overview

In this chapter, we present an overview of the Leadership for Transformational Learning course (LTL, hereafter)—including its content, design, processes, and intentions. As you'll recall from Chapter 1, LTL is the graduate-level course that the leaders we learned from in our research successfully completed in 2003, 2004, and 2005. This course was one in which leaders learned about adult developmental theory and the pillar practices that support adult development so that they could employ their learning to support adult growth and internal capacity building in their schools, districts, and workplaces after completing the course. By way of reminder, when we talk about supporting adult growth and internal capacity building, we are referring to increases in our cognitive, affective (emotional), interpersonal (self-to-other), and intrapersonal (self-to-self) capacities that enable us to better manage the complexities of leading, teaching, learning, and living.

You might be wondering *why* we taught this kind of course and *how* it might help you in your work. As mentioned in Chapter 1, the kind of content presented in LTL (i.e., learning about the importance of adult development and how to support it) and the immersive learning experience of the course design are essential in today's educational world, and in life for that matter. Given the increasingly adaptive challenges we encounter in schools, school systems, and university preparation programs every day, there is an urgent need to help adults develop the internal capacities necessary to better manage these complex **developmental demands**. While this is critically important on its own, it is also vital since we know that supporting adult development is positively linked to increases in students' achievement (Donaldson, 2008; Guskey, 1999, 2000). We hope that this book, which focuses on how leaders are actually using their learnings to courageously support adult growth in real-life practice, is helpful to you whether you serve in a school, district, university, or anywhere that you are caring for adults' professional or personal development.

You might also wonder why we are dedicating a chapter to describing the LTL course. We do so for several reasons. First, it's important to understand that while we are describing the content and processes employed in this particular fifteen-week, graduate-level course, what you will learn about in this chapter is representative of a *developmental model* that can be employed to enhance professional development and professional learning opportunities in schools, teams, districts, mentoring programs, and leadership preparation programs in districts and universities. We hope that some of the components of the course—content, processes, and practices—will be valuable to you as you enhance your professional learning initiatives, faculty meetings, math and literacy teams, district leadership cabinets, teachers teams, coaching relationships, and/or university classrooms with developmental structures and applications. In fact, this model has been employed in *all* of these contexts to create learning environments that support internal capacity building over time. More specifically, the professional development model undergirding the LTL course has been implemented, tested, and refined with aspiring and practicing superintendents, principals, assistant principals, coaches, teacher leaders, district leaders, and educators of all kinds in schools, districts, university leadership preparation programs (i.e., teachers and other educators who aspire to be principals, leaders who aspire to be superintendents), developmental leadership academies, long-term professional learning workshops (e.g., with math and literacy coaches, special education teachers and specialists, assistant principals aspiring to be principals) and long-term developmental institutes, as well as other venues since 1996.

In all of these contexts, regardless of duration or participants' roles, the biggest intentions of the "course" or learning enterprise are to (1) offer practicing and aspiring leaders and educators a chance to learn about theory and practices for supporting adult growth and (2) create opportunities within the context of the professional learning enterprise to actually *experience* and *engage in* the very practices and processes that support adult development while learning about them (Drago-Severson, 2012). This is important for many reasons and especially because we have learned that when educators participate in developmental practices and processes *firsthand*—and when they see them *modeled* in the context of their *own* learning—they are better able to introduce, facilitate, and sustain similar applications *in their own work contexts* when working to improve conditions and outcomes for all participants.

Toward these ends, in this chapter, we first provide you with an overview of the *content* that composes the LTL course. While Harvard psychologist Robert Kegan's constructive-developmental theory (1982, 1994, 2000) informs LTL's developmental course design and practices, we will save a detailed discussion of this theory for Chapter 3 (after you have a fuller understanding of the LTL course and its components). Below, though, just in case helpful, we outline the big ideas in this theory so that you can hold them in mind and heart as you read this chapter.

Second, in this chapter, we introduce the **pillar practices** for growth (i.e., teaming, providing leadership roles, mentoring, and collegial inquiry), which compose the **learning-oriented model for school leadership** (Drago-Severson, 2004b, 2009) that infuses the LTL design. Throughout the course, adults learn about these practices, design action plans for employing them in their own work contexts, and engage in them with classmates in support of their own and each other's learning. Our intention is to introduce the pillar practices as *developmental practices* for growth and to discuss how they can be employed to support adult development and internal capacity building. In addition, when we discuss constructive-developmental theory (Kegan, 1982, 1994, 2000) in Chapter 3, we will offer even more specific ideas about how adults who make meaning of their experiences in qualitatively different ways can grow from ongoing engagement in these pillar practices when provided with appropriate supports and challenges.

Third, in this chapter we share specific growth-enhancing practices and processes that leaders engaged in via the pillars when enrolled in LTL. These are practices that you may find very useful in your own practice as you work to create environments—regardless of context—that support adult development and capacity building. We hope that you find these strategies for enhancing professional learning and development helpful when creating conditions for supporting other adults' growth—and your own.

Constructive-Developmental Theory: A Sneak Peek

As promised, before describing LTL, we want to highlight a few of the foundational principles of Robert Kegan's constructive-developmental theory, which we will discuss in detail in Chapter 3.

First, constructive-developmental theory sheds light on the essential fact that adults make meaning of experiences in qualitatively different ways. We know, for instance, that adults can orient *differently* to the *very same* activity or event (say, for example, speaking in front of a group or receiving evaluative feedback). While a public presentation may be an exciting opportunity for one adult, it could easily be perceived as a dreaded burden for another. Similarly, while one individual may feel exhilarated and supported by direct, critical feedback on his or her performance, that very same feedback could leave a different—and equally competent—colleague in tears. While such diverse responses likely have many roots (i.e., based on one's personality, culture, prior experiences, and many other things), it is important to understand that each of us *also* has a particular, developmental **way of knowing** that guides our orientations to teaching, leading, learning, and life.

Briefly (for now), one's way of knowing is the filter through which we interpret all of our work and life experiences. It influences our capacities for perspective taking on self, others, and the relationship between the two. As we grow from one way of knowing to the next, the former becomes part of a new, more complex system. The **instrumental, socializing,** and **self-authoring ways of knowing** are currently the most common in adulthood (we will discuss these in detail in the next chapter).

You might be wondering, "OK, so why is this important?" Well, it's very important because our way of knowing—or meaning-making system—dictates *how* we take in, filter, and understand any initiative or professional learning opportunity. Understanding constructive-developmental theory and ways of knowing also helps us to better understand why diverse adults will experience the same events differently—and that they will likewise need *different* supports and challenges in order to grow, learn, and thrive. This kind of differentiation is something we naturally do when considering how to support children's and youth's learning and development. However, it is also the case that adults need something more than a one-size-fits-all approach when facing new challenges and opportunities.

While there is great hopefulness in this theory, we think—in the sense that it underscores the potential of *all* adults to grow and learn—it is important to remember that each way of knowing has developmental strengths and limitations and that one way of knowing is not necessarily better than another. Rather, it is the fit between personal (internal) capacities and one's environmental demands that is *most important*. That said, effective leadership (i.e., in the sense of being able to manage enormous amounts of ambiguity and complexity to meet the adaptive challenges we all face today) often requires some form of what we will describe in Chapter 3 as self-authoring capacities (Kegan & Lahey, 2009).

Leadership for Transformational Learning (LTL): Course Overview

As we have explained, the fifteen-week graduate LTL course at the center of this book is based on a developmental model for supporting adult growth and learning that we continue to employ in varied and diverse contexts. Accordingly, as teachers and facilitators of LTL, we sought to recognize and honor the qualitatively different developmental orientations, diverse internal capacities, and differentiated needs of individual learners in LTL throughout the course. Therefore, we next share an overview of key content, practices, and activities that we employed to support students' learning and growth. We hope that many of the ideas, processes, and practices described below will be useful to you in your noble and important work as well.

Developmental Intentions of LTL

LTL was designed with three big intentions. First, our aim was to teach Kegan's (1982, 1994, 2000) constructive-developmental theory since it informs *developmentally oriented school leadership*—or a model for supporting adult growth and internal capacity building—and the design of the course. It also informed the ways in which we offered feedback and structured pedagogy and practices employed in LTL to support learning and growth. Second, we sought to create a learning environment in which we, as instructors, simultaneously modeled how to support growth in general and through practices employed in the course. As we've shared, the course not only *taught* students about the theories of adult learning and development but also afforded students the opportunity to *experience* the theories in practice and in action in real time. Our third big intention was to structure LTL so that learners were engaging in the pillar practices in the classroom. We did so because we've learned that such firsthand experience better equips leaders to implement similar practices in their own schools, teams, districts, coaching practices, mentoring programs, and university classrooms.

Our goal in designing and structuring the learning environment in LTL was to scaffold students by bridging theory and practice. For example, both in the classroom and outside it we created opportunities for learners to reflect on their learning, to make connections between new ideas and their leadership practices, and to assume leadership roles within small learner teams. We provided theoretical frameworks and practices to enhance and extend educators' knowledge, experience, and skills. Writing, dialogue, shared reflection in pairs, triads, and teams, and personal case-based discussions (i.e., convenings, which we describe later in this chapter as an example of a practice that brings together personal writing, dialogue, reflection, and group work) served as the foundations of the course. You, too, may find these helpful in your own context as you work to support adult growth.

LTL Content: Knowledge Domains, Theory, Skills, and Promising Practices

Like the other developmentally oriented professional learning initiatives we facilitate, LTL focused on exploring the following questions: How can leaders create contexts that support adults' transformational learning (other people's and their own)? What practices support adult development? What developmental principles inform these practices? As shared in Chapter 1, LTL addressed these questions through lectures, readings, group discussions, case analyses, and interactive exercises, which we will learn more about in this chapter, and all participants examined five core components of developmentally oriented leadership:

1. Conceptions of leadership in support of adult learning and development (Donaldson, 2000, Heifetz, 1994)

2. Theories of adult learning and constructive-developmental theory (Brookfield, 1987, 1995; Daloz, 1983, 1986; Kegan, 1982, 1994, 2000; Mezirow, 2000; Osterman & Kottkamp, 1993, 2004; Schön, 1983)

3. Essential elements for creating positive learning environments for adults (Barth, 1990; Elmore, 2000)

4. Practices that support adults' transformational learning or growth (teaming, assuming leadership roles, reflective practice, and mentoring) and the developmental principles informing them (Drago-Severson, 1996, 2004a, 2004b)

5. The importance of caring for one's own development while caring for the learning of others (Ackerman & Maslin-Ostrowski, 2002)

While we discuss each of these five components in greater detail below, we have also included a list of topics discussed in LTL in Resource B and a reference list of readings from LTL in Resource C. In both cases, we have updated the content so that it includes more recent readings that we employ in teaching this kind of course and facilitating professional learning and development experiences for educators and leaders today. We hope you find these resources helpful when designing professional learning opportunities and enhancing initiatives aimed at supporting adult learning and capacity building.

Part 1: Connecting Theories of Adult Learning to One's Leadership Practice

LTL learners were purposefully exposed to a variety of adult learning theories and invited to contemplate their connection to leadership practices, supporting adult learning, and creating systemic change during the first sessions of the course. This was intentionally placed at the beginning of LTL so that leaders would understand that, while adult learning is vital in today's educational world, more than a focus on leadership—in its traditional sense—was needed.

Part 2: Understanding Adult Development

The second part of LTL focused on exploring Kegan's (1982, 1994, 2000) constructive-developmental theory in depth. As we shared earlier, we did so for several reasons, and namely because this theory

- illuminates the qualitatively different ways in which we as human beings make sense of and experience the world and our own and other people's teaching, learning, and leadership;
- helps us to understand the importance of a developmental perspective and approach when leading and designing professional development opportunities;
- highlights that adults need different forms of support *and challenge* in order to grow and increase our internal capacities;
- informs LTL course design, assignments, and feedback; and
- informs the learning-oriented leadership model and the pillar practices for growth (Drago-Severson, 2004a, 2004b, 2009, 2012), which were infused into the design of LTL.

To help you learn more about these important ideas, we discuss Kegan's theory in detail in the next chapter.

Part 3: Essential Elements for Creating Positive Learning Environments for Adults

This section of LTL focused on learning about the importance of creating healthy school and district cultures and why this is vital to supporting adults individually and to building growth-enhancing cultures (Barth, 1990; Elmore, 2000). In addition to discussing this in general, we offered spaces to discuss this in relation to developmentally oriented cultures that could support adults with a diversity of developmental orientations—or ways of knowing.

Part 4: Learning About and Employing Pillar Practices That Support Adult Growth

The next part of LTL focused on the four pillar practices (i.e., teaming, engaging adults in leadership roles, participating in collegial inquiry, and mentoring) that compose the learning-oriented model for school leadership and how these offer promising ways of facilitating adult growth in schools, teams, districts, professional development initiatives, and district and university leadership preparation programs.

While you may be familiar with these practices and even employ them in your practice, the distinguishing feature of the pillar practices is that they can be employed with developmental intentions. For example, many programs devoted to leadership development and professional learning for teachers and other leaders across the system invite adults to engage in reflective practice, share their perspectives, participate in cooperative/collaborative learning, work in teams, and collaborate and plan together. We also know that mentoring and coaching are common practices in schools today. However, the pillar practices involve *intentionally reframing these common practices* as contexts that explicitly support adult growth and internal capacity building. In other words, the **learning-oriented leadership model** and the pillar practices that compose it differ from common approaches to implementing these practices because they are informed by constructive-developmental theory and can support the growth of educators with different ways of understanding their experiences, work, leadership, and teaching. As you will see, these practices can be implemented in ways that offer developmentally appropriate forms of support and challenge to adults with a diversity of ways of knowing—ways of making sense of their experiences.

After learning about constructive-developmental theory, pillar practices, and other content discussed in the class, LTL learners had a chance to apply these ideas to real-life practice by reflecting on their own experiences and developing what we call an *action plan*. This is an opportunity to consider how they might transfer LTL learnings to their own practice. We discuss this in more detail toward the end of this chapter.

Part 5: Practices That Support One's Own Renewal and Development

Finally, toward the end of LTL, learners were invited to consider how they would care for their *own* growth and renewal as a way of ending well and moving forward in support of adult growth. To facilitate this process, we introduced literature related to the importance of caring for one's own renewal, development, and learning, while caring for others.

> **Reflective Moment:** After learning about the content and practices that compose this kind of professional learning and development initiative, what are two aspects of content (theory and/or practices) that support adults' capacity building that you would like to learn more about? How, if at all, do you think these will help you to better support adult growth?

Significantly, and regarding each of the five content domains described above, these same practices have proven effective in working with teachers, coaches, and school and district leaders in various professional development contexts and university classrooms.

A Few Words About LTL Learners and Meeting Times

While the LTL content and structures we describe in this chapter are representative of a larger developmental model of professional development and leadership preparation, it may be helpful to note that LTL was offered as an elective at Harvard's Graduate School of Education in 2003, 2004, and 2005. Graduate students from a variety of concentrations (e.g., school leadership, teaching and learning, human development and psychology, administration and social policy, schools and communities, principal preparation) in their master's and doctoral programs at the School of Education opted to join this course. In addition, each year, students from other professional schools at the university enrolled in the course as well (e.g., School of Government, School of Law). Thus, learners represented a range of perspectives, which contributed to a rich learning environment. In general, twenty-two to twenty-four learners enrolled in the course each spring. Each year, the LTL learners were diverse in terms of age, race, and other class demographics. They were also diverse in terms of current and hoped-for positions after graduation. For example, some were aspiring principals, practicing principals, aspiring and practicing teacher leaders, curriculum coordinators, leaders in ministry, and consultants. Their work contexts included K–12 schools, district level leadership, nonprofits, universities, and churches. And, LTL learners were diverse with respect to gender, ethnicity, prior educational background, and number of years in their current role.

LTL was a fifteen-week, semester-long course when the leaders in this study were enrolled. The course met once a week for three hours in the late afternoon or early evening on a weekday, although we now offer similar courses in nontraditional weekend and other formats in order to accommodate educators who work in schools and districts full-time. In addition, we use a similar curriculum when teaching educators in groups of diverse sizes (e.g., smaller university seminars, teacher institutes for schools and districts, and leadership preparation courses for 100 or more aspiring leaders).

During the years leaders in this study participated in LTL, each class session had two distinct parts. For example, we generally met first as a full group at the start of class to respond to questions by journaling and then engaging in whole-group discussion about the week's readings and their implications for learners' work as school leaders. On occasion, a course instructor gave mini-lectures (ten to fifteen minutes) about key highlights and ideas. Similarly, small-group (triads or quads) or partner discussions, free-writing or free-thinking time, and question-and-answer sessions were employed during this time as invitations for learners to think about, question, and apply course content to their own lives. Such practices supported students by offering them a chance to check, refine, and/or enhance their understandings with instructors and/or colleagues by discussing complex adult learning and developmental theories, pillar practices for growth, and different conceptual frameworks that were introduced in readings. These practices also intentionally offered a combination of private and different types of public settings (i.e., pairs, triads, quads, teams of five) because, depending on learners' preferences and/or developmental orientations, some found listening in private settings more supportive, while others preferred sharing publicly.

During the second half of class, learners were divided into two small groups. Each week, after the first two weeks of class, learners participated in a very special kind of case-based discussion, which we call "convening," during this second half. These two separate convening groups were composed of about twelve students each, and the groups remained stable throughout the semester. We will discuss convening as a practice supportive of growth and capacity building later in this chapter. This is a practice that many educators and leaders have adapted and now employ in the professional development opportunities they facilitate in support of adult growth.

In the next section we introduce the pillar practices since they were infused into the design, structure, pedagogy, and content of LTL. Our intention is to briefly introduce these practices now and then devote attention to the ways in which they can support adult growth after discussing constructive-developmental theory in greater detail in the next chapter. After describing the pillar practices, we share a few additional practices and processes employed in the course that are related to the pillars and that support growth and learning.

The Promise of Learning-Oriented Leadership

Four Pillar Practices for Growth

In this section we briefly introduce you to four pillar practices (Drago-Severson, 2004b, 2009, 2012) that can serve as structures and contexts—which we later will refer to as **holding environments** (Kegan, 1982, p. 115). These pillar practices can support adults with qualitatively different ways of understanding and interpreting experiences. Before describing the pillar practices, please allow us to offer a tiny bit more about the phrase "holding environment."

Earlier in this chapter we mentioned that, according to constructive-developmental theory (Kegan 1982, 1994, 2000), there are three ways of knowing most common in adulthood (i.e., instrumental, socializing, and self-authoring). Understanding these ways of knowing helps us to more effectively shape learning and growth contexts—or holding environments—for adults, since we can better appreciate the different kinds of supports and challenges individuals and groups will need to grow and learn. We will discuss this in more detail in the next chapter, but for now, it's important to underscore that the pillar practices we are about to describe are practices that, both independently and intertwined, can support adults with very different ways of making sense of their experiences.

Indeed, implementing the pillar practices with developmental intentionality enables us to honor and attend to adults' developmental diversity. It helps us understand that teachers, principals, assistant principals, coaches, learning specialists, superintendents, and district leaders—all of us—will make sense of our experiences in different ways and will need different forms of support and challenge in order to increase our internal capacities. It also has important implications for leadership because research has shown that developmental diversity will exist in any school, team, leadership cabinet, or district.

Next, we briefly introduce each pillar practice (for a full discussion, please see Drago-Severson, 2009) as *distinct yet mutually reinforcing* practices that you can implement in your schools, districts, and leadership preparation programs to facilitate adult development *and to strengthen capacity building* among educators and leaders of all kinds, regardless of their position (or yours).

Reflective Moment: Before reading about the pillar practices, please take a moment to consider one or both of the following questions:

- What is one way in which the practices you are currently implementing to support adult growth and internal capacity building recognize adults' different learning needs, preferences, and internal capacities? What do you feel is working well? What would you like to improve?
- Relatedly, what, if anything, have you found valuable about participating in teams, leadership roles, reflective practice, and/or mentoring? How has one or more of these practices supported your growth?

Pillar Practice 1: Teaming

Teaming brings adults together to engage in dialogue and, in so doing, creates opportunities for private and group reflection, reduces isolation, nurtures innovation, builds individual and group capacity, and establishes knowledge-based management systems (Barth, 2006; Wagner et al., 2006; York-Barr, Sommers, Ghere, & Montie, 2006). It often focuses on team teaching, pairing veteran and new teachers, forming leadership teams (both vertical and horizontal), examining student work, teacher practice, leadership challenges, and/or working collaboratively on reform or improvement initiatives. Researchers contend that teaming builds individual, school, and systemwide capacity for learning and improvement since it builds capacity within and across schools and school systems (Donaldson, 2008; DuFour, 2007). Many practitioners argue that in today's educational milieu, teaming—especially teaming designed to assess and improve student achievement—is at the heart of professional learning (McAdamis, 2007; City, Elmore,

Fairman, & Teitel, 2009). In fact, in Drago Severson's research (2004a, 2004b, 2009, 2012), teaming was the most common and most frequently implemented pillar practice.

From a developmental perspective, working in teams enables educators to question their own and others' assumptions, values, and philosophies about teaching, learning, and leadership processes—and provides opportunities for collaborative decision making and reflection. More specifically, teaming creates a context in which adults can examine and question their assumptions and beliefs about many aspects of schooling—including curriculum and student work, implementing the Common Core State Standards, accountability demands, and how a school's core values are reflected in the classroom. In addition to creating opportunities for educators to share their diverse perspectives and learn about one another's ideas and assumptions, it can be a space where educators challenge—or stretch each other—to consider alternative perspectives, and to test and revise assumptions toward growth over time. Learning to consider others' viewpoints can enable adults to more effectively manage situations with multiple sides and to develop broader perspectives on themselves, others, and the relationship between the two.

Of course, educators with different ways of knowing will experience and participate in teaming in different ways. Importantly, the extent to which adults are able to benefit from this practice depends, in part, on the availability of appropriate supports and challenges to facilitate growth, as we will discuss further in Chapter 3. For now, though, it might be helpful to recall that teaming was employed in LTL in multiple and overlapping ways. For instance, learners worked in semester-long convening groups that evolved and grew as extremely effective teams throughout the course. Learners likewise formed and re-formed smaller temporary "teams" when they gathered together in small groups to discuss questions, insights, and ideas related to course readings and ideas. Ultimately, these varied teaming opportunities also strengthened each cohort as a larger "full class team," and they helped learners establish trust and connections that lasted through the course and beyond.

Pillar Practice 2: Providing Leadership Roles

Schools are increasingly being called upon to establish and sustain cultures of shared responsibility and shared leadership that invite greater leadership and initiative among teachers and *all* educators in school communities (Farrington, 2007; Fullan, 2008, 2009; City et al., 2009). Unlike many common applications of *distributed leadership*, however, the pillar practice of *providing leadership roles* emphasizes the intentionality behind the new responsibilities. Instead of simply *assigning* or *delegating* duties, for instance, providing leadership roles involves offering emerging leaders appropriate supports and challenges (e.g., from a principal, coach, assistant principal, or colleague) so they can grow from the leadership experience—shifting the emphasis away from simple task designation or completion (Cochran-Smith & Lytle 2006; DuFour, 2007; Hord & Sommers 2008; Yost, Vogel, & Liang, 2009). Such an approach helps build collective capacity that enhances a community's ability to respond to increasingly complex educational changes and leadership challenges (Donaldson, 2006, 2008; Slater, 2008).

Additionally, providing leadership roles supports the collective work of all adults in schools, for we know that leaders need help to lead in today's multifaceted educational world (Dozier, 2007; Kegan & Lahey, 2009). We also know that leaders' modeling and behaviors influence the culture, that leading a school is complex work, and that there are many ways educators at all levels can work together toward larger, overarching goals (Leithwood & Riehl, 2003; Simons & Friedman, 2008).

As with teaming, however, leadership roles can be perceived differently (we will discuss this in more detail in Chapter 4) depending on an educator's way of knowing. For example, those who find assuming authority intimidating or challenging might initially require considerable support as they take on leadership, but other adults who make meaning in different ways might appreciate the opportunity to put their ideas into action. Either way, when appropriate supports and challenges are offered, leadership roles can serve as carefully tailored opportunities for growth—not just additional responsibilities— and they can help educators negotiate the oft-competing demands of providing and receiving support while attending to their practice and larger school needs.

In terms of the role of providing leadership opportunities in LTL, learners took up and shared multiple leadership opportunities throughout the course. Within small convening and consultation groups, for instance, learners assumed responsibility for timekeeping, facilitating discussion, and providing colleagues with detailed and thoughtful feedback. During larger group sessions, as well, students were always invited to share insights and experiences with the whole group, and their ongoing feedback and interests helped shape and direct course discussions.

Pillar Practice 3: Collegial Inquiry

We define *collegial inquiry* as a shared dialogue that purposefully involves reflecting on one's assumptions, values, beliefs, commitments, and convictions with others as part of the learning process (Drago-Severson, 2004b, 2009, 2012). Collegial inquiry is a developmental instance of a larger initiative commonly known as reflective practice, which can occur individually or in groups. While we can, of course, engage in reflective practice independently through reading or by reflecting privately, we need at least one partner to engage in collegial inquiry, for a number of growth-enhancing bene-fits arise from the synergistic interaction of diverse participants (co-inquiry). In addition, collegial inquiry, like teaming, creates a context in which adults can reflect on proposals for change, new initiatives, and schoolwide issues (e.g., sharing leadership), as well as grow indi-vidual, schoolwide, and district capacity. Creating supportive, rela-tional contexts in which adults can talk regularly about their practice—as well as their values, beliefs, challenges, and guiding philosophies—facilitates self-analysis and can enhance the individu-al's and the school's practice.

Practitioners and scholars mostly agree that professional learning opportunities for teachers, principals, assistant principals, coaches, specialists, and district level leaders should center on reflective prac-tice (Ackerman & Mackenzie, 2007; Byrne-Jiménez & Orr, 2007; Donaldson, 2008; Teitel, 2006; York-Barr et al., 2006). These educator-scholars and researchers believe that engaging in reflective practice will improve instructional and leadership practices and, in turn, enhance student achievement (Ackerman & Mackenzie, 2007; City et al., 2009; Elmore & Burney, 1999; Fullan, 2005; Johnson et al., 2004; Kegan & Lahey, 2009). Yet it is also true that we can more effectively shape positive educational communities (e.g., teams, professional learning communities, mentoring) and support adult growth if we engage in reflective practice *together*.

Of course, it is essential to establish trust and a safe context for adults to feel secure in sharing perspectives and assumptions and to engage in risk taking. It is also important to allocate appropriate resources (including time in the schedule) for collaborative meetings and to build structures for shared decision-making processes in order to support collegial inquiry.

Moreover, as you might imagine, participating in collegial inquiry is both a developmental practice and a *process*. Engaging in collegial inquiry over time creates a context for developing greater awareness of our beliefs, convictions, values, and assumptions. Reflecting with others can allow us to envision and test the validity of our assump-tions about leadership, teaching, learning, and practice and test alter-native ways of thinking or behaving. When leaders—principals, assistant principals, teachers, mentors, coaches, specialists, and superintendents—engage in collegial inquiry, a space is created for nurturing growth, and the process and context of engaging in this practice become a holding environment.

However, as you may suspect, educators will experience and engage in collegial inquiry *differently*, depending on their ways of knowing. For instance, offering and receiving honest and critical feedback is an essential part of collegial inquiry, but adults with different ways of knowing (i.e., developmental orientations) will experience feedback and collegial inquiry in qualitatively different ways. For example, and as we will discuss in further detail in the next chapter, some adults may experience a valued colleague's or supervisor's feedback as an indication of whether or not they are doing things the "right way." Others tend to understand feedback from valued others as expert advice—and these expectations for and judgments of their practice become their very own. Still others can generate their own expectations for their leadership, teaching, and practice in general. These adults have the internal capacity to weigh their colleagues' and supervisors' feedback against their own internal bench of judgment and to decide whether or not to implement others' suggestions. As these examples illuminate, attending to developmental diversity when structuring, supporting, and engaging in collegial inquiry is essential in order to meet adults where they are and to create a safe and productive implementation of this pillar practice.

As both a practice and a goal, collegial inquiry was infused into the LTL course design and experience. Convening, for instance, offered students a structured, developmental approach to collaboratively examining assumptions and challenges of practice. As we will discuss later in this chapter, after first establishing agreements about confidentiality and norms, convening group members helped each other to look deeply into their own and others' experiences and the underlying intentions guiding their actions. Similarly, pair-share and small-group discussions during class invited students to expand upon and consider with others the individual reflections they undertook after reflective writing prompts. In the sections that follow, we offer concrete strategies and suggestions for integrating these kinds of collegial inquiry experiences into any professional learning opportunity or initiative.

Pillar Practice 4: Mentoring

Mentoring, one of the oldest forms of supporting adult development, is a relational practice that customarily offers a more private way of supporting growth. This practice creates a context for broadening perspectives, examining assumptions, and sharing expertise. Put simply, mentoring is an opportunity for educators on both sides of the relationship—the person serving as mentor and the one in the mentee role—to broaden perspectives, examine assumptions and beliefs, and share expertise toward supporting growth.

For example, mentoring has been shown to support the retention of new teachers (Killion, 2000; Moir & Bloom, 2003; Saphier, Freedman, & Aschheim, 2001). Furthermore, mentoring relationships between new and veteran teachers, who are trained as mentors, have been proven to (1) enhance teacher performance and student learning by encouraging collegial dialogue (Jonson, 2008; Killion, 2000); (2) provide professional learning opportunities for both new and veteran teachers (Daresh, 2003; Holloway, 2004); (3) assist new teachers in effectively managing challenges and developing teaching practices through reflective activities and professional conversations about practice (Jonson, 2008; Moir & Bloom, 2003); and (4) create both career-related and psychosocial benefits for mentors and mentees (DeLong, Gabarro, & Lees, 2008).

In addition, scholars have recognized the crucial need for mentoring among principals, assistant principals, assistant principals aspiring to the principalship, and district level leaders to help them meet the multiplicity of challenges inherent in contemporary leadership and also reduce the isolation of what can feel like a solitary responsibility (Hall, 2008; Kegan & Lahey, 2009; National Staff Development Council, 2008).

While a great deal has been written about the importance of mentoring, and while mentoring can and does take varied forms, scholars have recently emphasized that no single mentoring relationship can meet all of a person's needs for growth. Instead, there is agreement in the field that mentoring relationships need to be nested in a larger developmental set of connections or constellations (Higgins, Chandler, & Kram, 2007; McGowan, Stone, & Kegan, 2007). Moreover, there is consensus that we need mentors throughout our lives and that our needs for growth change as we develop and are influenced by context. These contextual variables include the increasingly complex adaptive challenges we face as educators.

While LTL participants learned about mentoring in depth, and the course instructors did their best to serve as informed "mentors" to students when they reached out for additional suggestions, advice, or guidance (during and/or after the course), the limited fifteen-week duration of LTL made it difficult for students to fully experience the benefit of ongoing mentoring—which we consider a long-term process—within the class itself. Nevertheless, we did our best to offer a "sampling" of the pillar throughout and beyond the class through relationships with instructors and fellow classmates.

Summary of Pillars

In summary, four pillar practices for growth—teaming, providing leadership roles, collegial inquiry, and mentoring—make up the learning-oriented model for school leadership (Drago-Severson, 2004b, 2009, 2012) that we taught and modeled in LTL and other developmentally oriented professional learning opportunities afterward. While each of these practices was incorporated into the design and experience of the course, it is important to remember that adults with qualitatively different developmental orientations—and *capacities*—will orient to engaging in these practices *differently*. Yet with appropriate supports and challenges (which we will discuss more in Chapter 3 after describing constructive-developmental theory in greater detail), *all* adults can grow from participating in these practices, whether used independently or in combination. Indeed—and as we will highlight later when sharing LTL leaders' stories and experiences—employing the pillar practices can help us build capacity at both the individual and group levels, and it can help improve experiences and outcomes for children and adults alike.

A Close-Up on LTL Practices and Strategies

In this section, we offer rich descriptions of specific practices and processes we employed as *component parts* and *instances of* the pillar practices. These are strategies and applications that we employed in LTL and that we still use today in other similar professional learning opportunities to support educators' development and learning. Moreover, as we will describe in Chapters 5 and 6, LTL learners went on to employ many of these same practices in their own leadership, and we describe them in detail here in case helpful to you and your important work supporting adult development. In other words, we hope that you might consider employing and adapting these and similar applications as you continue forward in your own efforts to support adults' learning and growth. While we tease these specific strategies and practices apart here, in reality—and in the class—they worked synergistically to support learning and development. These practices were central to the very fabric of LTL.

Specific Pedagogic Strategies and Applications

While the design of LTL included many structures and practices to support and challenge aspiring school leaders, we share the following to provide a more detailed look at the kinds of practices we engaged with and in in LTL so that you are better able to (1) understand the context and rhythm of the class, (2) understand leaders' references to practices that they used and found helpful in the field, which they name in chapters that follow, and (3) see more clearly how these activities and applications work within the context of the pillar practices, regardless of context. We also offer them in case you find them helpful in your own noble work of supporting those in your care.

The practices incorporated into LTL were all intentionally employed to create developmentally oriented opportunities for reflection, sense making of learning, and transfer of theory to practice by inviting learners to engage in dialogue, writing, and sharing. In other words, we, ourselves, as instructors, and the learners in the course offered both support for and challenge toward gently pushing students to surface assumptions, seeing experiences in new ways, and considering alternative perspectives. During these times, instructors encouraged students to ask questions to more deeply understand their colleagues' perspectives—not simply advocate their own thinking or give advice. Students did the same to help each other while engaging in these practices and processes. They were asked to observe discrepancies in colleagues' and their own stated beliefs and actions, and we encouraged learners to pose questions to each other about how others involved in their leadership experiences felt, thought about, and experienced the encounters they shared without taking sides (i.e., being an advocate for their classmate). As instructors, we used course readings to help learners understand what developmental challenge and support looks and feels like to different learners and how they might think about these experiences from a developmental perspective. We also guided and joined students while they were practicing these newly developing skills during class and convening (i.e., personal case-based learning) by modeling supportive and challenging feedback and by helping learners shape their own comments through written and verbal feedback.

Practice: Writing in LTL

LTL was designed to include several types of writing as sources of developmental support and challenge to students' learning. Through both the process of writing and then sharing one's writing—or pieces of it—a person can gain new and broader perspectives (Brookfield, 1995). Research has shown that the practice of writing can help educators make sense of their pedagogy, teaching, leadership, and the process of education and change in new ways (Brookfield, 1995; Drago-Severson, 2009, 2012; Hashweh, 2004). In fact, as you know, writing can be a tool that helps educators—and all adults for that matter—to see and reflect on their experiences from a distance and to understand them from multiple perspectives.

Within the LTL class, student learners engaged in free writing, class assignments, and personal convening cases. We describe each of these practices below.

Free Writing. Free writing was an important pedagogical practice in LTL, one that took place during nearly every class. The lead instructor posed several questions to students and asked them to choose one or two to write and think through in a brief (e.g., three to five minutes) timed writing. For example, the following constitute a set of free-write questions presented to the class:

1. What are two powerful learnings, concepts, or ideas from this week's readings that you found meaningful?

2. What are two practical implications of these readings that you think will help you with your practice? How so?

3. How can you, as a school leader, create a context that you think will support adults' transformational learning?

To be even more specific about this process, free writing is an invitation to write down exactly what a person is thinking and/or feeling, giving no attention to self-censoring for a particular audience or for grammar and syntax. The central idea is to think honestly and openly on paper (we gave students journals) about whatever comes to mind in reaction to the prompt—a sentence stem (e.g., what I found confusing in this particular reading was . . .) or one of the questions listed above. After free writing, we invited learners to share whatever they felt comfortable sharing with a partner, small group, or large group (sometimes we invited them to share with one person, at other times with two peers, and still at others with a small group). We employed free writing to help learners focus their thinking and/or feelings and to clarify them before engaging in dialogue.

After learners engaged in private writing and then with a partner, triad, or team dialogue, we created a space for full group sharing. In other words, learners were invited to report out. For example, we invited them to share "one insight, question or learning based on their discussion and/or writing." Reporting out was helpful because it allowed instructors and the full class to understand students' questions, to help them engage with their own thinking about readings, and to focus follow-up discussions.

Over the years, we learned that LTL learners described and experienced the practice of free writing as supportive of their learning because, as they explained, it provided them with opportunities to hear and share feedback, develop their own thinking, make transfers to their own practice, and increase their self-confidence in their capacities to support other adults' learning.

Class Assignments. In addition to free writing in LTL, student-learners wrote several class assignments outside of class. These assignments—what we traditionally refer to as papers—were designed with developmental intentions. In other words, they were offered to provide learners with opportunities to further develop their thinking about supporting adult development, to transfer LTL learnings (i.e., theories discussed, practices presented) to their own real-life practice, and to synthesize new learnings, information, and perspectives gained from LTL readings, in-class discussions, and lectures. All LTL writing assignments were also designed to create and facilitate a conversation between instructors (lead and teaching fellows) and student learners through the written feedback provided by the teaching team.

We think it's important to know that the teaching team provided extensive written feedback on class assignments with particular attention to being both supportive and challenging and to helping the student learners examine their own assumptions in order to support development and offer alternative perspectives. As a teaching team, we read *all* student papers and discussed how we could support each learner. Doing so is an example of how we, too, engaged in collegial inquiry, teaming, leadership roles, and mentoring.

In summary, LTL writing assignments invited students to reflect on new developmental ideas and how they might help them to support others' and their own growth. Student learners were invited to consider how the readings and class discussions/exercises (see Resource B for readings)—and their experiences in LTL might inform their thinking and practice. All assignments encouraged students to choose something that was *meaningful to them and their practice.* We stressed this in our teaching and still do today. For example, in the guidelines for one of the assignments toward the end of the course, we invited student learners to develop an action plan so that they could think ahead to transfer their learning to their leadership.

This assignment was a two-page paper guided by questions to provide a structure. They submitted it to the instructors and to colleagues in their group so that they could learn from multiple perspectives. We offer the assignment guidelines in Figure 2.1 as a guide or model for implementing similar activities within your own context (Drago-Severson, 2004b, 2009).

All papers in the course gave us insight into the LTL learners' thinking and also allowed for developmentally mindful feedback that invited students to revise and refine their ideas. The written feedback offered supportive comments and posed questions (i.e., developmental challenges) intended to encourage student learners to consider theoretical lenses that were showcased in the course.

Personal Convening Case. In this section, we will share more about convening cases, a special form of class assignment, which were

Figure 2.1   Design Plan Assignment Guidelines

Design Plan. The main purposes of this assignment are to give you an opportunity to (a) develop your own ideas about how to best support adult development, (b) bring theoretical ideas to inform your described practice, and (c) receive consultation and feedback from colleagues. If you choose to, you may revisit this draft and elaborate on it for the final paper.
  In your design/action plan, please respond to the following prompts:

  1. Please sketch a *practice* that you would like to implement in your leadership in support of adult learning/development. The practice you discuss can be a practice that you invent or one that we have discussed or engaged with in class.

  2. Please discuss how at least one principle from adult developmental theory informs your thinking about how the practice can support adult learning or development. It is up to you to decide what theoretical concept will be most helpful in thinking through how the practice will support adult development. *Please provide at least one specific example of a connection between theory and practice.*

  3. What questions/challenges/dilemmas seem especially important for you to consider in terms of implementing this practice?

completed each week by one student in each small group and then shared with a small group of classmates during the convening process (Drago-Severson, Roloff Welch, & Jones, 2007; Drago-Severson, 2009). Students wrote a case based on an experience in which they were working to support another adult's development or someone was working to support their own development that did not go well, from their perspective. Learners in their team (approximately ten to twelve classmates and one instructor) read the case the week before it was discussed and were asked to provide written feedback to the "convener" (i.e., case author) that would be both supportive and developmentally challenging by probing assumptions and offering alternative perspectives. Convening groups met for about one hour of structured discussion during class time (i.e., students used a protocol) to dialogue with their colleagues on the convening case. During convening, the individual presenting his or her case listened to colleagues' feedback on the questions that were developed as part of the case-writing process. Again, in Figure 2.2, we offer the convening protocol in case helpful for your own very important work (adapted from Drago-Severson, 2009).

This pedagogical strategy was employed to create holding environments for growth in which students convened to reflect on problematic or puzzling cases from their own practice after establishing safe participatory norms. As discussed, the process of convening helps support learning, risk taking, and the examination of assumptions, and it can support development. Some examples of the complex issues or dilemmas that the cases centered on included (a) initial stages of a challenging initiative or project; (b) responding to upset or disappointed colleagues to support their development; (c) managing a complex task (e.g., evaluation) in support of another person's development; (d) attending to issues of diversity in an effort to support learning and development; (e) working through various sets of loyalties; and (f) making a tough decision.

Practice: Dialogue in LTL

Like writing, dialogue was purposefully built into LTL to provide learners with opportunities to share their perspectives, examine assumptions, and explore new ideas with their classmates. All of this was aimed at supporting growth and learning. As we have shared, opportunities for sharing and dialogue were built into personal, team, and small-group reflections to help learners more deeply understand the beliefs and assumptions that drive their actions and decisions.

Figure 2.2   A Protocol for Engaging in Convening and Consultation With Colleagues

Following is a protocol I ask school leaders in my classes to employ when engaging in the convening process. Given time constraints, we use a forty-minute time block for each convening. Depending on your context, you may choose to adjust the time frame for convenings. Many school leaders do adjust the time frame when conducting convenings in schools.

Brief Overview of Your Case and Questions   *Five Minutes*

This five-minute period of time is when the convener briefly reminds the group about the following: (1) focus of your case and (2) what questions you would like the group to address (i.e., what the group can help you with). At this time, the convener also addresses any clarifying questions group members may have about facts of the case.

Group Discussion/Consultation of Your Case   *Thirty Minutes (Total)*

This thirty-minute block of time is dedicated to group members' discussing and offering feedback on the convener's case and questions. The group will discuss the convening case, and all group members will listen closely to colleagues' thinking about the issues being highlighted. During this discussion, the convener will need to refrain from talking and, instead, focus on listening to each group member's comments. Group members will address case questions—developed by the convener and written in the case itself—and share their feedback and ideas.

Pausing and Checking in With the Convener   *Five of the Total Thirty Minutes for This Section*

Midway through the group discussion of the convener's case, the facilitator (who is also the timekeeper and an active group member) will ask the group to pause and be silent for three minutes so that all can reflect on (a) what has been said, (b) the type of feedback that has been offered, and (c) the questions the convener posed in his or her case. The last two minutes of this pause are reserved for the convener to talk and to let everyone know where he or she would appreciate the group's help during the next half of the convening. This is the convener's opportunity to redirect the group's focus.

Convener Reflections   *Five Minutes*

This period is reserved for the convener to share his or her reflections on the convening, learnings from the discussion, and any additional reflections as they relate to possible next steps, realizations, insights, or actions. The convener may wish to summarize what has been helpful and where he or she would like to go next with his or her thoughts, work, and/or questions.

Source: Adapted from Drago-Severson (2009, p. 204).

For example, after private time to think and write during the in-class free-writes, learners had opportunities to refine and share their thinking in multiple contexts (e.g., pair shares, small-group, and whole-group discussions) in order to talk through lingering questions, expand upon new insights, and offer and make connections between theory and practice. Dialogue was also central to students' learning in the context of convening. In particular, weekly discussions were structured to allow students ample time and opportunity to share their ideas. As we will discuss further when sharing graduates' reflections about convening in Chapter 4, students worked hard to support each other through caring, developmental dialogue, and aimed at once to respond to colleagues' comments and move the conversation forward with new thoughts and responses.

Practice: Guest Speakers

Students in LTL also had opportunities to interact with different kinds of educational leaders who visited class sessions. Both novice and experienced school leaders, for instance, discussed a variety of leadership challenges with the students, including the complexities of implementing successful professional learning initiatives, negotiating department and schoolwide reform, and facing resistance from colleagues and supervisors. Providing aspiring leaders with opportunities for candid, safe conversations with experienced leaders currently working in the field, we have learned, can help students further consider potential connections between course ideas and practice and also learn from the noble and important work of leaders working to support adult development in diverse contexts.

Chapter Summary

In this chapter, we presented an overview of the Leadership for Transformational Learning (LTL) course that the leaders in our study completed in 2003, 2004, and 2005—and that is representative of a developmental model that can be used in your own practice—including its content, design, processes, and developmental intentions. While we focused throughout on key ideas and pedagogical strategies employed when the leaders in this study were enrolled in the course to help contextualize their sharings, which will be presented in the chapters that follow, it is important to emphasize that the content, theories, practices, and processes described in this chapter are very similar in nature to those that aspiring and practicing leaders and educators engage with and in other professional learning experiences that we continue to facilitate in schools, districts, professional learning communities, teams, coaching, and university classrooms.

In particular, this chapter

1. Offered an overview of the *content* that composed the LTL- course

2. Introduced the pillar practices that were infused into the LTL course

3. Shared specific practices and processes, which support growth and learning, that leaders engaged in and with via the pillars when enrolled in the LTL course

We hope that you have found this overview of the LTL developmental model to be helpful and that the processes, content, and pillar practices for growth are useful to you as you continue with your noble work of supporting adult development and capacity building in your work context.

In the next chapter, we introduce Harvard psychologist Robert Kegan's constructive-developmental theory and highlight the developmental intentionality of the learning-oriented model for school leadership and the four pillar practices that compose it (i.e., teaming, engaging adults in leadership roles, inviting educators to engage in collegial inquiry, and mentoring), which we introduced in this chapter. Both Kegan's constructive-developmental theory and the pillar practices informed LTL course design and pedagogy to support educators' learning and growth. These also infuse professional development experiences that we facilitate in schools, districts, and university classrooms.

Reflective Questions

We offer the following questions as an opportunity for you to reflect on learnings from this chapter as well as ideas you might have in terms of enhancing the opportunities you offer to adults in your care—and yourself—to support growth and capacity building. Please take a moment to reflect on these questions. You might want to respond to them privately first and then engage in collegial inquiry with a partner or group of colleagues. We hope you find these useful.

1. How would you describe professional learning and development opportunities in your workplace? How do you think other adults would describe these professional learning and development opportunities?

2. What do you consider to be the most important features of designing professional learning opportunities? Why? What are two practices you engage in regularly by yourself or with colleagues in professional development to support your own growth? How are they working? What are two practices you employ in any kind of professional development you design to support other people's growth? How well do you think these practices are working?

3. In professional development that you either lead or participate in, what, from your perspective, is working well? What is challenging? What kinds of practices do you or others currently employ to support adult learning and capacity building? How do you think they are working? What, if anything, would you like to improve? Why? What kinds of supports would be helpful to you in terms of making these improvements?

4. In what ways, if any, do the ideas and practices discussed in this chapter help you think about ways you might improve professional learning opportunities that you either lead or participate in? What, if anything, resonates with your own experience?

5. After reading this chapter, what is one new ingredient—or practice—that you feel will help you and other adults grow?

6. Before reading Chapter 3—a chapter that focuses primarily on adult developmental theory—please take a moment to consider your current ideas about how adults grow. How do you think growth is supported?

3

A Close-Up on Constructive-Developmental Theory

Using Theory to Guide Adult Learning in Schools, Districts, and University Preparation Programs

Introduction and Overview

In this chapter, we offer a detailed discussion of Harvard psychologist Robert Kegan's constructive-developmental theory to further illuminate the developmental underpinnings of the Leadership for Transformational Learning (LTL) course model, the pillar practice for growth that are informed by this theory, and also to illuminate the great *hopefulness* of understanding and applying this theory and related practices in your leadership. As you know, adults' different ways of knowing have implications for the different kinds of supports and challenges we need to offer in any teaching, leading, or professional development opportunity. Therefore, we describe in this chapter the three ways of knowing most commonly found in adulthood—instrumental, socializing, and self-authoring—and explain how the pillar practices and the learning-oriented model (Drago-Severson, 2004b, 2009, 2012) can help you simultaneously support the **growth** of adults who make meaning with *any* of these ways of knowing.

For example, after exploring constructive-developmental theory in more detail, we outline the developmental underpinnings of the four pillar practices for growth (e.g., teaming, providing leadership roles, collegial inquiry, and mentoring) that we introduced in Chapter 2—as well as specific supports and challenges you can embed when implementing these practices so that they can support the growth of adults with different developmental orientations. As you will soon see, this theory helps us understand that (a) as adults we make sense of our experiences of everything in qualitatively different ways; (b) in order to support growth, we need to differentiate the kinds of supports and challenges we offer to others; and (c) to facilitate growth, we all need a mix of *both supports* and *challenges.*

In addition, in the chapters that follow, you will soon learn that the LTL graduates we learned from spoke a great deal about how this theory has made a big difference in how they support adult growth and capacity building, how they design professional development for adults in their workplaces, how they work with adults in teams and professional learning communities (PLCs), and also in their professional and personal lives. We hope that you similarly find this theory helpful and informative, and hope, too, that reading more about it will help you better understand its influence on LTL leaders' thinking about and on-the-ground practices for supporting adults' capacity building in their schools and districts. In addition, we truly hope that you find this theory helpful in your leadership practice and life, as LTL leaders have, and as we have.

For example, many leaders in our workshops and professional development initiatives over close to two decades have shared how understanding constructive-developmental theory and the ways it informs the pillar practices has helped them to better understand adults' developmental needs and orientations, to offer better and more meaningful feedback to adults on their instructional practice and/or leadership, and as one leader recently commented, "to have a bigger heart and be a better leader." As mentioned earlier, and as you will see in the chapters that follow, this theory and the pillar practices have helped educators and leaders *differentiate* their leadership in support of adult growth to better meet the needs of the adults they serve.

In addition to the reasons we outlined, there are other important reasons why you might find learning about this theory and how it informs the pillar practices useful, meaningful, and helpful. First, given the mounting demands of the current educational climate, we *need* to support the growth and development of all educators so that they can better manage the rising tide of challenges and imperatives—together. Understanding how adults make meaning of their teaching, leading, professional development experiences, work in teams, participation in PLCs, and experiences of leadership roles—as well as what they need in order to contribute most effectively to the work—can help us build capacity at both the individual and organizational levels. In addition, it can help us create schools, teams, districts, PLCs, preparation programs in districts and universities, and coaching relationships that serve more authentically as growth-enhancing contexts.

Finally, we hope this understanding helps you, as a leader and facilitator of learning, to understand *your own needs for growth*, how to better support yourself, and how to secure supports and conditions that will contribute to your own development. This is essential, as you know, because our capacities influence how we can support others and are important to renewal and sustaining ourselves. Accordingly, as you learn more about this theory, we invite you to consider these ideas in terms of not only how they could help you support others' growth, *but also how they could shed light on ways to support your own growth.* We talk more about this in the final chapter and truly hope you find this discussion meaningful and helpful.

Ultimately, a knowledge of constructive-developmental theory can help you shape any professional learning opportunity—whether a formal professional development initiative, teaming session, faculty meeting, collegial conversation, feedback debriefing, or university course—as an endeavor not only in which the work gets accomplished but also in which adults feel alive, supported, and "well held" in the developmental sense. (Drago-Severson, 2012, p. 1). *This, we hope, will be of use regardless of your role—as teacher, assistant principal, principal, coach, district leader, professional learning leader, or special education specialist.*

While we trust you understand that there is much more to this theory than we can share within this chapter, we offer what we see as the *most important principles of this theory* to be of good help to you and your practice. Our hope is that we can provide you with a workable understanding of this theory so that, should you find it a meaningful lens, you can employ it in your noble practice of supporting other people's and your own growth. In essence, this chapter is an invitation for you to "rent" this theory—and this is the very same invitation we extend to learners in LTL when we present these similar ideas.

To be of best help to you, we've organized this chapter as follows. First, we offer an important distinction between **informational learning** and **transformational learning**. Next, we provide an overview of the foundational principles that compose Kegan's theory (1982, 1994, 2000), the three most common ways of knowing in adulthood, and the importance of "holding environments" (Kegan, 1982, p. 115) in order to support adult growth. We mentioned the importance of a holding environment in Chapter 2, but here we discuss it in more detail to (1) help you understand the three functions it serves and (2) connect it to how the pillar practices are real-life holding environments that you can employ—should you wish to do so—in your own work. Then we circle back to the pillar practices, briefly, to illuminate how they can offer supports and challenges to adults who have different ways of knowing. Please know that all we share is offered with great respect and care for you and your noble commitments and with hope that you find this chapter useful in your efforts to support other educators' growth—and your own.

Acknowledging Strengths and Limitations of This Theory

Importantly, constructive-developmental theory, like all theories, has both strengths and limitations. No one theory can help us understand all aspects of our lived experience, nor can any single theory help us understand all of the dimensions of another person's lived experience. What a theory *can do* is shed light on particular features of life. In the case of constructive-developmental theory, it is a theory that helps us understand the process of **meaning making**, the different ways in which we make sense of our experiences, that we need different forms of developmentally appropriate *support and challenge* to grow, and that we grow within the context of relationships. This theory does not illuminate the ways in which racial identity, gender, religion, or age might influence our development or meaning making, for example. Yet, we still find it very promising—and our hope is that you will too.

You might wonder—as some educators do—where did this theory come from? The constructive-developmental family of theories stems from more than forty-five years of research about how we grow from the moment we are born to the moment of our last breath (Basseches, 1984; Baxter-Magolda, 1992, 2009; Belenky, Clinchy,

Goldberger, & Tarule, 1986; Kegan, 1982, 1994, 2000; Knefelkamp & David-Lang, 2000; Kohlberg, 1969, 1984; Perry, 1970; Piaget, 1952). While Kegan's constructive-developmental theory is a powerful lens for understanding how to support adult development in K–12 schools, districts, university leadership preparation programs, for-profit organizations, and professional learning initiatives, it is only recently beginning to be applied in schools. Nevertheless, it is a power-ful and hopeful lens—and, as we have explained, one that we invite you to "rent" and consider applying.

To offer a little more context, constructive-developmental theory is a Neo-Piagetian theory. The Swiss psychologist Jean Piaget (1952, 1963, 1965) dedicated his life's work to understanding the develop-ment of children's cognition and their moral and social reasoning. Kegan extended Piaget's theory in several ways. First, Kegan exam-ined development across the life span. Second, his theory includes cognitive as well as other lines of development, namely affective, interpersonal, and intrapersonal. Kegan, like Piaget, describes dis-crete stages of development and illuminates the processes involved in movement from one stage of development (i.e., what we refer to as a way of knowing) to the next. Kegan's theory also attends to the com-plex interplay between an individual's way of knowing and his or her psychosocial context in order to describe and highlight the important interaction between the two.

Informational and Transformational Learning: Why Might This Distinction Matter to *You*?

In today's complex educational world, with the increasing demands of caring for children and youth, the Common Core State Standards, new evaluation systems, and other challenges that you encounter every day, there's a need to prioritize learning that can help educators better understand, meet, and exceed evolving expectations. Before learning more about the important distinction between infor-mational and transformational learning, however—which we consider key to designing and facilitating professional learning today—we invite you to consider the reflective question on the right.

> **Reflective Moment:** In your own professional development—and/or the kinds of opportunities for development and learning that you offer to other adults in your care in your practice—how much of what you offer is oriented toward teaching new skills or content—which is very important—and how much of it is oriented toward increasing adults' internal capacity?

As we define it, informational learning relates to learning facts and important skills. Put simply, this type of learning centers on increases in *what* we know (Drago-Severson, 2004b, 2009, 2012; Kegan, 2000). It might be helpful to think about informational learning in terms of increasing "encyclopedia" forms of knowledge, which we of course need to help us manage many demands we face as educators and leaders—especially *technical challenges* (Heifetz, 1994) that require specific expertise or know-how. Ultimately, informational learning helps us to increase our skills, change our attitudes, and develop our competencies (e.g., understanding how to create a budget; learning skills to help us work in today's technological world; having skills to analyze data in order to understand and assess students' test scores and academic achievement over time). However, informational learning is not enough to help us manage the complex *adaptive* challenges we encounter with increased frequency as educators and leaders. And, it will not equip us to build our own or other adults' *internal* capacities in teams, schools, PLCs, districts, and leadership preparation programs.

As we discussed in Chapter 1, within schools and across school systems, we are currently facing more and more adaptive challenges (Heifetz, 1994), which require us to manage enormous amounts of complexity and ambiguity. These challenges, as you know, are challenges in which the *problem itself* is murky—and for which there are no known solutions. Such challenges require new and more complex internal capacities in order to address them—and they require that we "solve the problem *in the act of working on it* [italics in original]" (Wagner et al., 2006, p. 10). While educators and leaders might need support in tackling technical aspects of their work (e.g., data analysis, budgeting, scheduling), new demands without clear or simple solutions indicate that many of the challenges we are currently facing are *adaptive* in nature.

To manage these kinds of challenges, we need to learn new approaches that will enable us and those we care for to *grow*. We need to shape professional development opportunities as contexts for growth and opportunities to increase internal capacities. In order to engage with the complexity of these situations and the adaptive challenges we face, we require a different kind of learning—transformational learning.

As mentioned, throughout this book we use the terms growth, transformational learning, developmental orientation, and internal capacity building interchangeably. As emphasized earlier, we define transformational learning as increases in our cognitive, emotional (affective), interpersonal (self-to-other), and intrapersonal (self-to-self) capacities that enable us to better manage the complexities of learning, leading, teaching, and living (Drago-Severson, 2004b, 2009, 2012; Kegan, 2000). Transformational learning actually changes *how* a person knows and understands the world, his or her experience in it, and other people.

To support the process of growth or transformational learning, we must first understand a person's current meaning-making system or way of knowing, because it shapes how a person interprets—or makes sense of—all life experiences. This means meeting a person where he or she is in his or her current way of *constructing* the world. When a person grows—and when transformational learning occurs— there is a qualitative change in a person's way of knowing. This means that there is an internal change in the *structure* of a person's meaning-making system and that a person is able to take a broader perspective on himself or herself, other people, and the relationship between the two (Kegan, 1982, 1994). As you might suspect, this kind of learning is essential in today's world, and better understanding constructive-developmental theory is one promising way to build developmental learning experiences into professional development opportunities of all kinds.

Foundational Principles of Constructive-Developmental Theory

Kegan's theory, which centers on both the structure and process of a person's meaning-making system or way of knowing, is based on three central principles: *constructivism, developmentalism,* and *the subject-object balance* (which composes a person's meaning-making system). In case helpful, the subject-object balance is all about perspective taking. By this, we mean that what is very close to us—what is so close that it cannot yet be seen—actually "runs" us (we are **subject** to these aspects of ourselves, so to speak). On the other hand, those things that we *can* reflect on, control, and not be "run by" are the things we can hold out and see as **object**.

The first principle of the theory, constructivism, points to the importance of understanding that we actively put things together— we interpret and *construct* experience—every minute of our lives. Our constructions create our realities with respect to cognitive, affective, intrapersonal (the self's relationship to itself), and interpersonal (the self's relationship to others) lines of development. The second principle is developmentalism, and it helps us to understand that the ways in which a person makes meaning and constructs his or her reality can develop—grow more complex—over time and throughout one's life, provided that he or she benefits from developmentally appropriate supports and challenges. It is essential to have both supports and challenges in order to grow. The third major principle is what Kegan (1982) refers to as the "subject-object balance." A meaning-making system— or way of knowing—hinges on this balance. As mentioned above, this balance centers on the relationship between what we, as human beings, can take a perspective on and control (i.e., hold as "object") and what we are identified with, cannot see about ourselves or others or the relationship between the two (i.e., are "subject to"). These three big ideas illuminate the developmental underpinnings of the learning-oriented model for school leadership and the ways in which the pillar practices can support transformational learning.

As shared earlier, a person's way of knowing, or meaning-making system, is the lens through which *all* life experience is filtered—it is the window through which a person *sees* the world and actively interprets life. One's way of knowing organizes how a person understands one's self and one's experience of others, and of work and life situations. In the context of education, our way of knowing shapes *how* we understand our roles and responsibilities as teachers, assistant principals, principals, superintendents, coaches, professional learning specialists, and learners and the way we think about what makes a good leader, a good teacher, or a good superintendent. A person's way of knowing is not random; instead, it is stable and consistent for a period of time and reflects a coherent system of logic. A way of knowing might feel more like the way we *are* rather than something we *have* (Drago-Severson, 2004a; Kegan, 1982, 1994; Kegan, Broderick, Helsing, Popp, & Portnow, 2001).

Three Most Common Ways of Knowing in Adulthood

Kegan's constructive-developmental theory is composed of six qualitatively different stages, meaning-making systems, or ways of knowing, as we call them. You might be wondering whether or not a way of knowing is associated with gender, for example? Well, according to research (Broderick, 1996; Goodman, 1983; Kegan, 1982, 1994; Kegan et al., 2001; Lahey, 1986) one's way of knowing has not been found to be associated with gender, age, or life phase.

The instrumental, socializing, and self-authoring ways of knowing are most common in adulthood. Because of this, here we provide an overview of the key characteristics of these three ways of knowing. There is, however, a fourth way of knowing beyond self-authoring. It is known as the *inter-individual* (Kegan, 1982) or **self-transforming way of knowing** (Drago-Severson, 2009, 2012). It's important to note that while this meaning-making system is becoming more prevalent in society today than it was in the 1980s and 1990s because of the complex implicit and explicit demands of work, leadership, and life (McCallum, 2008; Nicolaides, 2008), the percentages of adults making meaning with this way of knowing remain smaller than the other three more prevalent ways of knowing. (For a fuller description of our ways of knowing, please see Drago-Severson, 2009, 2012; Kegan, 1982; Kegan & Lahey, 2009; Lahey, Souvaine, Kegan, Goodman, & Felix, 1988.)

Below and throughout this book, we focus on the three most common ways of knowing in adulthood because we feel this will be most helpful to you and your practice. It's also important to note that the LTL leaders focused on these three more common ways of knowing while in the LTL course. Table 3.1 summarizes the essential characteristics of these three ways of knowing.

Growing From One Way of Knowing to Another—and the Demands of Leadership

Before providing a snapshot of the key characteristics of the three ways of knowing most common in adulthood, it is important to state that there are also distinct and identifiable *transitional stages*. We will share a little bit about *the process of growing* from one way of knowing to the next here (for an in-depth discussion of this, please see Drago-Severson, 2004a, 2009; Kegan, 1982; Lahey et al., 1988).

Growing from one way of knowing to another is a process by which there are increases in an individual's cognitive, affective, intrapersonal, and interpersonal *internal* capacities. Each new way of knowing incorporates the former into its more expansive meaning-making system as a person grows.

Although this theory, like other stage theories, is hierarchical in nature, one way of knowing is not necessarily better than another, unless the implicit and explicit demands of the environment call for higher-level internal capacities. We think the best way to look at this question is in terms of the match between our internal capacities and the demands of our work and the different roles we have in life. In other words, for us this is really a question about the **developmental match** or **goodness of fit** between our way of knowing (i.e., the internal capacities we have), the challenges we face, and others' expectations of us.

Table 3.1 Ways of Knowing Most Common in Adulthood According to Kegan's Constructive-Developmental Theory

Stages →	Stage 2	Stage 3	Stage 4
Kegan's (1982) terms →	Imperial	Interpersonal	Institutional
Drago-Severson's (2004b, 2009) terms (way of knowing) →	Instrumental	Socializing	Self-authoring
How does the person orient to experiences (e.g., to teaching, collaborating, sharing in decision making, learning, leading, and living)?	Rule-based self	Other-focused self	Reflective self
What is the person's underlying thought structure? *Subject (S):* What a person is identified with and cannot take perspective on or see about self—what "runs" the person. *Object (O):* What a person can reflect on, manage, be responsible for, and take perspective on	S (can't see about self): Needs, interests, wishes O (can take a perspective on): Impulses, perceptions	S (can't see about self): The interpersonal, mutuality O (can take a perspective on): Needs, interests, wishes	S (can't see about self): Authorship, identity, psychic administration, ideology O (can take a perspective on): The interpersonal, mutuality
How does the person define one's self?	Orients to self-interests, purposes, and concrete needs	Orients to valued others' (external authorities and supervisors') expectations, values, and opinions	Orients to self's values (internal authority) and standards
What are the person's orienting (preoccupying) concerns?	Depends on rules and the "right" way to do things and act; is concerned with concrete consequences. Decisions are based on what the self will acquire. Others are experienced as helpers or obstacles to meeting concrete needs. Person does not yet have the capacity	Depends on external authority, acceptance, and affiliation. Self is defined by important others' judgments and expectations; it is oriented to inner states. Self feels responsible for others' feelings and holds others responsible for own feelings.	Self generates and replies to internal values and standards. Criticism is evaluated according to internal standards and bench of judgment. Ultimate concern is with one's own competence and performance. Self can balance contradictory feelings.

Kegan's (1982) terms →	Imperial	Interpersonal	Institutional
Drago-Severson's (2004b, 2009) terms (way of knowing) →	Instrumental	Socializing	Self-authoring
	for abstract thinking or generalizing from one context to another.	Criticism and conflict threaten the fabric of the self.	Conflict is viewed as natural and enhances one's own and others' perspectives to achieve larger organizational and systemic goals.
What are the person's guiding questions?	"Will I get punished if I don't follow rules or do something wrong?" "What's in it for me?"	"Will you (valued other/authority/ supervisor) still like/value me?" "Will you (valued other/authority) approve of me?" "Will you (valued other/ authority) still think I am a good person?"	"Am I maintaining my own personal integrity, standards, and values?" "Am I competent?" "Am I living, working, and loving to the best of my ability?" "Am I achieving my goals and being guided by my ideals?"
What are the "Tasks" at the person's growing edge?	Grow to be open to possibilities for multiple "right" solutions and pathways to resolving issues and problems Grow capacities for abstract thinking	Grow to generate one's own internal values and standards Grow to understand that conflicting perspectives and points of view can enhance collaboration and shared decision making without threatening interpersonal relationships	Grow to become open to seemingly opposing points of view, perspectives, and ideologies Grow to embrace diverse problem-solving approaches
In what ways can the person be supported in his or her growth?	Set clear and explicit expectations and goals; share step-by-step procedures for accomplishing tasks, goals, and practices; offer and model specific skills, concrete advice, models of best practices	Model how to engage in conflict and disagreement without threatening relationships; create opportunities for growing one's voice, sharing one's expertise with colleagues and assuming leadership roles with support; acknowledge and confirm person's thoughts and encourage and support development of self's own standards and internal values	Create opportunities for person to critique and analyze one's own perspective and ideology; invite person to assume role of facilitator; encourage consideration of seemingly diametrically opposed perspectives

Source: Adapted from Drago-Severson (2004b, 2007, 2009, 2012). "Underlying Thought Structure" (Row 3) is from Kegan (1982), *The Evolving Self*, pp. 86–87.

That being said, it is nonetheless critical to acknowledge that there are certain kinds of positions—including leadership positions—that do demand the ability to *spontaneously demonstrate* more complex internal capacities. For instance, leaders in schools, districts, and other organizations must be able to understand others' perspectives while simultaneously having the capacity to hold on to their own (Kegan & Lahey, 2001, 2009). Importantly, Kegan and Lahey (2009) have also argued that many of the demands of modern life and leadership outpace adults' developmental capacities.

In 1994, Kegan conducted an analysis of the rates at which people demonstrate the different ways of knowing based on a composite from three studies (Dixon, 1986; Goodman, 1983; Greenwald, 1991). He found that only approximately 18% of adults demonstrate a self-authoring way of knowing. While this percentage has likely increased today, it's important to note that the demands of leadership often require these kinds of self-authoring capacities.

In general, according to constructive-developmental theory, people tend to demonstrate the same way of knowing within different roles and across different contexts (for a more detailed discussion of rare exceptions to this, please see Kegan, 1994, p. 371). However, it is also important to note that *context matters*. There are some contexts and conditions that are not conducive for us to demonstrate our most complex selves. For example, McCallum (2008) found that under periods of extreme stress some adults tended to "fall back"—that is, they temporarily demonstrated less complex ways of knowing. This kind of temporary falling back was also noted in work by Knefelkamp and David-Lang (2000).

Next we present a discussion of the central features of the three ways of knowing most common in adulthood.

The Instrumental Way of Knowing: "Rule-Bound Self"

An educator with an instrumental way of knowing has a "what do you have that can help me/what do I have that can help you" orientation to learning, teaching, leading, engaging in teams and PLCs, and living. Importantly, instrumental knowers understand that observable events have realities separate from their own but generally understand the world in concrete terms. Instrumental knowers orient toward rule following and feel supported when others provide specific, explicit advice.

These adults are aware that their preferences and feelings remain consistent over time, but they lack the capacity for abstract thinking (in the psychological sense) and making generalizations from one context to another. Instrumental knowers are able to take perspective on and control their impulses; they hold these as objects. They do not, however, have this same sense of perspective on their needs, wishes, and interests. Instead, they are subject to their desires—*they are run by them*. Other people are perceived and experienced as either helpers or obstacles to getting one's own concrete needs met. In addition, another person's needs and interests are important only if they benefit or interfere with the needs of the instrumental knower. For example, an instrumental knower might think, *I'll have a better chance of getting your help to get the things I need if you like me. If you don't like me, you will not help me get what I want.*

Adults with this way of knowing have dualistic thinking; they believe there are "right" and "wrong" ways to do things, "right" and "wrong" answers, "right" ways to think and "right" ways to behave. They generally want to learn "the rules," whether the rules dictate how to perform a task as an educator, solve a problem, or help their students with an assignment. While these adults orient toward focusing on achieving their *own* concrete goals and interests, they are not self-absorbed. It's important to note that they can be as kindhearted as anyone else. In other words, instrumental knowers will feel supported by concrete, more tangible expressions of support, such as direct suggestions, step-by-step guidelines for completing tasks, and models of best practices.

As Table 3.2 shows, creating situations wherein these adults are encouraged to open up to multiple perspectives will help them to broaden their perspectives and grow over time.

Table 3.2   Instrumental Knowers: Supports and Challenges for Growth

Supports	*Challenges (Growing Edge)*
• Setting clear goals and expectations • Providing explicit step-by-step procedures for dialogue and working with other colleagues as well as explicit directions for tasks • Sharing examples of rules, purposes, and goals—and how to share them with others • Engaging in dialogue that provides concrete advice, specific skills, and information and instructions about practice—including best practice models	• Providing opportunities to learn about multiple perspectives through dialogue • Creating tasks that require abstract thinking (in the psychological sense) and scaffolding instrumental knowers through the process • Encouraging movement beyond "correct" solutions and toward other perspectives—and modeling the process • Discussing how multiple perspectives could build abstract thinking and increase perspective broadening on self, others, and the relationships among them

Source: Adapted from Drago-Severson (2009, p. 279).

The Socializing Way of Knowing: "Other-Focused Self"

Educators with a socializing way of knowing have developed more complex developmental capacities for reflection. Unlike instrumental knowers, socializing knowers can think abstractly and reflect on others' actions. In fact, socializing knowers have developed the capacity to think abstractly and to make generalizations from one context to another. These educators can reflect on their actions and the actions of others. Their orientation is *other-focused*, and they often subordinate their own needs to those of others. When people have grown into a socializing way of knowing, they can identify with and internalize other people's feelings. An educator might ask himself, "What does my coach think I should do? Will my principal still like me if I disagree with her?"

Socializing knowers are able to subordinate their own needs and desires (they are held as object) to the needs and desires of others. However, they are not yet able to have perspective on their relationships. They feel responsible for others' feelings and hold other people responsible for *their* feelings. Interpersonal conflict is almost always experienced as a threat to the self, and acceptance by authorities is of the highest importance. For example, a valued authority's expectations and judgments become one's *own* expectations and judgments. In other words, if you as my superintendent think I am doing good work in my role as principal, then I think the very same about myself. Valued others, authorities (e.g., a spouse, principal, team leader, superintendent), and often societal expectations (e.g., religious or political ideologies), are understood and experienced not simply as resources to be used by the self (as they are for educators who are instrumental knowers), but rather as the source of internal confirmation or authority (Drago-Severson, 2004b, 2009).

As Table 3.1 indicates, a socializing knower is most concerned with abstract psychological consequences, asking, "Am I meeting your expectations? Do you still like/love and/or value me?"

When supporting the growth of socializing knowers, principals, team leaders, coaches, and supervisors can encourage and create opportunities for such knowers to voice their *own* opinions before learning about authorities' (e.g., supervisors, coaches, mentors, principals) perspectives. Often, it is helpful to invite educators with this way of knowing to share their perspectives in pairs or small groups *prior to* large-group discussions (you may recall this strategy from our discussion of LTL free-writes and pair-shares in Chapter 2). This helps them clarify their own beliefs, values, and standards rather than adopt those of others before addressing larger audiences. Table 3.3 describes several supports and challenges that will help socializing knowers to grow.

Table 3.3   Socializing Knowers: Supports and Challenges for Growth

Supports	Challenges (Growing Edge)
• Ensuring that these learners feel known and accepted • Feeling that authorities and valued others confirm, acknowledge, and accept these knowers' own beliefs • Supervisors and valued colleagues and/or loved ones show acceptance • Providing opportunities for these educators to share perspectives in pairs or smaller groups before sharing with larger groups • Ensuring and modeling that interpersonal relationships are not jeopardized when differences of opinion arise	• Providing opportunities to develop *own* beliefs, becoming less dependent on others' approval • Encouraging this knower to construct own values and standards independently, and move away from coconstructing them • Supporting the acceptance of conflicting points of view without feeling threatened • Supporting this knower in separating own feelings and responsibilities from another person's • Supporting this knower in distinguishing own perspective from need to be accepted

Source: Adapted from Drago-Severson (2009, p. 279).

The Self-Authoring Way of Knowing: "Reflective Self"

Educators who make meaning primarily with a self-authoring way of knowing have developed the capacity to take perspective on their interpersonal relationships and society's expectations. In other words, they are no longer run by or subject to these; instead, they hold them as object, meaning that they can *look at* them, *manage* them, *evaluate* them, *prioritize* them, *reflect on* them, and *regulate* them. Accordingly, we refer to self-authoring knowers as having a "reflective self." Moreover, they have the capacity to generate their own value system, standards, and personal philosophy, and they take responsibility for and ownership of their own internal authority. They can identify abstract values, principles, and longer-term purposes and are able to prioritize and integrate competing values. Self-authoring knowers can assess other people's expectations and judgments of them and compare these with their own. Demonstrating competency, achieving goals, and working to one's fullest potential are of primary concern for adults with this way of knowing.

A limitation, or area for growth (*growing edge*), for these educators is that they are made up by—or "subject to"—their own ideologies, self-system, and theories. As Kegan (1982) explained, "The self is identified with the organization it is trying to run smoothly; it *is* this organization" (p. 101). To support the growth of self-authoring knowers, one could offer ideas for consideration that do not coincide with their own and encourage them not to dismiss those ideas without consideration. Helping these adults to become less invested in their own perspectives and more open to opposing views will support their growth over time. In other words, leaders can support self-authoring knowers' growth by gently challenging them to let go of their own perspectives and embrace alternative points of view. Table 3.4 describes some of the developmental supports and challenges that will help these knowers grow.

Table 3.4   Self-Authoring Knowers: Supports and Challenges for Growth

Supports	Challenges (Growing Edge)
• Providing opportunities to learn about diverse points of view • Offering opportunities to analyze and critique ideas and explore own goals • Ensuring that learning from the process takes place and modeling this • Supporting learning about and demonstrating own competencies • Emphasize competency • Inviting demonstration of competencies and dialogue	• Challenge knower to let go of own perspective and embrace diametrically opposing alternatives • Support this knower in accepting diverse problem-solving approaches that differ from own • Challenging knower to set aside own standards for practice and open up to others' values and standards • Encouraging educator to accept and learn from diverse ways to explore problems

Source: Adapted from Drago-Severson (2009, p. 280).

The Holding Environment: The Context in and Out of Which We Grow

Constructive-developmental theory helps us understand that growth—in particular the growth and internal capacity building involved in transitioning from one way of knowing to the next—always takes place in some context, which is referred to as the "holding environment" (Kegan, 1982, p. 115). A holding environment is the context in and out of which a person grows.

Before sharing the three primary functions of a holding environment, we think it might be helpful to remind you of the explicit link between the construct of a holding environment and the learning-oriented model of school leadership that informed the LTL course design—especially because the pillar practices that comprise the model serve as holding environments for adults with different ways of knowing. In other words, holding environments can be created *within* these practices so that engaging in them can support the growth of adults with diverse ways of making sense of the world and their experiences.

D. W. Winnicott (1965) originally used the term holding environment to refer to the different kinds of care and challenges needed to support an infant's development. Winnicott maintained that these environments need to be responsive to a child's rapidly changing needs as he or she grows out of infancy. Kegan (1982) extended the application of the holding environment to a human being's *entire* life span, arguing that we need different forms of support and challenge (i.e., holding) in order to continue growing throughout our lives. In light of this, holding environments must change as we develop if they are to offer appropriate forms of support and challenge.

As teachers, principals, assistant principals, superintendents, and educational leaders of all kinds, we need to shape teams and schools as holding environments for children's growth, adults' growth, and *our own*. Doing so can enhance the ways in which we learn and work together and improve the design and implementation of professional learning opportunities. More specifically, holding environments can consist of a relationship with one person, a series of relationships, any one of the pillar practices, or a complex organization like a school.

In shaping a holding environment that will support adults with different ways of knowing, there are two fundamental ideas to consider. The first is that effective holding environments need to offer a healthy balance of both *high support and high challenge*. The important point here is that in order to support growth we need *both support and challenge*. The second big idea concerns something we mentioned before introducing the different ways of knowing—the importance of goodness of fit. We mention it here for a different reason, though. It is crucial to consider the goodness of fit, or developmental match, between the holding environment and an educator's way of knowing. For example, if educators participating in leadership or teaching teams are expected to take a stand for their beliefs or to exercise authority, the socializing knowers among them will need to be gently supported and challenged to develop these capacities since socializing knowers generally look externally (e.g., to a supervisor, authority) for approval.

Similarly, good or effective holding environments serve three functions (Kegan, 1982). First, and as with any effective teaching and learning endeavor, a good holding environment needs to "hold well" by meeting an individual where he or she is in terms of how *he or she is currently making meaning of experience*. This means it must recognize, honor, and confirm who the person is, without an urgent need to push for or demand change. Second, and only when the person is ready, good holding environments "let go" by offering developmentally appropriate challenges that help the person grow toward a new way of knowing. Last, a holding environment needs to "stick around" to provide continuity, availability, and stability as a person is demonstrating newly developed internal capacities during the growth process.

The sticking-around function of a holding environment is sometimes challenging to offer for a variety of reasons, one of them being the prevalence of shorter-term professional learning initiatives. However, the pillar practices can serve as holding environments that fulfill all three functions to help a person move from one place to the next on the developmental continuum. We know that the process of growth is not often comfortable or easy. Instead, it is frequently painful as we let go of what we held tightly to—our old self—and strive to rebalance who we are growing to become.

Why Ways of Knowing and Holding Environments Matter

As we emphasized earlier, understanding Kegan's constructive-developmental theory and the ways of knowing, as well as the importance of shaping holding environments for growth, is important when conceptualizing the developmental basis of the learning-oriented leadership model and the pillar practices, which we introduced in Chapter 2 and will say a little more about here. Before we do, though, we want to offer a few points for your consideration.

First, the pillar practices, informed by constructive-developmental theory, incorporate developmental supports and challenges in order to facilitate transformational learning or growth. Second, all that we have discussed thus far helps us understand the value of adopting a developmental stance—and a developmental model—when considering how to support our own and other people's growth. Third, developmental mindfulness also helps us to move away from labeling adults on the basis of behaviors alone (Drago-Severson, 2004b, 2009; Levine, 1989). It offers a lens through which we can better and more deeply understand adults' attitudes, behaviors, and expectations and better understand how to support growth for individuals with different ways of knowing.

For example, it can help us to remember that adults with different preferences, needs, and developmental orientations require *different* forms of support and challenge to participate effectively in practices intended to support professional and personal growth. Providing developmentally oriented support means recognizing, acknowledging, and affirming a person and how he or she makes sense of experiences. Providing developmentally oriented challenges, as we mentioned earlier, means posing helpful questions and/or offering alternative perspectives to gently push the edges of a person's thinking or feeling. We refer to this as "standing at the edges" of someone's thinking or meaning making (Drago-Severson, 2009).

Consider, for example, how educators with different developmental orientations make sense of what constitutes a good leader and the kinds of expectations these adults have for leaders. As Table 3.5 shows, educators with different ways of knowing conceptualize and have different expectations for their leaders.

Table 3.5   Educators' Expectations of Good Leaders

Way of Knowing	Expectations of Good Leaders
Instrumental knowers	For educators who make meaning in this way, good leaders are those who show them how to learn and who offer explicit directions as to how to complete work and/or tasks. Effective leaders *give* instrumental knowers their knowledge and the rules they need to follow to do their work the *right* way so that they can be rewarded. These educators know that they have performed well because they can do something (demonstrate a behavior) and because they achieve intended results.
Socializing knowers	For these educators, good leaders are those who care about them as human beings (not just as workers). Effective leaders are patient and explain things to help them understand. Good leaders really listen and offer support—*they know* what is good for these educators to know and *tell* them what they *should* know. Socializing knowers describe "good" and effective leaders as kind, patient, and encouraging. Socializing knowers can feel, internally, when they have learned something, and they value and appreciate the leader's acknowledgment of that.
Self-authoring knowers	For these educators, effective leaders are one source of knowledge, and they see *themselves* and peers as equally valid sources. Self-authoring knowers have the capacity to offer feedback to leaders to help them improve their leadership practices—and they expect that leaders will listen to them. Good leaders help self-authoring knowers meet their own internally generated goals. These educators know when they have demonstrated proficiency—they assess this according to their own internal benchmarks. When they have learned/mastered something or some skill set, they can then think of and create *on their own* different ways to teach what they know and understand to support others.

This variety of developmentally different expectations has important implications for leadership because, as we explained in Chapter 2, research has shown that developmental diversity will exist in any school, team, leadership cabinet, group, or system.

Revisiting the Pillar Practices: Developmental Supports and Challenges

The ways in which we engage in the pillar practices—or any form of learning or collaborative work—varies according to *how* we make sense of our experiences. With appropriate supports and challenges, however, we can grow and participate in these processes, professional development experiences, teams, PLCs, and leadership preparation programs more effectively.

Table 3.6 suggests supports and challenges that can facilitate capacity building for adults with each of the most common ways of knowing as they engage in the pillar practices. As you may notice, many of the strategies described below align with specific practices from the LTL course design presented in Chapter 2 (e.g., free writing, small-group discussion, norm setting, the use of protocols). In the LTL course, we *intentionally* implemented, modeled, and *made transparent* these supports and challenges (and their developmental underpinnings) so LTL learners would be both supported and appropriately challenged—and so they would be better prepared to support growth and learning in their own contexts as leaders. Please note that

Table 3.6 Engaging in Pillar Practices: Supports and Challenges for Growth

Pillar Practice	For Instrumental Knowers	For Socializing Knowers	For Self-Authoring Knowers
Teaming	*Supports:* Provide clear conversational guidelines, concrete goals, step-by-step procedures and directions, and clear due dates. *Challenges:* Gradually introduce tasks requiring abstract thinking; encourage movement beyond "right" answers.	*Supports:* Demonstrate acceptance of individuals; model disagreement without threatening interpersonal relationships. *Challenges:* Encourage perspective broadening and internal value generation through supportive dialogue.	*Supports:* Provide opportunities for promoting, analyzing and critiquing one's own goals, theories, and ideas. *Challenges:* Encourage acceptance and consideration of conflicting or discordant ideas and perspectives, especially those that are diametrically opposed to one's own.

Pillar Practice	For Instrumental Knowers	For Socializing Knowers	For Self-Authoring Knowers
Providing leadership roles	*Supports:* Offer concrete goals signaling success; model sharing rules, purposes, and goals with others. Provide models of best practice. *Challenges:* Encourage consideration of multiple perspectives, as well as the testing/analysis of alternative solutions and/or pathways.	*Supports:* Confirm feelings of value and confidence; encourage sharing one's voice and recognize person's achievements and risk taking. *Challenges:* Encourage individual generation (rather than coconstruction) of values, standards, and goals. Safely introduce and scaffold conflict.	*Supports:* Provide opportunities to demonstrate competencies, critique proposed ideas, and initiatives and contribute to developing vision. *Challenges:* Gently push these adults to consider alternatives, perspectives, and problem-solving approaches not in direct alignment with their own.
Collaborative inquiry	*Supports:* Facilitate the sharing of concrete examples of practice; provide specific advice, skills, directions, and information; set definitive outcomes. *Challenges:* Promote dialogue and discussion of multiple perspectives; Push for transferability of concepts and abstract thinking.	*Supports:* Create safe and accepting group norms that allow for difference and disagreement; provide opportunities to share perspectives in pairs or triads before sharing with larger groups of colleagues or authorities/supervisors. *Challenges:* Encourage the toleration of conflict, model engaging in and with it, and encourage the development of individual beliefs.	*Supports:* Create structures for demonstrating competencies and free dialogue; encourage self-reflection and open sharing of opinions. *Challenges:* Emphasize the importance of tolerance and openness during debate; encourage sincere consideration of opposing viewpoints and opposing perspectives.
Mentoring	*Supports:* Name purposes and objectives for mentoring relationship; offer expertise and advise; share reasoning behind perspectives. *Challenges:* Encourage movement beyond "correct" solutions; facilitate abstract discussion and consideration of others' needs/perspectives.	*Supports:* Explicitly acknowledge and confirm others' beliefs and perspectives; suggest "best" solutions to complex problems and challenges. *Challenges:* Encourage mentee to recognize and establish own values and standards and to tolerate conflict without feeling threatened.	*Supports:* Allow mentee to demonstrate own competencies, critique own work, and move forward with self-determined goals. *Challenges:* Engage in dialogue and offer additional goals, viewpoints, and problem-solving alternatives for contemplation.

Source: Adapted from Drago-Severson (2009) and Drago-Severson & Blum-DeStefano (2011).

by implementing and adapting suggestions from across the ways of knowing below, you too can support the learning and growth of diverse individuals *simultaneously* by employing the pillar practices.

Chapter Summary

In this chapter, we described Robert Kegan's constructive-developmental theory (1982, 1994, 2000) since it informed course design and the learning-oriented model of school leadership—composed of four pillar practices—which were employed in LTL to support adult growth and learning. This theory also informs professional development initiatives that we have facilitated and currently facilitate in our work with educators and leaders in schools, teams, districts, and leadership preparation programs.

More specifically, we emphasized the important distinction between informational and transformational learning and described the foundational principles of Kegan's theory (1982, 1994, 2000)—including the three ways of knowing most common in adulthood (the instrumental, socializing, and self-authoring), and the important role of holding environments for supporting growth. We shared the three main functions holding environments serve and illuminated how the pillar practices *are* developmental holding environments that you can employ in your practice to support capacity building in others and yourself. We also offered specific strategies for supporting and challenging adults with different ways of knowing *simultaneously* by employing the pillar practices.

In the next chapter we explore the changes in thinking and understanding that LTL leaders attributed to their learning and experiences in the course. We hope you find this useful as well as you work nobly and courageously to support adult learning and growth in your own unique contexts.

Reflective Questions

We offer the following questions as opportunities to reflect on and consider ways you might apply learnings from this chapter to enhance the kinds of opportunities you offer to adults in your care—and to yourself—to support growth and capacity building. Please take a moment to reflect on these questions. You might want to respond to them privately first and then engage in collegial inquiry with a partner or group of colleagues.

1. How would you describe professional development in your school, grade level, team, district, and/or university? What do you think is working well in terms of supporting adults' capacity building? What do you feel is not working as well as it could? If there were one thing you could change about professional development in your team, school, district, or university, what would that be? Why? How do you think altering it would help with supporting other adults' growth and/or your own?

2. How do you create holding environments for supporting other adults' growth in your practice? How do you think they are working? What would you like to improve? What are two insights you've gained from reading this chapter that you could employ to make contexts for growth even more effective?

3. How do you currently offer different kinds of supports and challenges to adults who have different needs, preferences, and experiences? What would you like to improve? What are two insights you've gained from reading this chapter that you could employ to differentiate supports and challenges for adults in your care?

4. Each of us has a dominant way of knowing. Which way of knowing do you think best describes how you make sense of the world? What do you see as your growing edge? What are two ways you can work to support and challenge your own development? You might want to revisit Table 3.1.

5. What are three big takeaways that you've gained from reading this chapter? How would you like to use them to enhance your practice?

PART II

Lessons and Examples From Leaders in the Field

4

Learning About Leadership for Adult Development

LTL Ideas and Practices That Made a Difference for Leaders

Introduction and Overview

> *With our thoughts we make the world.*
>
> —The Buddha

We begin this chapter with an inspiring quote from the Buddha that illuminates the power of *thinking*—in terms of how it guides our behavior as we work to help support growth and build capacity in adults. Indeed, the promise and power of thought as a call to action has long been recognized by philosophers, researchers, and educators (Argyris, 1982; Kegan, 2000; Gardner, 2006). In other words, we know that it is only by changing our minds as well as our hearts that we can truly reshape our behaviors to address the many complex adaptive challenges facing the world—and educators of all kinds—today

(Drago-Severson, 2009, 2012; Heifetz, 1994; Wagner et al., 2006). In light of this, in this chapter, we discuss educational leaders' sharings about how their learnings and experiences in the Leadership for Transformational Learning course (LTL)—which, as we discussed in Chapter 2, is representative of a larger, developmental approach to leadership development—informed their *thinking about and understanding of leadership* during, immediately after, and years after successfully completing the course. While the leaders we learned from in this study were enrolled in LTL as graduate students in 2003, 2004, and 2005, we offer here their descriptions of the course ideas and practices that were most meaningful to them—as they related in surveys and interviews at the time of the course *and* years after the course—in order to highlight how those ideas and practices can be applied in broader contexts. We also offer important takeaways for practice and application.

To help illuminate these leaders' new understandings of leadership after the course *and in actual practice*—and the ideas and practices in LTL that, together, helped bring them about—we organize this chapter into four main sections.

First, we address leaders' descriptions of the changes in their thinking about leadership and supporting adult development, both immediately following the course and years afterward, including the importance of their new ideas about how to help adults grow. For example, many leaders in this study—who went on to serve as principals, assistant principals, teacher leaders, educational consultants, and university faculty—shared the importance of understanding, as we often do intuitively for children and adolescents, that adults make sense of the world in very different ways. The fact that we are all united by a common human need to learn and grow was a key learning, and one that, as they explained, had a powerful and lasting influence on their leadership work.

In the second section, we highlight key LTL *learnings and ideas* that these leaders reported as helpful to their leadership development and to their understandings of how to support the growth and learning of adults. In particular, we focus on their descriptions of how learning about constructive-developmental theory (Kegan, 1982, 1994, 2000)—which we discussed in Chapter 3—was a powerful influence in terms of helping them understand and support adults with different ways of knowing. We also present their sharings about the related concept of creating holding environments (Drago-Severson, 2004, 2009, 2012; Kegan, 1982) as an important takeaway for their own practice in terms of how they learned to care for and support adult growth in their work contexts. We conclude this section by offering an overview of additional concepts and ideas that were introduced in LTL and that a number of leaders continued to find relevant and important, years after completing the course.

In the third section, we raise up educational leaders' descriptions of *practices* employed in the context of LTL that made a difference for their thinking about and understandings of leadership for supporting adult development. We focus first on the practice of convening (Drago-Severson, 2009), a carefully crafted opportunity to engage deeply in teaming and employ collegial inquiry around personal cases, which we described in detail in Chapter 2. In this section, we also share leaders' recollections of the power of experiencing instructor modeling of key practices while leaders were in the process of learning about them. For many of these leaders, recognizing and experiencing this **developmental intentionality** (Drago-Severson, 2009, 2012) helped them learn to demonstrate the power of these ideas for actual leadership work and helped them feel the very real potentiality of bridging theory and practice. We conclude this section by offering an overview of related course practices that made a lasting impact.

Finally, in the fourth section, we offer key takeaways and an opportunity for you to apply these ideas to your own practice. Here, we aim to highlight what these learnings might mean for you, as an educational leader in a school, district, leadership preparation program, or educational practice of any kind, and also how they might be of future help and use.

Chapter Context

> *[I]t's easier to talk about changing minds in general than to effect enduring changes in any particular mind.*
>
> —Howard Gardner (2006, p. 62)

> *[LTL] helped me to see the world through a very different lens. . . . It was a paradigm shift in the way I saw myself and others, and I became a much more grounded, diplomatic, objective communicator.*
>
> —Brooke, School Principal,
> Former University Professor

As Harvard professor and psychologist Howard Gardner (2006) explained in the above passage, it is not an easy task to change our minds, and many factors help or hinder our ability to do so. He also wisely reminds us that enduring change may be the most elusive and important of all.

Nevertheless, when, in 2009, we spoke with leaders who had successfully completed LTL four, five, or six years earlier, we learned that nearly all of these LTL graduates now serving as educational leaders (19/20) still attributed important changes in their thinking about leadership in support of adult growth and learning to their experience in the course. In fact, more than half (13/20) described deep, fundamental changes in their understanding of what it means to effectively lead. In terms of both duration and scope, then, the LTL experience seemed to have made a dramatic difference.

Just as Brooke, a school principal and former university professor, shared in the quote above, LTL catalyzed an important "paradigm shift" in her thinking about herself—both as a leader and in terms of how she cares for and interacts with others. In addition, and importantly, many course graduates explained how LTL helped transform their approaches to leadership.

Indeed, these leaders shared that LTL course ideas—in combination with the developmental design of the class (i.e., carefully attending to students' ways of knowing in structure, design, and implementation)—supported transformational thinking about how they conceived the very nature of leadership, their roles as leaders supporting adult development, and the urgency of facilitating adults' real growth in schools, school systems, and classrooms. This chapter helps explain, from these leaders' perspectives and experiences, why a developmental approach to supporting their learning and leading was so meaningful for them and how it altered the ways in which they thought about leadership in support of helping other adults grow.

New Understandings of Learning-Oriented Leadership and Supporting Adult Development

I'm confident that [LTL] . . . was the first time I thought about the fact that if you were going to increase the expectations on adults, they would need help to learn these new things. And that they could. [S]o it was pretty revolutionary for me.

—Melanie, Currently Pursuing Doctorate in
Education Leadership, Former Middle School
Principal and Instructional Leader

As Melanie, like many leaders, shared above, LTL helped highlight the important idea that adults are *learners*. Reconceptualizing adults in this way, and understanding that they both *can and want* to learn, helped Melanie and others recognize the need to offer different kinds of supports to help adults meet new expectations, build capacity—and grow.

While this key principle remained at the forefront for leaders during their semester-long experiences in LTL in 2003, 2004, and 2005, respectively, these educational leaders also reported enduring shifts in their understandings about how to support adult development. Before describing how they went on to use LTL ideas in their actual practice, however, we first want to share a little more about what we learned from these leaders early on—through surveys and interviews conducted before, during, and soon after the class. For instance, just after successfully completing LTL years ago, the leaders described a number of key insights (Drago-Severson, Asghar, Blum-DeStefano, & Roloff Welch, 2011), including developing

- deeper understandings of the importance of recognizing that adults make meaning in qualitatively different developmental ways,
- realizations that adults need different kinds of supports and challenges to learn, grow, and exercise new competencies, and
- understandings of concrete and practical applications for using developmental theories to enhance their leadership.

As we explain next, these ideas continued to grow and inform these leaders' caring efforts to support other adults' development in their unique contexts, years after the end of the course.

Leaders' Thinking and Hopes Prior to Enrolling in LTL: Meeting Students Where They Were

As we describe in greater detail in the Research Appendix, before each offering of LTL, we administered a pre-course survey so that we could understand leaders' incoming hopes, expectations, and understandings of supporting adult development. In these surveys, many of the educational leaders—all of whom were graduate students at the time—expressed a belief in the power of adult learning for improving schools and education but placed great emphasis on encouraging *self-directed* learning and other adults' ability to address and solve problems *independently*. Adults, they explained, needed to take responsibility for their *own* learning and professional improvement. However, as we will describe, these leaders were able to broaden and deepen their understandings of what it means to support adult learning and growth. For instance, they came to see—through learning about and experiencing developmental principles and practices in LTL—that adults orient *differently* to self-direction and need different kinds of supports and challenges to grow, learn, and thrive.

An Incoming Focus on Self-Direction

Like many other aspiring and practicing leaders before the course, Svetlana, who planned to become a university professor in a developing country, came to LTL with a strong interest in supporting adults through her work. In her pre-course (i.e., pre-LTL) survey, for instance, she explained that she cared deeply about supporting teachers and parents of children—seeing the two as inextricably linked—and also indicated that she thought supporting adults meant assisting them "to gradually become *able to learn on their own and in groups . . .* so that they can continuously improve their practice [emphasis hers]." Likewise, Jane, who at the time of LTL served as a middle school teacher and department head and who aspired to lead districtwide professional development, felt a strong "belief in responsibility" in terms of encouraging adults to initiate and monitor their *own* learning. For many of these leaders, increasing adults' "intrinsic motivation" was a key part of supporting adult development, and this foundational idea grew more complex and sophisticated as they learned in LTL what it means to support adults at different developmental places. In other words, as we describe below, these leaders grew to understand through the course that leadership in support of adult development means *more* than challenging and empowering colleagues to stand and think on their own. Rather, as they explained *after* successfully completing LTL, effective leadership involves carefully tailoring developmental supports and challenges to best help adults meet the many complex demands and challenges they face as educators today.

Margaret, for instance, who served as a high school language teacher and adult educator before taking LTL, characteristically shared the following important insight just after the course. As she explained,

> Now I get that we are all in one stage [of development] or another, that although personality is important, I can't dismiss people as "not getting it." Now [after LTL], I can be more compassionate with myself and others as being in a stage that will morph as we are supported and challenged [to grow throughout our lives].

Below, we highlight a few of the key insights these leaders shared just after the course experience, including

- the importance of understanding adults as learners, rather than "finished products,"
- the promise of balancing both supports and challenges when working to help adults grow, and
- the power of differentiating supports and challenges so that adults with different ways of knowing can grow and learn together.

Leaders' Insights Just After LTL: Learning and Growing Together

As just described, in post-class surveys and interviews conducted soon after leaders successfully completed LTL—meaning after grades were submitted for the course—these leaders explained that their new learnings about developmental diversity helped them understand the importance of supporting and challenging adults in different ways to build both individual and organizational capacity. After all, they explained, adults can continue developing just like youth with the proper care and support. As Lana, a high school teacher who created a nonprofit organization, representatively described,

> When you think of schools, you think of children's learning, but you never think of adult learning. But adults are learners. And that's something that I realized in this course, that it's important to . . . support and challenge the students as well as the adults.

Moreover, immediately after the course, LTL graduates emphasized the importance of *balancing* supports and challenges across a spectrum of learners. While some students in the graduate-level class initially prioritized high support *or* high challenge in their ideas about leading adult learning, most now realized that support and challenge *together* most effectively move individuals and groups forward. As Jane related, attending to both through differentiation can help:

> In this class, I learned a lot about how to support the needs of different [developmental] levels and that [adults are] just like kids. I think a lot about my own teaching in high school. Not all kids learn alike, and it is interesting to see that adults are the same way—that all adults learn differently. But, by creating a variety of opportunities for learners, then everyone should be able to find appropriate challenges and supports.

Ultimately, after completing the graduate course experience, the leaders in this study shared that they felt better equipped to handle and more excited about opportunities to lead adults' personal and professional learning and development. For instance, being able to "witness," as Lana described, adult developmental theories in action really helped drive home and spark her learning. Similarly, Matt, an elementary school teacher at the time of the course, felt that experiencing firsthand the "possibilities" of a developmentalized learning environment gave him, like many LTL graduates, a "greater toolkit of ideas" for implementing learning-oriented leadership in his future leadership work.

As we describe in the remainder of this chapter, these initial developmental insights carried over and grew to inform leaders' understandings of supporting adult development *years later*, as they took up their own leadership positions in schools and other organizations.

Leaders' Reflections Years After Completing the Course: New Understandings of Supporting Adult Development

I have to say I carried that class with me all the time and . . . I feel like every day there's something that speaks to me, that brings me back to something that we either discussed or practiced [or] read about. . . . I feel like it's just . . . so relevant.

—Tara, Middle School Assistant Principal

While LTL graduates reported important insights and learnings—and also great enthusiasm for their new ideas—immediately after the course, those we learned from four, five, and even six years later, who went on to become educational leaders in various contexts, affirmed the lasting influence of what they learned in LTL on their conceptions of leadership in support of adult development. They shared, for example, that they

- internalized developmental ideas and principles,
- found LTL both professionally and personally meaningful,
- recognized the importance of growing oneself to better support others, and
- understood the power of including, respecting, and celebrating others in their leadership.

Indeed, of the twenty leaders we interviewed years after the course—including principals, assistant principals, teacher leaders, educational consultants, university professors, and a district leader—nineteen described LTL as having a continued and meaningful influence on their thinking about and understandings of leadership. The single participant not represented in this count explained that, while she was sure that she used ideas consistent with LTL in her current leadership work as an assistant high school principal, it was "very hard to pinpoint" specific attribution, given the length of time that had passed since the conclusion of the graduate class.

"It Becomes Part of You": Internalizing Developmental Ideas

Describing the power of her LTL experience and related learnings, Marisa, an adult educator and therapist in South America, explained, "once you learn it [the promise of developmental mindfulness], it becomes part of you. I think it's something like a seed that, once it's put inside of you, it keeps growing forever." This type of internalization, especially around the promise and hopefulness of understanding adults—like all people—as learning, growing beings, resulted in what thirteen of the twenty leaders described as *fundamental reimaginings* of what it means to effectively lead and support both one's own and others' growth.

Both personally and professionally, the LTL experience helped participants reframe their thinking about their own and other adults' lives. It challenged them, for instance, to truly understand that, in the most hopeful and positive sense, who we are today isn't necessarily who we have to be tomorrow. All of us, after all, have the potential to grow toward our biggest, best selves—and this growth orientation held important leadership implications for these educators and leaders.

Sharing, in a very powerful example, how LTL "really helped change [her] world," Brooke, a school principal who was serving as a university professor at the time of our study, reflected:

> [A]t the time [of the course], in my personal life, I was at a very critical juncture in terms of being a gay woman, and that was my biggest fear holding me back from . . . wanting to be a head of school, because I was so scared about what people thought of me. And so [the course] really helped me, learning the theory and learning what kind of knower that I am. I said I don't want to . . . be stuck in this place that I'm in worrying—and the only part I worried about [was] what they thought of my sexuality. So it really helped me get past that. I came out to more people that year than I can even

really recall. And . . . every job interview I went to . . . I was very open and honest and I wanted to make sure that they didn't hire me under any false pretenses.

Just as LTL helped Brooke to grow herself and gain the objectivity she needed to confront her fears about sharing her sexuality, her personal journey made possible her more effective leadership in service to others as well.

Marisa, too, noted this connection between growing oneself and helping others. As she explained,

[T]he class really helped me to not only become aware myself of this situation, this personal growth through experiences, and different ways of knowing, but also to help others to become aware of that too in their own personal life.

Describing her work as an adult educator and therapist in South America, she went on to express her now innate enthusiasm for developmental ideas and practices, given the profound influence of her LTL experience:

I feel like I want to implement these things [developmental practices], and I notice that they come out naturally because they're kind of embedded in me right now. Maybe not under the title of holding environment [or] reflection, but in my behavior, it's like I was able to incorporate some of that [the LTL experience]—I hope most of it—within myself.

For Marisa, like many of these leaders, LTL provided a framework for thinking about and seeing oneself and others in new ways. Moreover, now "naturally embedded" in their worldviews, these leaders' developmental understandings drew strength from their convictions "within," deepening their commitment to LTL-inspired ideas and practices.

Leadership With and for Others

Leaders also shared with us years after LTL that they continue to value collaboration as a key imperative for and support of effective leadership. For example, Brenda, a graduate student in education leadership who had served as a language teacher and academic dean since completing LTL, reflected on the lasting influence of the course, including her enduring belief in the beauty of leadership with and for others:

[LTL] shaped my leadership style in that I recognized that you needed to create a shared vision, that you had to be collaborative. . . . You need to provide the support, but then things need to grow organically in a way. . . . [Y]ou can't just come in top-down and tell people what to do. If they're sharing in the practice and you meet them where they are, then they're going to take off on their own and do things that are far beyond what [others are trying to make them do].

As many of these educational leaders shared with us, learning-oriented leadership cannot be realized alone. We need others to make the changes we wish to see in ourselves and our workplaces, for our students and for our world, and it is only by sharing ideas—and our best and truest selves—that we can move forward in this important work together.

As Matt, who, after LTL, went on to serve as the head of a lower school, explained,

[I]t is a really deep belief of mine that everybody is really valuable in some way and has something that they can really offer us that, were they not with us, we would be different. [Something that] we could only get from that person.

As an important complement to this belief, Matt also felt deeply the importance of earnestly sharing his own knowledge and expertise as a leader, and he described this reciprocity as follows:

[T]here are a lot of people that weren't lucky enough to go through [LTL], and so as someone who was, who was able to benefit from that learning, then I have a real responsibility to share that learning with other people.

New Understandings of Supporting Adult Development: Summary

Ultimately, nearly all (19/20) of these educational leaders attributed significant shifts in their thinking about and understandings of educational leadership and supporting adult development to their learning and experiences in LTL, years after course completion. While the leaders described many insights, including the internalization of developmental ideas and practices, the importance of growing oneself to help others, and the very real value of honoring and respecting individuals as key to systemwide capacity building, Jane perhaps summed up the hopefulness at the heart of this study:

> [T]his stuff is so clear in my head is because I'm really using it. . . . [I]t was one of those courses that I really had no idea [of] the impact that it would have on me, and just how I think about adult learning. I mean it was really tremendous.

As with all kinds of learning, we remember best what we use most often—and for these leaders, developmental mindfulness and intentionality have proven effective and key parts of their leadership lives and work in support of adult development.

Helpful and Meaningful Course Learnings

In the sections below, we share educational leaders' reflections on key course learnings that proved most helpful and important to their personal understandings of leadership in support of adult development. First, and in particular, we focus on leaders' lasting takeaways regarding Kegan's (1982, 1994, 2000) constructive-developmental theory, as well as the related concept of crafting and sustaining holding environments to support the learning and growth of both children and adults. Next, we present a concise overview of additional course-covered concepts that a number of leaders mentioned as helpful, including espoused theories and theories-in-use (Argyris & Schön, 1974), reframing resistance by understanding the "language of complaint" as an indication of care (Kegan & Lahey, 2001), the important difference between technical and adaptive challenges in education (Heifetz, 1994; Wagner et al., 2006), and the power of avoiding assumptions by grounding thought and action in what can actually be seen and observed (Argyris, 1982; Senge, Kleiner, Roberts, Ross, & Smith, 1994). While not mentioned as frequently as constructive-developmental theory or holding environments, these ideas continue to inform and inspire leaders' important work supporting adult development.

As all of the leaders featured below have shared, these concepts—together—have continued to inform their leadership thinking and practice, even years after the course, and they have played an enduring role in their understandings of the importance of honoring and attending to developmental diversity. We offer leaders' powerful examples here to illustrate some of the ways these ideas can support and inform leadership development and practice in real-life leadership contexts.

Constructive-Developmental Theory: The Promise of Experiencing This Theory in Action

> *Before this class [LTL], any thinking I had about adult learning was derived from my own experience—mostly traditional practices, workshops, seminars, et cetera—and generally remained nameless. I didn't really know what it meant when people were* learning/transforming *[her emphasis]. Now I understand, to some extent, the kind of change in thinking that can/does happen.*

> —Amy, Elementary School Teacher,
> Post-course Reflection

Just as Amy, immediately after the course, described the power of finding words and ideas in which to ground her thinking about and understanding of learning and growth in adulthood, the educational leaders we learned from years later shared similar reflections about the value of their LTL learnings and experience. In particular, almost all (17/20) shared that learning about constructive-developmental theory helped establish a common language for talking and thinking about transformation, growth, and capacity-building that remained powerful and with them years later—and also provided a useful lens for looking at both themselves and others.

Recognizing, for instance, that the developmental model applied to adults as well as children and adolescents was an important and lasting takeaway for the leaders. As Jane, now an educational consultant, described, the principle that "all kids can learn" was "really clear" to her as a teacher, "and that felt really good." Yet, as she took on more leadership roles in her school, this "developmental model" began to have new implications for her work with adults:

> And then I started to be a department head, and it started to occur to me as you run into the teachers who are resisters. . . . It really started to make me wonder if that [developmental] model was applicable to an adult relationship as well. In other words, can we think of adults as [being] on this developmental learning continuum in the same way that I did kids? . . . And so the biggest overarching, general lesson that I took away from [LTL] was that that is indeed the case.

Moreover, *experiencing* the developmental intentionality of the course design helped drive home both the promise and power of meeting adults where they are in a developmental sense, and it brought the theory to life in memorable and meaningful ways. As Lauren, researcher in cognitive science and former teacher, explained, "the activities that we did [in LTL] have just led to, in an everyday kind of way, . . . greater acceptance of where people are [developmentally]." More specifically, learning about constructive-developmental theory in LTL helped these leaders

- find a language for thinking and talking about developmental diversity,
- understand that, in a developmental sense, adults make meaning of the world in very different ways,
- discover that resistance may be developmental in nature, and
- feel the power of attending to ways of knowing by experiencing teaching informed by developmental principles.

Below, we discuss these themes in greater detail, drawing from leaders' reflections and sharings.

Understanding and Embracing Developmental Diversity in Leadership

Years later, as was the case soon after the course, understanding adults as growing and active meaning-makers—with qualitatively different orientations to learning, living, teaching, and leading—has remained central to the graduates' leadership philosophies and thinking. Sarah, for example, who went on to lead as an assistant professor at a graduate school of education, explained that her "big takeaway" was "really understanding that people are in different places in how they understand the world around them."

Palia, too, who currently serves as a high school assistant principal and professional learning leader, reflected that she now understood the developmental diversity inherent in most any group or team as a gift to be nurtured. "Some people," she explained, "are really good at very different kinds of things, and we want to be able to not just celebrate that, but really, really develop that."

This fundamental reframing of what it means to lead, serve, and support adults continued to inform the thinking and work of LTL graduates in meaningful ways, and it was one of the most frequently offered (17/20) examples of the power of the course experience. Lucy, for instance, who now works abroad as a Foreign Service officer, described the practical value of this principle in her varied and expansive work supporting adults:

It was really helpful for me to keep in mind the ways that—since it was adults I was working with [in sensitive immigration experiences and professional conversations]—the ways that adults were making meaning out of the ways that we were presenting information. So that has remained very important and at the forefront.

Likewise, in her work as dean and teacher in schools, Brenda continued to value "the idea that teachers are all at different stages . . . and that you can't just 'teach' teachers." Rather, she explained, "You need to meet teachers where they are and have a framework for understanding . . . that." Indeed, by naming, explaining, and valuing developmental diversity, constructive-developmental theory helped give leaders a language for thinking about and understanding adults' qualitatively different ways of knowing—and, accordingly, helped them to see the promise in leadership that embraced and supported adults of all kinds.

Reframing Resistance

In addition to the important insights above, leaders shared that constructive-developmental theory helped them better understand—and therefore manage—the resistance they sometimes encountered in their schools and organizations. Jane, for instance, realized during the class that many of the teachers she experienced as "resisters" as a science department chair might actually have needed different supports and challenges in order to succeed and meet the new expectations she was laying out for them.

Brenda, too, took to her leadership work in schools after LTL an understanding that "difficult teachers aren't necessarily difficult." Resistance, she explained, may in fact have developmental roots, and teachers' lack of buy-in into new initiatives and ideas may stem from a misalignment between expectations and capacities. Sometimes, Brenda noted, "they're [the teachers] not responding well to whatever tasks you're putting in front of them, or whatever mode you're using to help [them] improve," so you need to try something different rather than blame them for mistakes. For Brenda, like many of the leaders in our study, the constructive-developmental framework helped her "see where teachers are" in terms of their ways of knowing, and accordingly, lead more effectively with and for *all* members of her school—children and adults alike.

As Jane similarly shared, understanding the work in this way "just gives you some perspective." It makes resistance, she explained, "less 'ouchy' and personal," and it allows you to reach out to people in ways they really appreciate.

Experiencing the Power of Learning-Oriented Leadership

For many of the leaders, too, LTL provided a practical, on-the-ground demonstration of the power of attending to developmental diversity, because—as we described in Chapters 2 and 3—the course structures and instruction were informed by constructive-developmental theory. By caring for ways of knowing openly and tangibly, LTL helped leaders *feel as well as learn* the promise of leading with developmental mindfulness. Along these lines, Brooke, now a school principal, explained how the class helped bring theoretical ideas to life: "I got it [the theory] on a very intellectual, philosophical level, but . . . what [LTL] did was ground it in reality and practice," making it very "adjustable and real." While the merging of theory and practice was an important theme for many of these leaders, we offer more of their sharings about this takeaway in the next main section of this chapter.

Ultimately, nearly all of the leaders we learned from years after the course (17/20) described constructive-developmental theory as a powerful learning that helped shape their understandings of and approaches to leadership. By (a) providing a language for thinking and talking about the different ways adults make sense of the world, (b) illuminating the promise of understanding adults as learning, growing beings, (c) introducing the possibility that colleagues' resistance can have developmental roots, and (d) demonstrating the power of developmental theory through course pedagogy and structures, LTL helped foreground the great potential of a developmental perspective, and it made a lasting contribution to leaders' thinking and future work.

Holding Environments: A Lasting Hope for Practice

Related to the leaders' evolving understandings of constructive-developmental theory and the importance of attending to adults' developmental ways of knowing, more than half of these educational leaders (13/20) described both the experience and the concept of a holding environment as a powerful influence on their approaches to leading in their unique contexts. As described in Chapter 2, in ways both large and small, LTL provided examples of intentionally crafted holding environments—in whole-group, small-group, and pair-share interactions—as well as student-student, student-instructor, and instructor-instructor exchanges. Experiencing this feeling of being "well held" (Drago-Severson, 2012) in diverse ways—both individually and in combination—made a lasting impact on LTL graduates, and it inspired many of them to prioritize growth-enhancing holding environments in their leadership work years after the course. For example, leaders described the importance of

- establishing safe, trusting, and respectful learning environments with and for others;
- respecting adults' individual expertise and experience;
- balancing supports and challenges to meet people where they are in a developmental sense; and
- attending to developmental diversity with purpose and intentionality.

The Importance of Safe and Respectful Environments

Elizabeth, for instance, now a high school math teacher and department head, explained that "creating an atmosphere where people feel safe" is now a priority for her in her work with teachers. Thinking back to LTL, Dana, currently a high school English teacher, department chair, and professional development leader, similarly appreciated that she and her classmates "were given a very comfortable and safe learning environment" in LTL, as this was "really important." Looking ahead, Dana likewise reflected that the support and respect she felt in the course "as an adult" who "brought [expertise] to the table" was something she aspired to replicate in her own leadership. She described how she remained cognizant of not "forcing" ideas on others when working with the teachers at her school:

> I think one of the things that I appreciated in the course that I try also to carry out as a leader is [that] I never felt like ideas were forced upon me . . . and I feel like that's really important when working with adults. I think it's important to treat [teachers as adults] . . . and respect them and the knowledge that they bring and to . . . help them develop. So those are the things that I really appreciated, and those are things I hope that I'm bringing into my style of leadership at our school.

Support and Challenge as Developmental Support

For other leaders in the study, a resonant takeaway was the need to balance both supports and challenges in effective holding environments. As Jenai, an educational consultant who has also served as a school administrator, explained,

> The other big concept [from LTL] that I always talk about [is that] . . . adult learning happens at the intersection between challenge and support. And I *always* [emphasis hers] think about that in all of my program designs, and in thinking about systems for human resources.

Just as immediately after the course LTL graduates realized that high support or high challenge alone may not be enough, many educational leaders continued to understand, years later, that an appropriate blend of caring attention and gentle push—in a developmental sense—is important for building both capacity and trust.

As Jane shared with us, experiencing the holding environment in the course—and learning about its developmental underpinnings—helped lay bare some powerful strategies for creating and sustaining the trust essential to any growth-enhancing relationship or context. As we described in Chapters 2 and 3, whether in whole groups, collegial inquiry teams, or one-on-one with a partner, these strategies can help demystify the process of creating safe spaces for learning, and they can help leaders build both capacity and trust. Rather than simply an "x factor" or "magic quality," as Jane described once thinking about the ability to foster respect and commitment, a leader's effectiveness involves *purposefully attending to developmental diversity*. In fact, the leaders shared that intentionally tailoring supports and challenges to meet the needs of adults with different ways of knowing was *key* to structuring safe, respectful contexts in and out of which others—and the leaders themselves—could grow.

Other LTL Learnings That Made a Difference for Leaders

In addition to key LTL learnings about constructive-developmental theory and holding environments, the educational leaders talked about other course concepts and ideas that also made a difference for their leadership work in support of adult development. Below, we offer in Table 4.1 an overview of other learnings and takeaways that a number of course graduates described as meaningful to their important leadership thinking and work, including

- the power of working to align espoused theories and theories-in-use (Argyris & Schön, 1974),
- further reframing resistance by understanding the deep feeling and commitment underlying the "language of complaint" (Kegan & Lahey, 2001),
- the relevant distinction between technical and adaptive challenges in education (Heifetz, 1994; Wagner et al., 2006), and
- the great importance of avoiding assumptions by grounding leadership thought and action in what can actually be seen and/or heard (Argyris, 1982; Senge et al., 1994).

Table 4.1 Other LTL Concepts and Learnings That Made a Difference

Concept/Learning Discussed in LTL	Key Takeaways From These Concepts
Espoused theory v. theory-in-use (Argyris & Schön, 1974)	• Recognizing that gaps can sometimes exist between what leaders—like all people—believe and value and what they actually do in practice • The importance of working to better and/or best align one's beliefs with actions
Language of complaint (Kegan & Lahey, 2001)	• Reframing complaints and frustrations with an awareness that people get most upset about things they value deeply • Listening carefully to and acknowledging others' grievances to help develop an understanding of their deep values and commitments
Adaptive and technical challenges (Heifetz, 1994; Wagner et al., 2006)	• Understanding the difference between *technical* challenges (those for which someone, somewhere has an answer—even if we ourselves do not) and *adaptive* challenges (those that are hard to pin down and require the capacity to learn as we manage them) • Recognizing that not all problems can be solved quickly and easily (or simply with expertise) • Understanding that change is a process that requires individual and organizational capacity building
Using observable data (Argyris, 1982; Senge, Kleiner, Roberts, Ross, & Smith, 1994)	• The importance of avoiding assumptions by grounding thinking and actions in observable data (i.e., what was said and/or what was done) • Remaining mindful and cautious of running up the Ladder of Inference (Argyris, 1982; Senge et al., 1994) and the temptation to jump to conclusions based on surface behaviors and/or our assumptions

While leaders referenced these ideas with less frequency than constructive-developmental theory and the related concept of the holding environment, it was clear from the number of leaders who spoke passionately about these key learnings that they continued to play an important role in their leadership work and their efforts to support their own and others' development.

Helpful and Meaningful Course Practices

In this section, we present the course practices—activities and general experiences—that the educational leaders described as most helpful and meaningful for their learning and leadership development, from the vantage point of their real-world leadership roles. First, we focus on leaders' reflections on convening, the case-based collegial inquiry activity described in Chapter 2. Next, we detail their recollections of the power of the instructor's modeling of developmental principles and practices while students were in the process of learning about them.

While we discuss these practices separately, it is important to realize that no single practice was presented in isolation or as a stand-alone activity. Rather, developmental principles were threaded through every one of these practices *and every other element of the course itself.* Much like a tapestry, in which individual strands are woven together to create a complex and complete image, LTL was designed to bring together and bring to life many complementary practices in a full-color display. That being said, convening and modeling are two examples of developmental practices that can be applied more broadly in diverse contexts and two practices that leaders specifically recalled as helpful for their own leadership development. Chapter 2 provides more detailed information about how to create the conditions and lay the groundwork for the kinds of meaningful experiences the leaders describe below.

Finally, we provide an overview of additional practices that a number of these leaders described as helpful and meaningful to their leadership development and current approaches in the field.

Convening: Experiencing the Power of True Collaboration

> [O]ther people's insights into dilemmas I'd struggled with [were very helpful], because sometimes I think that the same dilemmas just show up in our lives in different forms.
>
> —Lauren, Cognitive Researcher, Author, Former Teacher

For nearly all the educational leaders (17/20), convening and the convening experience came up as important and lasting practices. As we described in Chapter 2, convening is a form of *teaming and collegial inquiry* centered on personal case-based learning. In particular, and looking back on convening, the leaders recalled

- the power of applying course learnings to their own lives and challenging work experiences,
- an appreciation of the safe, trusting environment in which convening took place (both within their groups and in the class), and
- the value of true collaboration and collegial inquiry.

As Lauren described above, convenings made a lasting impact because of the deep self-learning many were able to achieve and also because of the reciprocal spirit of giving that pervaded convening groups. Looking carefully at oneself—and aspiring to really see and be with others—was part of the learning journey for many of the leaders we learned from. After all, just as the "same dilemmas" often reappear in our own lives in different forms, so too do we frequently share experiences, frustrations, and challenges with others in similar roles and situations. As many of the leaders shared, and as we discuss in more detail below, examining and reflecting on their values, beliefs, assumptions, and commitments in this way—and in the company of trusted others—was a powerful support for their personal and professional learning.

"Real-World" Learning: Applying LTL Ideas to Personal Cases

The powerful "real-world" applicability of convening was highly valued by leaders, including Rachel, who serves now as a vice president of a charter management organization. "[O]ne of the things I really appreciated about the class," she told us, was "that it forced us to apply the ideas that we were learning to something from our own lives." Such a practical and personal focus helped her think about developmental diversity "in a different, more robust way than just reading about it and talking about it." Marisa likewise shared that convening brought her and her group "a tremendous sense of awareness about our ways of knowing and how we were developing" because it allowed them to look at their own experiences through a developmental lens.

Sharing in Safety: Trust and Norms in Convening Groups

Relatedly, the leaders also recalled the trusting, respectful environment they were able to cocreate with convening group members, given the opportunities for norm setting and trust building in their groups and in the course. Elizabeth, for instance, described this safety as an incredibly powerful feeling and one of her biggest takeaways:

> I don't know that I've ever been in another learning environment where I felt as safe and respected. . . . And the reason I felt safe . . . is that I had so much faith that people would not be making negative assumptions about me. . . . I mean, we all come into every interaction with our own prejudices, but

> I really felt in that environment like I could be very honest and I could express what was troubling to me, and people would not assume the worst.

Lucy, too, recalled the power of working collaboratively with a group of people she could really trust and count on:

> I found it helpful to be sitting in a circle with a group of very thoughtful, well-intentioned people who I had no reason to believe harbored any ill feelings or other agendas—where people are really just focused on the issue at hand and trying to create or to think about or think in different ways about a problem that was presented, and pulling together to develop and share different perspectives.

Of course, as Jane noted, "there were a lot of conditions and structures . . . in place" that helped set the stage for convening successfully. We outlined a number of these in Chapter 2, including a protocol for engaging in convening and consultation that you could use in your own school context, and we also offer below, in Figure 4.1, a general guideline for establishing team ground rules that can be used to help establish norms in any group or team.

As you know, and as these leaders shared, building and sustaining a safe context for sharing and learning together is essential for effective collegial inquiry and for safely exploring and growing from case-based analyses like convening.

There for Each Other: Experiencing Real Collaboration

Ultimately, the safe and respectful convening environment described by leaders allowed them to show up with and for each other in important and powerful ways. Experiencing *real* collaboration—without the guarded or competitive undercurrents that complicate many professional and academic relationships—highlighted promising possibilities for many of these educational leaders. For example, Jed, now the head of a K–12 charter school, explained that convening reinforced his belief that "bringing real dilemmas and using structured protocols to critically examine what's going on . . . is the most significant and profound way for adults to be together."

Indeed, convening supported and challenged leaders to learn and grow as individuals, but it also reinforced the power of doing this important work together. Learning, like leadership, was not a solitary act for the leaders in LTL, and showing up for others became

Figure 4.1   Protocol for Establishing Team Ground Rules

While the amount of time is not included below, it is wise to allocate specific amounts of time for each part of the process—for example, for a team of eight, fifteen minutes for initial introductions and twenty-five to thirty minutes for discussion of safe learning environments and confidentiality. Of course, times will vary depending on the number of team members. A general guideline for how to go about establishing team ground rules follows.

1. Invite members to free write (i.e., write what comes to mind without censoring one's thinking) for two to three minutes in response to the following questions: What constitutes a safe, productive, and supportive team learning context for you? What makes a team learning space unsafe for you and your learning?

2. Before each team member has a chance to share—whatever he or she feels comfortable sharing with the group—one team member will want to volunteer to take notes on what is discussed, type the notes, and *provide hard copies for all team members*. Our idea here is not to capture every word verbatim but rather to capture the essence of what is said, with direct quotations when possible.

3. Invite team members to share their thinking with each other. Doing so helps develop ground rules or norms for engaging in team discussion and for creating a safe learning environment. This is especially important because team members will be sharing their personal experiences.

4. At the next team meeting, distribute the notes from the previous meeting so that all team members can add to them, if needed. Periodically revisiting this ground rule document and checking in with team members around these important issues can strengthen collaboration and support learning and development.

5. After the safe and productive team learning environment discussion, if the topic hasn't come up already, the team will want to come to a shared understanding of what kind of confidentiality agreement they'd like. After the team has agreed how to handle confidentiality, the person who is taking notes will want to restate the agreement for the team and add it to the document, along with the team's thinking about what makes a safe and productive team learning environment. Team members may want to discuss how they want to handle confidentiality around issues discussed in the team with others within the school, for example.

Source: Drago-Severson (2009, p. 93).

just as—if not more—important than one's own traditional, competition-driven performance in class. As Lucy related, after describing the many gifts she felt her convening group members had given her, she hoped she had been "contributing in the same way when other people came with their questions as well."

Ultimately, even after many years, these leaders looked back on their convening experience as a powerful support for their learning and leadership development. By (a) applying course learnings to their own lives and leadership dilemmas; (b) experiencing the safe, trusting, and respectful support of colleagues; and (c) benefiting from true collaboration in their teams and inquiry groups, leaders challenged themselves—and others—to grow in ways they hoped to translate to their own important work in support of adult development.

Instructor Modeling: Seeing Is Believing

Instructor modeling of learning-oriented practices similarly resonated with many of these leaders, both as students in the class and as they looked back on their course experiences years later. Intentionally designed to demonstrate developmental principles and the pillar practices in action as students were learning about them, LTL was taught as a team, and the instructor and teaching fellows modeled and described many aspects of teaming, collegial inquiry, providing leadership roles, and mentoring within the class and in their planning meetings. Moreover, the instructor carefully attended to students' diverse ways of knowing in all aspects of the course pedagogy, as described in detail in Chapters 2 and 3.

As Jed explained, from his current vantage point as a school head, LTL was so powerful in large part because it was taught "in a manner that mirror[ed] the importance of the content." Because "the course itself was set up in a manner that reflected the theories of adult development," he shared, it allowed "different people to enter in in a way that provided the right balance between support and challenge." Moreover, he continued, "just from that [the modeling] alone, the credibility of [the instructor's] teaching and leadership was incredibly powerful." Indeed, like Jed, more than a third of the leaders we learned from (7/20) recognized this type of modeling as an important course practice and as a powerful lesson in what it looks and feels like to lead effectively.

Matt, for instance, now a lower school head in an independent school, reflected on the instructor's modeling of developmental principles and on what he described as the powerful alignment between theory and practice. Given his own value for honoring diversity and the unique contributions of individuals, LTL, he explained, helped him better understand how to do this in the field as an educational leader. "Part of it," he shared, "was about the structural elements of it [the course], and part of it was about . . . modeling for me what it looks like to go through that process [of leading developmentally]." Indeed, for many of these leaders, witnessing and experiencing developmentally oriented leadership while learning about it proved a powerful support for learning and their own practice years later.

"Training the Trainers": Passing Developmental Intentionality Forward

Jane likewise realized that, as a leadership development course, LTL "was training the trainer, so to speak," and preparing leaders to support adult development in their future roles and contexts. In her current work as an educational consultant, for instance, Jane faces similar challenges and opportunities—in terms of preparing adults to support others in their own contexts—and she appreciated the LTL instructors' careful modeling of growth-enhancing practices. As she explained, LTL instructors knew that they were "presenting the content to the students, but also that they [the students] were going to be leading the work." They needed, accordingly, "the opportunity to reflect on ... what was behind [pedagogical] decisions" and how they "connect[ed] to the theory." This kind of explicit modeling, we learned, made a powerful difference for Jane and other LTL graduates working to support adult development in their own contexts.

Indeed, instructors provided opportunities for students to peek behind the curtain and understand the purposeful nature of the course design, and we have offered similar sharings and explications throughout Chapters 2 and 3. While, as the educational leaders shared, such transparency was helpful for LTL students on two levels—as both learners and as future leaders—it is our hope that laying bare some of these strategies and leaders' current thinking about them will likewise prove helpful for your important work in support of learning and growth across the life span.

Other LTL Practices That Made a Difference for Leaders

> [O]kay, that's think-pair-share, but I never would have thought about that before from a developmental perspective and really understood how important that is. And I do think that by being sensitive ... as a designer of the work, that creates conditions where trust can be built because ... people's stress levels come down, and you are meeting them where they're at.
>
> —Jane, Educational Consultant

In addition to convening and instructor modeling, a number of these leaders shared other important course practices that made a difference in their thinking about and orientations toward leadership.

For example, eight out of twenty specifically identified, as Jane did above, how the combination of differentiated class activities described in Chapters 2 and 3—such as free-writes, journaling, small- and large-group discussions, and pair-shares—helped model how intentional developmental differentiation can support adults with different needs and ways of knowing. Additionally, more than one-third (7/20) explained that examining assumptions in ways additional to convening—such as completing Kegan and Lahey's (2001) Four-Column Exercise—supported their growth and thinking as leaders. In particular, we focus on

- Differentiating opportunities for thinking and sharing
- Written assignments/Developmental feedback
- Providing reflective opportunities
- Readings

We present an overview of these practices, and leaders' key take-aways, in Table 4.2.

We hope that sharing leaders' reflections about these important practices, as well as their experiences with convening and modeling, helps illustrate the kinds of structures and activities that infused LTL with developmental intentions and that continue to feel important to leaders working for nurturing their own schools and organizations as contexts supportive of adult development. We hope, too, that these ideas and practices can be employed more broadly—in schools, teams, professional learning communities, districts, as well as leadership preparation and professional learning programs—to help educators of all kinds meet the mounting demands and pressures of leading, teaching, learning, and living today.

Chapter Summary

Well, what I think I really do is look at it as people are growing, people are learning, and that's something that I took away from [LTL] . . . to help people develop and learn, and to understand where they're coming [from] and then try and help them in their journey of growth.

—Diane, State Department
of Education Consultant

Recognizing the beauty, vulnerability, and hope inherent in all human beings—and adults in particular—was a central message of

Table 4.2   Other LTL Practices and Experiences That Made a Difference

Powerful Practice for Growth Observed and Experienced in LTL	*Key Takeaways and Implementations*
Differentiating opportunities for thinking and sharing	• Offering opportunities to "free-think or free-write" (Drago-Severson, 2012) before sharing with others helped leaders feel comfortable in LTL and demonstrated the power of attending to developmental diversity when leading large groups. • Inviting adults to share in pairs or small groups, before sharing with whole group, likewise helped establish comfort and trust. • Providing leaders safe opportunities to explore their thinking and feeling helped them understand how to structure meeting times and discussions in their own work contexts.
Written assignments/ Developmental feedback	• Applying course ideas to real-life experiences in writing assignments helped bridge theory and practice and suggested the importance of allowing adults to pursue personally meaningful questions, projects, and goals. • Receiving developmentally supportive and developmentally challenging (i.e., "stretching") feedback verbally and on writing assignments helped leaders grow and highlighted the importance of carefully crafting feedback to meet people where they are (developmentally speaking) and support growth.
Providing reflective opportunities	• Offering quiet times for journaling and reflection created space for LTL leaders to push their thinking forward and demonstrated the value of carving out time for pause moments. • Reflective opportunities likewise supported leaders' growth and development and helped them examine assumptions and set goals.
Readings	• Reading about theory and practices for supporting adult learning and development helped leaders establish a common language for discussing ideas. • Readings were also easy to share and discuss with others in order to teach ideas. • Learning from others' expertise, both practical and theoretical, was meaningful for many leaders.

the LTL experience, and one that helped leaders embrace the urgency and importance of supporting adult learning and growth in their own unique contexts. Given the potent connection between thinking and action (Argyris, 1982; Kegan, 2000; Gardner, 2006), and the all-too-familiar challenge of "changing minds" (Gardner, 2006), the educational leaders' shifts in understandings of leadership presented in this chapter—like Diane's above—suggest the great promise of learning about adult developmental theories in conjunction with experiencing a developmentalized curriculum. For many, after all, seeing is believing, and together, the course concepts and practices described in this chapter seemed to have made a difference for the leaders who graciously shared their thinking and experiences with us.

Indeed, nearly all of the educational leaders we learned from years after the course (19/20) attributed important changes in their thinking about leadership to their experience in LTL, and more than half (13/20) described deep, fundamental changes in their understanding of what it means to lead effectively—including more sophisticated emphases on growing capacity by meeting adults where they are in a developmental sense and attending to developmental diversity. While such a stance is admirable and important for its own sake, the documented connection between adults' learning and growth and the improved learning and achievement of students (Guskey, 1999; Kaser & Halbert, 2009; Moller & Pankake, 2006; Wagner, 2007) makes the promise of learning-oriented leadership even more timely and urgent—especially given the growing demands of our accountability-driven climate and the challenges of meeting new standards and expectations.

To help illuminate some of the factors that supported these leaders' shifts in thinking, we divided this chapter into four main sections. First, we described educational leaders' reflections on their changes in understandings of leadership as a result of LTL, including the importance of recognizing adults as learners—with different competencies, strengths, experiences, and ways of knowing. Just as they were able intuitively to do with and for their students as teachers, the leaders we learned from in this study shared their evolving appreciation for adults' diverse capacities and orientations to the world.

In the second section, we outlined additional course learnings—including constructive-developmental theory and the related concept of a holding environment—that stood out for LTL graduates. Similarly, in the third section, we shared leaders' reflections on specific LTL practices—including convening as a powerful form of teaming and collegial inquiry and the value of instructor modeling of developmental principles in action. While it is difficult to tease apart the integrated elements of the LTL experience and while it is important to note that these principles and practices were presented together in class as parts of a larger whole (as described in Chapters 2 and 3), we offer the educational leaders' sharings about these specific components as they represented commonly voiced reflections in our interviews and to help illuminate *some* of the factors that supported leaders' shifts in thinking.

In this, the final section, we offer below a number of concluding considerations gleaned from the leaders' sharings. First, though, we invite you to engage in the reflective opportunity presented in Figure 4.2 to help connect these ideas with your own experiences.

Figure 4.2   A Reflective Application Opportunity

After now having read Chapters 1, 2, 3, and 4, we invite you to consider the following questions, as an opportunity to reflect on the connections between your own professional experiences and the ideas presented in these chapters.

1. Can you think of a time when you worked with a leader who you felt was a good role model? How do you think his or her leadership affected your own? What, for example, are the kinds of things you're doing today that might link back to that experience?

2. What events, situations, or experiences in your professional and/or personal life helped you shape your thinking about what it means to support adults' growth and/or learning?

3. What elements do you feel are most important in order to create contexts that help adults grow and learn?

What Does This Mean for You, and What Might You Do With It?

While the educational leaders we learned from shared many earnest and powerful reflections about their learning and thinking, both immediately after and years following the LTL experience, their insights informed their efforts to lead in support of adult learning and growth in their unique contexts, as we describe next in

Chapters 5 and 6. This direct connection between learning and application suggests the long-lasting influence of the course experience and leaders' related thinking, and it also suggests some important takeaways for creating learning contexts of all kinds that support leadership development and practice.

Below, we offer a collection of key takeaways to highlight what these learnings might mean for you, as educational leaders and practitioners of many kinds, and to illuminate how they might be of future help in your noble work. We very much hope that learning about these educational leaders' LTL learnings and reflections will prove helpful in your own efforts to affect hearts and minds in support of adult growth and learning and that their sharings demonstrate, at least in part, how honoring adults as valuable and unique individuals can help create the conditions for personal and organizational transformation. As the leaders learned,

- Approaching adults as learners, and understanding principles of adult developmental theory, can inform leadership orientations in powerful ways.
- Experiencing developmentally oriented teaching and leadership *while learning about them* can help demonstrate the importance and power of attending to developmental diversity in our multiple roles and responsibilities.
- Creating the conditions and setting the groundwork for authentic collaboration takes time and effort, *and the benefits* are deep and long lasting.
- Crafting environments in which adults feel respected and "well held" (Drago-Severson, 2012) can inspire individuals to shape and create similar experiences for others.
- Growing ourselves, as educators and leaders of all kinds, can make a big difference for those in our care—both children and adults.

In the next two chapters, we share concrete examples of how the educational leaders went on to use these ideas in their unique work contexts. We offer, for example, an overview of the specific LTL-related practices they are using in their schools, districts, and organizations in Chapter 5, and then we take a deep look into three of the leaders' sharings in Chapter 6 to help illustrate some of the ways these ideas are being applied in combination by real-life leaders in their important work.

Reflective Questions

We offer the following questions as a chance for you to reflect on ideas from this chapter. We invite you to consider how, if at all, you might apply learnings from this chapter to enhance the kinds of opportunities you offer to adults in your care—and to yourself—to support growth. Please take a moment to reflect on these questions. You might want to reflect on them privately first and then engage in collegial inquiry with a partner or group of colleagues.

1. What stands out for you as one important learning from this chapter?

2. How, if at all, do you think this learning might be useful to you in your practice?

3. What is one step you will take to improve your already growth-oriented practice for others and for yourself?

5

Transferring Powerful Learnings

Supporting Professional Growth From University Classrooms to Real-Life Practice

Introduction and Overview

Knowing is not enough; we must apply. Willing is not enough; we must do.

—Johann Wolfgang von Goethe

Energized and excited by their powerful learning experiences in the Leadership for Transformational Learning (LTL) course, the leaders we learned from in this study went on to implement, adapt, and invent learning-oriented practices as school principals, assistant principals, teacher leaders, educational consultants, district administrators, and university professors. When we checked with LTL graduates four, five, or even six years after they successfully completed the course, we were inspired as they shared compelling insights and examples from their own practice about their work to support colleagues'—and their own—learning and growth in light of the many complex challenges and demands facing schools and education today. In this chapter, we describe the innovative ways in which these leaders transferred their insightful learnings about developmentally oriented leadership practice from LTL to their workplaces. Put most simply and powerfully, this chapter is about *applying and doing*, as the above quotation suggests. There is great power in these things, as you know, and we also hope that you find the stories and examples presented throughout this chapter meaningful within the context of your own important work.

To help you understand how these leaders transferred their learnings from LTL to their actual leadership practice, in the first section, we offer an overview of the hopes and ideas for developmentally oriented leadership that graduates expressed *immediately* after completing the course years ago. Next, in the following three sections, we describe *how they are actually using and adapting* the growth-enhancing practices and strategies that they learned about and experienced in LTL. More specifically, we focus on three important aspects of their practice that emerged from leaders' sharings about supporting adult learning and internal capacity building:

1. Leaders' initial and ongoing strategies for establishing trust, respect, and buy-in, which we describe below as *preconditions* for instituting practices with developmental intentions

2. The ways in which they are using the pillar practices and adaptations of them for supporting adult growth and capacity building

3. Their efforts to differentiate developmentally appropriate supports and challenges within the pillar practices to support adults with diverse developmental capacities (i.e., ways of knowing)

Finally, we conclude by sharing larger takeaways—ideas and strategies—and questions for reflection that you might find useful, given your interest in developmentally oriented leadership practice.

Chapter Context

While new approaches to leadership development are emerging (Browne-Ferrigno, 2007; Byrne-Jiménez & Orr, 2007; Donaldson, 2008; Drago-Severson, 2012; Stoll & Seashore-Louis, 2007), the question still remains: how do aspiring and practicing leaders actually *use* what they learn in university preparation and professional development programs about supporting adult growth in their own work? Which practices and strategies, for example, effectively prepare leaders for the complex and daunting challenges of leading in the twenty-first century? How can we help leaders build their capacities to support adults with different developmental needs and preferences in our schools, professional learning communities, teams, districts, and district and university leadership preparation programs?

As we shared, this chapter immediately addresses these questions, as it explores how and why leaders were able to transfer their LTL learnings to actual practice years after successfully completing the course. While in Chapter 4 we presented the important *conceptual* changes leaders attributed to the course—or their new understandings of leadership and their role in supporting others' growth and learning—we focus here on what leaders hoped to do *after* completing LTL and then on practices *they actually went on to implement* in their schools and organizations.

While, as you might suspect, the leaders we learned from are at different points and phases regarding the implementation of learning-oriented leadership—composed of four pillar practices (i.e., teaming, inviting adults to assume leadership roles, engaging in collegial inquiry, and mentoring)—we hope that the examples that follow help illustrate what it looks like *in real life* to begin to lead, learn, and grow in this way.

Hopes for Developmentally Oriented Leadership Practice

> *[Wherever] I go, my first year I'll spend a lot of time listening . . . and a lot of time trying to learn the culture of the school. . . . [I]deally what I would [like] would be to try to create space in the day, regardless of what I'm doing, that allows time for personal reflection and allows time for collaborative reflection.*
>
> —Matt, Current Head of School,
> After Completing LTL in 2004

Immediately after the course, many of the LTL graduates, like Matt above, shared big and important hopes for carrying forward what they learned and experienced in LTL. As they shared in interviews and surveys immediately after the course (please see the Research

Appendix for more details about this phase of the study), they wanted to use their LTL learnings to build growth-enhancing spaces in their workplaces to support their colleagues' and their own professional learning and development.

While in Chapter 4 we illuminated fundamental shifts that LTL learners experienced in terms of their understandings of developmentally oriented leadership, in this section, we share their hopes and plans for implementing learning-oriented leadership strategies in their own educational contexts immediately after completing LTL. As you will see, their hopes centered on providing appropriate structures and opportunities that would support adult professional growth in their work settings. These ideas centered on the following larger themes:

- Creating opportunities for sharing, dialogue, and collaboration among colleagues that would bring adults together
- Developing safe contexts for collegial inquiry and reflection on practice
- Building mutually respectful and trusting relationships
- Differentiating supports for individuals with diverse developmental capacities (i.e., ways of knowing)

Below we elaborate on these big hopes to help frame the sections on transfer that follow.

A Hope for Creating Structures That Would Bring Adults Together

Just after successfully completing LTL, nearly two-thirds of the graduates emphasized the importance of creating safe spaces and structures (e.g., nonthreatening and respectful environments) *to bring adults together* to engage in collegial inquiry about their instructional practice. To achieve this goal, many underscored the value of creating an environment based on "mutual trust and respect" in which adults would feel comfortable and *safe* sharing their ideas and voicing their concerns about and vulnerabilities in practice. Allocating time to foster interactions and to build relationships among colleagues was an essential element of this practice in their view, and they accordingly hoped to create professional learning teams, book clubs, curriculum writing groups, and collaborative inquiry groups. Similarly, nearly all aspiring and practicing leaders hoped at the time to employ and "differentiate" practices and professional development in order to attend to the diverse developmental needs (in relation to ways of knowing) and internal capacities of adult learners in their care—regardless of setting. Having experienced this in LTL, they wanted to offer the same to other adults in order to support their growth and instructional and leadership practice. For example, as Margaret, a teacher leader at the time of the course, shared,

> People are at all different stages and levels of learning. [That's] something I've really become cognizant of this year. And it's important in developing programs or . . . environments that [are] conducive to adult learning to really . . . provide people with many different ways to express their learning . . . [to] really try to appeal to learners at all different levels and stages.

A Hope for Building Safe Learning Contexts for Dialogue and Reflection

After learning about and experiencing the safe learning context of LTL, nearly all of the graduates emphasized in surveys and interviews just after the course that they hoped to build similarly safe and supportive spaces—like the collaborative dialogue and reflection groups they valued in class—in their future leadership practice.

More specifically, they explained that they hoped to create spaces for people in which they could feel safe to talk about their feelings and ideas for improving instruction and in which teachers and other adults could safely share and examine the beliefs, values, and assumptions that guide their practice. Collectively discussing "good" teaching and "effective" leadership with colleagues—and addressing their concerns and disagreements in candid and respectful conversations— they believed, would help them better learn, grow, and meet the challenges they face together as educators. They explained that allocating time in faculty meetings for thinking together about practice and benefiting from troublesome cases (like personal convening cases) would be very helpful and could help with student achievement. For example, Elizabeth, a social studies teacher and educational leader at the time, described the power of carefully and intentionally structuring collaborative reflective practice:

> Enabling and nurturing and helping to create and develop an environment that promotes reflective practice is huge, and I think I never realized the magnitude of power that reflective practice can have [when you reflect together with colleagues]. . . . I think the emphasis on that time, and structuring that time, and needing that time is something [very important].

A Hope for Building Respectful and Trusting Relationships

Similarly, after the course, nearly all of the aspiring leaders emphasized the importance of careful listening and honest sharing to build respectful relationships based on mutual trust with their colleagues. They told us that they firmly believed that these relationships would help open dialogues and enable colleagues to work collaboratively—in the truest sense of the word (i.e., turning toward each other) to address issues related to their instructional practice.

Establishing trust was noted by a majority of leaders as being an essential precursor to engaging in collegial and critical inquiry into improving instruction and practice. As Deniz, who was an aspiring educational leader from Turkey while in LTL and who now serves as a school leader, explained, his big hope involved

> Building activities so that people trust each other. . . . [For example, I want to encourage and create opportunities for] going out, having picnics, dinner, and . . . self-disclosure . . . [because] those kinds of things build trust. When people start to trust each other, [that can] . . . move to improving instruction.

Like his LTL classmates, Deniz valued the role of formal and informal interactions among his colleagues to help establish trusting relationships. Similarly, reflecting on the intimate connection between trust and engaging in "critical reflection" to improve teachers' instructional practice, Jane, a science teacher and department head at the time of the course, noted the importance of building a "climate of trust" to facilitate dialogue and reflection in her work. She believed in the crucial significance of developing a "common ground" for dialogue by listening to and understanding other's viewpoints. This, in her view, fosters trust and reflection through dialogue and sharing.

A Hope for Differentiating Supports for Professional Development

Additionally, nearly all of the LTL graduates talked about how they hoped to implement what they learned in LTL about the significance of differentiating supports and challenges to make professional development relevant and meaningful for adults with different ways of knowing.

For example, Margaret, a lead teacher in an adult literacy program at the time, shared her hope of making group discussions more meaningful for teachers with different ways of knowing. Doing so would "get people to talk to each other and just make sure that everybody had a reason for being there," as she put it. She further explained that she planned to differentiate professional development by (a) articulating the purpose of discussions and focusing them around "specific topics" so that instrumental knowers would feel comfortable and "grounded," (b) recognizing various viewpoints during discussions to engage socializing knowers, and (c) encouraging self-authoring knowers to "facilitate the group" so that "they would also feel challenged."

Similarly, to differentiate supports and challenges for nurturing adult growth, about two-thirds of the LTL graduate-leaders emphasized just after completing the course that they wanted to identify their colleagues' particular needs in order to help them grow. In other words, they hoped to provide a variety of developmental supports and challenges to meet their colleagues where they were. For example, Matt, an elementary teacher at the time of LTL, noted that his knowledge of adults' different ways of knowing would now help him "figure out the type of supports and challenges" he could put in place to help particular adults with different developmental orientations.

Transfer to Practice

> *Knowledge is of no value unless you put it into practice.*
>
> —Anton Chekhov

As we describe in detail in the Research Appendix, we also surveyed and interviewed graduates several years after their successful completion of LTL to learn how they were actually employing ideas and practices learned in LTL. In the next sections, we illuminate the developmentally oriented practices that these graduates shared from their actual leadership work several years after completing the course. Specifically, we discuss the LTL-inspired strategies and practices—and adaptations of them—that these leaders are now employing to support adult development, build human and organizational capacity, and grow in their unique contexts.

As we explained earlier, we divide this topic into three thematic sections: (a) descriptions of leaders' efforts to lay the groundwork for collaborative developmental practices, (b) their implementations and adaptations of the pillar practices, and (c) their specific strategies for differentiating within the pillar practices. Below, we begin with a discussion of leaders' efforts to build mutually trusting and respectful relationships with colleagues as fundamental **preconditions** for their learning-oriented leadership practice. As noted earlier, we refer to these as preconditions because these leaders describe them as essential first steps toward supporting adult growth.

Preconditions for Supporting Development: Building Relationships Based on Understanding, Trust, and Respect

> When I think about [LTL], I think about making sure that I'm always building in time for relationship[s] . . . and trust to be built. . . . [That's the] foundation to be laid before anything else can be accomplished.

—Tara, Middle School Assistant Principal

In this section, we share how, years after completing the course, LTL graduates described building mutual trust and respect with colleagues as essential *preconditions* to their work supporting adult learning and growth in their unique educational contexts. When we checked in with leaders four, five, and even six years after LTL, nearly all (18/20) described the vital importance of developing mutually respectful, trusting relationships in their work and designing, crafting, and leading safe holding environments that support the learning and growth of colleagues. In other words, for these leaders, developing trustworthy and caring relationships was fundamentally linked to the success of their learning-oriented (i.e., growth-enhancing) leadership efforts and initiatives. It's important to note that nearly all LTL leaders emphasized that it is not possible to create safe learning environments without these essential elements, or *preconditions*, as we call them. These preconditions, they explained, are significant and essential to establish *before* and to nurture *during* programs and practices that challenge or stretch—in a developmental sense—colleagues' thinking, feelings, and work. Doing so not only alleviates anxiety and instills a sense of confidence and safety for all participants, but also builds a shared vision and contributes significantly to the overall success of improvement efforts in general.

Accordingly, to build mutually trusting, respectful, and safe learning contexts for their colleagues, these leaders employed a number of promising strategies in their leadership work in schools and educational organizations. For instance, they shared the importance of

- carefully listening to teachers and striving to understand their points of view and concerns,
- avoiding assumptions about colleagues' intentions or work to better engage in genuine, critical conversations about practice, and
- seeking and valuing teachers' honest input on school policies and programs.

In the following sections, we share leaders' examples of each of these strategies to build meaningful, trusting, and respectful professional relationships with their colleagues in their current leadership practice. Caring for these kinds of authentic exchanges allowed the leaders, in their view, to better create contexts in which they could *then* implement the kinds of practices—the pillar practices—that support adult growth and capacity building.

Listening Carefully and Caringly to Colleagues to Show Respect and Demonstrate Trust: An Essential First Step

> *One of the things I try is, a lot of times, people just need for you to listen [to] how things are going. . . . [P]eople need to just talk or feel like they can vent. Really just considering listening [is key].*

> —Dana, Department Chair

Even years after LTL, when we talked with graduates about what felt most important to them in terms of what works when supporting adult growth, the majority pointed toward the vital role of shaping "caring and safe spaces" that support continued professional growth. They emphasized the importance of *really listening* when crafting holding environments in which adults can share and ask for help with instructional practice and other needs. Listening, they explained, is a fundamental first step in the *how* of creating a caring environment for learning based on mutual trust and respect.

For example, in a representative response to our question about the strategies that help in developing safe contexts for effective learning, Matt, who now works with a large cohort of elementary teachers as a division head, talked about the power of listening to and honoring colleagues' ideas. Matt explained that he did not believe in imposing his ideas on teachers. "Shouting" them down or forcing his "edict" on teachers would mean losing their trust, as he described below:

> If I just [go] . . . to a meeting and sort of give my edict, I'd be shouting a teacher down, right? . . . I would lose them, right? They wouldn't be on board; I've lost their trust.

Likewise, Tara, a middle school assistant principal and instructional leader, stressed the importance of listening to her teachers' views about what is important to them in terms of their professional development. Listening—rather than imposing her agenda—lies at the core of her leadership practice. "Building in time" to learn about and understand what her teachers are thinking is extremely important to her, and she explained her thinking about attending professional learning group meetings at her school during her early tenure as leader. As she noted,

> [At first] I attended all of the [meetings] to make sure that they were happening and to just kind of facilitate them . . . just kind of establishing trust and relationships. . . . [G]iving it space to happen is simply a matter, a lot of the time, of me just sitting and being quiet at a meeting and not trying to direct it or impose my agenda on this team, this teaching team.

Like Matt, Tara has learned to avoid the temptation of providing all the answers as a leader. Sometimes, she shared—like other leaders we learned from—that inviting adults to find their own way, and really listening and being present as they do so, can support learning and practice and build internal capacity in both the individuals involved and the school or organization as a whole.

Avoiding Assumptions: Demonstrating Respect and Attention by Using Data to Guide Critical Conversations

Two-thirds of the LTL leaders we learned from emphasized that avoiding assumptions about teachers' intentions—and actions based on these assumptions—was another vital precondition for developing trusting and caring relationships. A safe environment based on trust, transparency, and respect, they explained, requires that leaders avoid interpreting people's work, actions, and attitudes based on surface behaviors and their own assumptive lenses—or what they think is or should be happening. About two-thirds described how they strive to build trust and safety in their professional relationships by looking beyond their first or immediate impressions and by using observable data to inform their collaborative discussions with and evaluations of colleagues.

For example, Jane, an educational consultant working with district administrators and teachers, described the importance of using data to avoid jumping to inferences based on one's preconceived notions. She referred to the **Ladder of Inference** framework (Argyris, 1990; Senge, Kleiner, Roberts, Ross, & Smith, 1994), which she learned about in LTL. She described how it informs her practice in building open and trusting relationships with her colleagues. In her leadership role as a data analyst, she strives to rely on concrete data on teachers' instructional practice or student performance and invites other people to examine it with her and to look at it from alternative viewpoints. In doing so, she consciously avoids the potential tendency to make meaning of people's intentions and actions in light of her assumptions and tries to construct her conversations in a "descriptive voice." As she elaborated,

> [T]he meaning that you make of the data that you've selected is [necessarily] dependent upon your experiences, beliefs, and assumptions. And so the theory behind [using] the descriptive voice is that you increase the amount of data that you're able to select, either through reflection or having other people look with you, but you increase what you're able to see or speak [so] that you'll make ultimately more informed decisions.

Like Jane, Gina, an instructional leader and a counselor, prioritizes descriptive data while assessing and providing feedback about teachers' instructional practice. Using "pure descriptions" of teachers' instructional practice helps in evading "subjective" and "judgmental" interpretations of their actions, she emphasized.

As a school leader, Matt also attempts to understand and attend to his tacit assumptions about teachers' work by grounding his feedback on teachers' instructional practice in observable data. He carefully observes teachers in their classrooms and records their actions, activities, and instructional decisions (what is called "directly observable data" in the Ladder of Inference framework). Later, in his conversations with teachers, he refers to those observed actions and offers his thinking about any teaching-related issues. As he described,

> And I think that I'm always trying to think about how I'm observing things, and how I'm using what I'm observing . . . to move to a place that is getting the most clean data so that I'm in a position, then, that I can make the best types of decisions in terms of addressing a situation or in terms of setting a vision.

While in Chapter 6 we will further detail Matt's efforts to ground his leadership practice in observable evidence, it is important to note here that a developmental approach to using data involves both sticking closely to the facts as one can see them and then looking further and beyond numbers, observable actions, and surface behaviors to individuals' feelings, meaning making, and understandings. As you know, both *talking with* and *listening to* individuals about data and their experiences are an important part of supporting growth and development, and one that becomes particularly relevant given the strong emphasis placed on data in many current initiatives and systems.

Seeking Teachers' Input on School Policies and Programs: Building Trust and Respect by Modeling True Collaboration

Inquiring about teachers' responses to school policies and programs also emerged as an important practice for developing mutual trust and understanding. Slightly less than one-half of the participants noted the importance of seeking their colleagues' input on curricular innovations and new academic programs to foster a climate of care and trust in their workplaces. Doing so, they shared, demonstrates a leader's commitment to collaboration and respect for individual perspectives and contributions.

In a powerful and representative example, for instance, Elizabeth, a math department head and secondary mathematics teacher, highlighted her efforts to consult with teachers and honor their suggestions before making decisions about curriculum programs and policies. Doing this, she explained, helped build a shared vision for change and nurtured meaningful professional relationships with and among her colleagues. At the time, Elizabeth was planning to introduce a new preassessment system at her school. While she and her principal thought that it was a sound plan, other teachers seemed to have concerns about it. Initially, she tried to pull resisters onboard with her logical arguments, but ultimately felt this strategy was not effective. Therefore, she decided to reach out to the teachers individually to probe and better understand their concerns about the strengths and limitations of the new plan. This strategy was helpful in developing a shared vision of assessment and a joint plan for implementing the new program. As she shared,

> [W]e actually left at the end of the summer with [the idea] kind of up in the air. We hadn't settled anything when we came back in August. . . . [But] I was much better prepared,

and I think our team [of teachers] was much better prepared
to talk about what types of assessment they [feel] comfortable
with . . . What [the teachers] see as strengths, what they see as
weaknesses in the plan, and how can we build on those. And
really try to reach out to them on a much more individual
level. I think it was much more successful than just sitting in
a room with all the faculty and saying, "You're going to do
this" [preassessment plan].

Similarly, Dana, a department chair, tries to establish trust by
inviting teachers in her department at different times during the year
to provide feedback about what programs are going well for them
and what support they need from her. Seeking frequent feedback
from teachers about their practice and struggles, she explained,
assures them that she and the school leaders are serious about hearing their voices and addressing their problems when necessary.
Additionally, because much of the feedback is provided anony-
mously, the teachers can feel free to offer honest feedback that informs
Dana and her school head about the effectiveness of their leadership
practices. On a more informal level, Dana also regularly seeks teachers' feedback to find out what is working well and identify further
appropriate supports and reinforcements. As she explained, this
strategy both builds on and strengthens her trusting, respectful relationships with the teachers she works with:

I have a strong relationship with the teachers in my department, so . . . I ask them at the end of the year or during the end
of the semester [for different] types of feedback for things that
they need from me or things that have been going well for
them, things that they maybe are struggling with.

As you know, and as we describe in further detail in the example
below, feedback and input can be gathered in many ways, but—as
these leaders attested—most important when seeking feedback is a
willingness to learn from the wisdom, experience, and perspectives of
others. Leading for adult development, after all, is as much about
growing oneself as supporting others, and the hard and important
work of growth is all the more meaningful and productive when we
can do it with others by our side.

Meeting Before the Meetings. Offering a slightly different and useful
strategy for seeking input from teachers and key stakeholders, Jed, who
supervises and supports three principals and three assistant principals

of different divisions (lower, middle, and upper school) on his leader-ship team in his role as the head of a large, urban K–12 charter school, shared his practice of meeting individually with lead team members before holding large, important administrative—leadership—team meetings. Jed explained that his intention in these premeetings is "to get the landscape of what people are feeling and thinking" in relation to "complex" and "potentially contentious" issues that they may not be comfortable discussing for the first time—and in a large group—at bigger administrative meetings. Therefore, in an attempt to understand and care for colleagues' concerns, he engages in individual discussions with them to establish *a foundation for mutual understanding and trust before the formal meeting itself.*

During our interview, Jed described how he attends to the concerns of his team of administrators by making a conscious effort to under-stand their thinking in order to carefully and sensitively tackle contro-versial issues without surprising anyone. His careful planning to meet individually with administrators creates a sense of mutual trust and respect between him and his colleagues. As Jed described this practice,

> [O]ne strategy that I've employed much more deliberately recently . . . is the importance of *meeting before the meeting* [emphasis his]. . . . [W]hat I've been doing in the last couple years is making the rounds to people individually before the [administrative] meeting to establish some common ground, and so I can sort of take the ombudsman perspective going into the meeting having already vetted people's concerns so that they don't surface in a way that is surprising or uncomfortable.

Jed believes that this strategy for seeking out his administrative team's views before meetings is effective in dealing with intricate issues and making important decisions about the school—and, of course, that it helps build and nurture trusting and respectful colle-gial relationships.

Summary: Trusting, Respectful Relationships as Preconditions for Supporting Adult Growth

For nearly all of these leaders, the importance of establishing and maintaining trusting, respectful relationships emerged as a clear and important takeaway from LTL. It was also an essential *precondition* for supporting adult development in their schools and work contexts years later. In LTL, they learned that people develop best in safe environments where they feel comfortable voicing their concerns and developing their ideas further—and they learned that growth-enhancing practices, like the pillar practices that we will discuss in the next sections, are rooted in and grow out of trustworthy and respectful relationships. Importantly, LTL graduates shared several concrete, course-inspired strategies that they employ in their current leadership work to create safe and nurturing contexts for growth. For example, respectfully listening to colleagues in a non-judgmental environment, working to avoid assumptions when engaging in critical conversations, and inviting and honoring colleagues' thinking, concerns, and understandings of important issues and organizational policies emerged as useful strategies for fostering mutual trust in schools and organizations.

They explained that employing these practices helps those in their care understand that their leader is genuinely interested in their professional growth and will respond positively to constructive comments and suggestions aimed at enhancing their instructional practice. Taken together, these strategies also lay the necessary groundwork for implementing other kinds of growth-enhancing practices, like the pillar practices, as the leaders share below. Table 5.1 presents the concrete steps and strategies that most of these LTL leaders are employing to listen to colleagues respectfully, seek teachers' input on school policies and programs, and avoid imposing their assumptions on their colleagues.

Creating Powerful Holding Environments Through the Learning-Oriented Pillar Practices

> *I've learned that people will forget what you said, people will forget what you did, but people will never forget how you made them feel.*
>
> —Maya Angelou

Very importantly for the LTL leaders, *simultaneously learning about and experiencing* the robust holding environments in the structures and practices of LTL demonstrated the possibility and promise of re-creating and adapting these practices for the adults they care for in their current leadership work. As we discussed in the earlier sections about leaders' hopes, most carried from the class a strong desire to craft similar kinds of developmentally oriented opportunities to help teachers and other adults reflect on practice, build capacity, and strengthen practice—together. Years after successfully completing the course, and from the vantage point of their own work as educational leaders in different contexts, the LTL graduates explained that they now center their leadership thinking, intentions, and practice on shaping holding environments (Drago-Severson, 2004a, 2004b, 2009, 2012; Kegan, 1982, 2000) in

Table 5.1 Preconditions for Supporting Adult Development: Building
Professional Relationships Based on Mutual Trust and Respect

Listening to Colleagues Caringly and Respectfully	• Creating a climate of open communication where people's ideas are respected and valued and where people are not afraid to voice their concerns • Recognizing and acknowledging teachers' fears, concerns, and inhibitions about the change process • Meeting with colleagues regularly to engage in dialogue aimed at exploring their concerns about complex issues • Taking colleagues into confidence—to build trust—before discussing any potentially contentious issues at meetings • Understanding teachers' concerns about their practice
Avoiding Assumptions	• Questioning one's own beliefs, convictions, and assumptions • Using concrete observations (i.e., data) to inform thinking and decisions • Drawing on data to collectively guide critical conversations
Seeking Teachers' Input on School Policies and Programs	• Establishing a common ground for dialogue and decision making by inviting and carefully considering teachers' input on professional programs • Building a shared meaning of organizational mission • Developing a shared vision for improvement in professional practice • Developing mechanisms to receive teachers' feedback on the supports provided to them

their workplaces that support adult growth and internal capacity building. They emphasized how important this is in general and also how vital it is given today's many complex leadership and teaching challenges.

In particular, these leaders emphasized how the four pillar practices for growth—teaming, collegial inquiry, providing leadership roles, and mentoring—serve as powerful holding environments for supporting growth and capacity building for the adults in their care. Inspired by how these practices "held" them so well (in the psychological sense) as aspiring leaders in LTL, they described the different and meaningful ways they have been able to translate these practices to their own schools and organizations to support the growth and learning of their colleagues—and themselves. While we introduced these practices in detail in Chapter 2—and offered a developmental view of how they serve as contexts for supporting the growth of adults with different ways of knowing in Chapter 3—we thought it would be useful to offer a brief summary of these pillar practices here, by way of gentle reminder (please see Table 5.2).

Table 5.2   Pillar Practices: A Framework for Creating Developmentally Oriented Holding Environments

Pillar Practice	How It Is Developmentally Oriented
Teaming	Teaming is a pillar practice that can be employed to support personal and organizational learning through adult collaboration. Leaders have described how teaming decreases employees' sense of isolation, opens up and improves communication, enables them to include other adults in leadership, enhances chances for achieving organizational and instructional goals, improves implementation of new initiatives, and enhances instructional improvement and internal capacity building. Teaming supports growth in adults who have different ways of knowing. While working with others in a team, adults have the chance to share and learn from each other's perspectives and more fully understand and question their *own* and other adults' thinking, assumptions, and beliefs that guide instructional and leadership practice. The context of a team can be one in which adults experiment with new ways of thinking to support one's own and other adults' growth. As discussed in Chapters 2 and 3, adults need different forms of supports and challenges to engage effectively in this practice and to grow from their engagement.
Providing leadership roles	School and district leaders report that inviting teachers, staff, and administrators to assume leadership roles creates growth opportunities. Adults grow from assuming responsibility for the development of an idea, the implementation of a proposal, and various other types of leadership positions (e.g., leading teams, leading meetings, spearheading change initiatives). Providing leadership roles, however, is more than simply assigning tasks or delegating. For example, the purposive phrase "providing leadership roles" moves beyond "distributive leadership" because of the *developmental intention* that accompanies these roles. When a leadership role is offered, someone is there to facilitate the growth of the person assuming the role by offering supports and challenges to facilitate and scaffold growth. Offering support as a person assumes a leadership role creates a holding space for growth as the person takes on new responsibilities and bumps up against the complexity of enacting the new role. This helps people better understand their own thinking and underlying assumptions and can help them move forward as they test out new ways of acting. Providing leadership roles to teachers and other educators invites the sharing of authority and expertise. Providing leadership roles also allows leaders and educators to modify forms of support and challenge in order to support growth and build individual capacity. In sum, inviting adults to assume leadership roles supports growth and internal capacity building, provided that developmentally appropriate supports and challenges are offered to the adult assuming the role.

(Continued)

Table 5.2 (Continued)

Pillar Practice	How It Is Developmentally Oriented
Collegial inquiry	Collegial inquiry is a shared dialogue directed toward helping adults become more aware of their thinking, perspectives, and assumptions, and those of their colleagues (Drago-Severson, 2004b, 2009). Collegial inquiry differs from reflective practice, which can take place in isolation, in that a person needs at least one partner in order to engage in collegial inquiry. Leaders in our research have shared that they employ collegial inquiry for a variety of reasons and in diverse contexts, including collaborative decision making and conflict resolution. Many of these leaders structure faculty, department, and team meetings to facilitate reflection and discussion regarding practice, goals, and instruction through collegial inquiry. Doing so, from their perspective, encouraged self-reflection and built individual and organizational capacity.
	Over time, engaging in collegial inquiry can help educators listen to and learn from diverse perspectives. It also enables adults to clarify their own thinking and to better understand the influence of their assumptions on thinking and behaviors. The following are examples of how school leaders successfully employed collegial inquiry: (1) inviting adults to reflect privately in writing in response to probing questions, followed by team discussion of their ideas; (2) collaborating as they worked to set annual and team goals and evaluate programs, new initiatives, and instructional practices; (3) responding to questions related to a mission and instructional practices individually and then developing shared understandings of next steps; and (4) reflecting privately and then collectively to engage in resolving conflict.
Mentoring	Mentoring is arguably the oldest form of supporting adult development. It is a private, relational way of supporting growth. Participating in a mentoring relationship is an opportunity for broadening perspectives, examining assumptions about instruction and leadership, and sharing expertise. Importantly, mentoring supports the development of both partners in the mentoring relationship. In schools and districts, mentoring has a variety of forms and purposes. These include pairing experienced or deeply knowledgeable teachers and leaders with novice or struggling ones, pairing faculty to teach and implement technology, and team mentoring. More generally, mentoring programs meet a number of organizational and district needs, including the transmission and reinforcement of mission, the proliferation of expertise, and the provision of emotional and professional support to both new and experienced educators within schools and across school systems. When structuring mentoring programs, however, it is important to consider the goodness of fit between the mentor and mentee *and the developmental supports* and *challenges* necessary to foster adult development (please see Chapters 2 and 3 for a more detailed description).

After experiencing the pillar practices in action and also learning about their developmental underpinnings in LTL, nearly all of the leaders went on to employ these practices in different combinations and different forms, as we will describe below. Their implementations of the pillars provide a unique opportunity to see what developmental practices look like and feel like in real-life leadership practice. Significantly, nearly all twenty of the leaders who participated in interviews with us emphasized the promise of implementing the pillars in some form. Some focused on implementing one or two pillars deeply in their practice, while others choose to employ all of them. What we offer below are representative illustrations of how these leaders went on to implement, adapt, and refine each of the pillars as holding environments that support adults' internal growth.

Teaming: Bringing Adults Together to Enhance Learning and Practice

> In the classroom, it can be a very lonely profession, and that's why I draw my teachers out and form professional learning communities for them online and face-to-face . . . [M]y whole school is a professional learning community, but I organize my teachers in professional learning teams. . . . [T]hey have a face-to-face [meeting] to talk about different ideas week after week.

—Adrian, Secondary School Principal, Singapore

As Adrian points out in the above passage, teaching can be a "very lonely profession." Like many of these LTL leaders, Adrian strives to bring teachers together in teams to strengthen practice, build community and capacity, and foster adult growth and learning—which can help educators of all kinds better meet the urgent demands of new professional and performance standards and also positively impacts student performance. In this section, we focus on the ways in which these leaders employed the pillar practice of *teaming* as a safe holding environment for learning and growth in their educational organizations.

Please recall that teaming—in the developmental sense—involves prioritizing space and *time* for adults to collaboratively examine their ideas, assumptions, ideologies, and practices, experiment with and learn from new perspectives, and support and improve each other's professional work (Drago-Severson, 2004b, 2009, 2012). Nearly all of the LTL leaders in this study wholeheartedly emphasized the importance of collaborative work in their current leadership practice and explained that teams now enhance their colleagues' professional and personal learning. For instance, important features of how they are using teaming as leaders to engage colleagues in collaborative practice include

- creating teams as holding environments to build relationships and promote growth through collaboration (nearly all, 18/20), and
- crafting teams as truly safe learning contexts (18/20).

As we discuss in more detail next, these leaders have embraced teaming as a developmental practice that fosters and sustains nurturing, collaborative learning contexts supportive of individual and organizational growth. To help illustrate how they have transferred these ideas to their actual leadership, we next present a few representative examples from the field.

Teams as Holding Environments: Building Relationships and Promoting Growth Through Collaboration. Constructively challenging adults to further develop their professional knowledge, internal capacities, and skills by working collaboratively is a significant feature of teaming as a developmental pillar practice. Adults grow and learn— and can grow closer to one another in the professional sense—when they pool their efforts, energy, and expertise in teams toward common goals and purposes. Nearly all of the LTL leaders (18/20) emphasized the importance and promise of building collegial relationships through collaborative work. In particular, they shared, working in safe, productive teams allows adults to learn from each other, grow together as individuals and as a group, and enhance practice.

For example, Lucy, a diplomat working in U.S. embassies abroad, attempts to create safe teaming opportunities for reflecting and learning in her unique organizational context because it is "designed to be in constant flux." In her leadership role as a diplomat, Lucy focuses on facilitating educational and learning opportunities either for Americans going abroad or for people abroad traveling to the United States. She leads her peers at the embassy in her consular work and also oversees some local employees. She explained that her organization is not a "stable entity" because the job description of employees and the location of their work changes constantly. Nevertheless, Lucy still finds ways to create "mechanisms for reflection" in teams—as holding environments—to support her staff's professional development in this special and "fascinating" context. Talking together about their work in safe teams helps Lucy and her colleagues think about ways to improve their performance in Foreign Service contexts, and it helps to foster a more collegial, collaborative approach to the unique challenges they face.

Similarly, Palia, a high school assistant principal and professional development leader, brings her teachers together to discuss and reflect on various issues of concern related to curricular and instructional practices. These discussions focus on talking about important challenges and students' academic struggles—for example literacy issues—and reflecting on ways to engage and support their students. She also encourages teams of teachers to observe each other's instruction and record their observations. Later these observations and reflections inform their team discussions and help them look at their intentional—and sometimes "unintentional"—instructional strategies, challenge their routine ways of approaching issues, and work collaboratively to support each other in addressing those challenges. Teaming, Palia explained, helps her teachers discover different aspects of their own classroom practices and also helps them really connect and talk with each other about important issues that might otherwise go unexamined. In particular, visiting each other's classrooms and observing classroom practice helps teachers learn from diverse perspectives and also notice and talk about taken-for-granted instructional routines and behaviors. As Palia explained,

> We have teachers in each other's classrooms all the time, so it's like we'll write down every single question out of a teacher's mouth in the course of an hour and twenty minutes, and suddenly people are realizing, wow, a lot of the questions that they're asking are really fact based, they're really recall based . . . [and] that's not their intention.

For Palia and her teachers, like many of the other leaders we learned from in LTL and other professional learning initiatives we have had the honor of facilitating since then, teaming provides adults with the opportunity to learn with and from each other, while simultaneously honing in on agreed upon ideals and visions for successful practice.

Strategies for Crafting Teams as Safe Learning Contexts. In addition to these important ideas, the majority of the leaders (18/20) we spoke with in interviews years after the course emphasized the importance of creating teams as truly safe spaces for collaborative reflection and dialogue about practice. Their own experiences in LTL and their reflections on instructor modeling, they shared, helped them transfer the practice and experience of teaming to their own schools and leadership contexts. In particular, many detailed the specific strategies they are using to build and sustain teams as safe collaborative environments. Below, for example, we describe how two leaders are currently using norming processes when engaging adults in teamwork in their work contexts. We hope that these particular examples help highlight the different, creative ways teaming can be used to promote collaborative practice and reflection in diverse settings.

In her work with teachers and administrators as a counselor and consultant, for example, Gina invites adults to establish norms and ground rules as part of the process of creating safe contexts for dialogue and respectful listening. Inspired by her experiences as a learner in LTL (please see Chapter 2 for a detailed discussion of the importance of creating norms and Figure 4.1 for a sample protocol to guide this process), Gina adopted the practice in her work to develop a culture of collaborative reflection in a safe environment. She said that creating structures and scaffolds for teachers helps them really reflect on their practice *with* each other. At the time of our interview, for instance, Gina was beginning work with a new team of instructional leaders. Establishing norms, she explained, was the very first item on the agenda when she recently gathered the group together for a book study.

Establishing these norms and openly considering and evaluating goals were important, Gina explained, for these agreed-upon norms and rules for dialogue allow for a candid, critical, and respectful exchange among the adults on her team. In contrast with some of her less successful experiences as a member of prior teams, where at times the work "didn't go very far," Gina hoped that developing these norms at the outset would help establish a common and safe ground for the mutual exchange of ideas and practices for meaningful teamwork. This was a lesson she learned from LTL, as the shared norms she experienced in the class helped her feel free and safe to share in that context.

In a related example, Jane, who consults with district-level teams around data-driven instruction, described her concrete efforts to structure and facilitate collaborative thinking and reflection with adults on teams. When leading and guiding teams, for example, she challenges individuals to agree to more than social niceties and conventions when setting norms. "I know that typically norms are about things like 'let's be on time' and 'turn your cells phones off' and 'don't e-mail while we're talking,'" she explained, but as she also shares with the adults she works with, these things are "not really going to help us change our behavior or talk about things in a different way." As she explained further,

> Being respectful and being supportive of other people in a team setting [often] means that you sort of find opportunities to agree with them, that you don't question their reasoning . . . that you just sort of nod along even if you disagree. . . . [Similarly,] to be strong and maintain integrity, which is sort of the advocacy piece of this, means that you stick to your point and that you don't cave in and you hammer it home. . . . [But, from a more productive, growth-oriented perspective] being respectful and supportive actually means that we assume that people want us as their colleagues to help us identify our hidden assumptions, the gaps in our reasoning and logic. They want to be asked how did I get from A to B? So that being respectful in that world as a colleague in a group is not just always nodding along and agreeing but is asking those questions.

Of course, and as we discussed in more detail in Chapter 3, adults will orient to norm setting and teaming differently depending on their different ways of knowing. With this in mind, Jane encourages the adults on her teams to really talk about how meeting the norms should look and feel. In addition to further clarifying expectations and uniting the group, this process allows individuals to express to their teammates the kinds of responses and procedures that would feel helpful and supportive. Below, Jane describes her thinking and approach further:

> And I also pushed them [the adults on her teams] to give examples, which is a different kind of norms conversation. So if I say I'm going to advocate while inviting inquiry, how are you going to do that? What are you going to say? What are the words that you would use to do that? Give me an example. So that's sort of one difference in terms of how they're going to set norms, and then . . . they need to make some decisions about how are they going to know if they're meeting the norms. Because typically you set norms, and then that's the end of it, so what I really encourage them to do is to make some concrete decisions among their members about, to some extent, what are we going to do if someone

violates a norm? What do we do? And what are ways, again, concrete things that you can say or do to indicate that we're either meeting or not meeting our agreement about how we're going to talk to each other? And really encourage them, at least for the first number of meetings, to set aside some time to do that.

Jane felt that this clear and strategic focus on creating and monitoring norms better enables people to participate in and benefit from team discussions in accordance with their particular needs. As we have seen, and as you know, developing and implementing mutually agreed-upon norms, rules, and protocols are crucial to engaging in productive teaming experiences—and Jane, like many of these leaders, has found significant success with their implementation in the field. As she shared,

> People have said back to me a number of times how powerful that [norm setting] was, and we've even had someone listening in on a session recently that was not a participant, they were just there observing, and they came up to me and they said, Oh my, I just set norms with this other team a week ago, and they were all [social] norms, so we are actually going to go back . . . and redo norms the way you just taught us!

As Jane's and Gina's examples suggest, carefully structuring collaborative work—and establishing and upholding agreed-upon norms—is key to the successful implementation of this pillar. Moreover, as many of these leaders' experiences revealed, meaningful and effective collaboration on the *team* level can help translate into more effective and unified *organizational* progress—even in the face of the many adaptive challenges educators face in their schools and systems. As we discuss in the next section about how leaders employed the pillar of collegial inquiry in their current work, effective teaming practices also lay the groundwork for deeper, collaborative dives into fundamental and complex questions of teaching, learning, and leadership.

Collegial Inquiry

I don't believe that there are quick-fix solutions to complex problems, and so I like to think of it more as managing dilemmas rather than solving problems.

—Jed, Head of Urban Charter School

In addition to teaming, the leaders we learned from intentionally employed forms of *collegial inquiry* in their work to collaboratively address the complex challenges they face as educators. As discussed in Chapter 2 and Table 5.2, collegial inquiry is a developmental practice that can support individual and organizational growth by engaging colleagues in a critical and collaborative inquiry into their practice (Drago-Severson, 2004b, 2009, 2012). Some of the most important and prominent features of collegial inquiry that emerged from these leaders' practice include

- providing appropriate structures (e.g., protocols) to encourage teachers to engage in difficult conversations around their dilemmas to foster critical inquiry into practice, and
- critically and collaboratively examining practice to better see, understand, and grow from intentions, assumptions, goals, and actions.

By carefully scaffolding collegial inquiry, and carefully and caringly supporting colleagues in critically examining their professional thinking, feeling, and acting, these leaders were able to translate their LTL learnings and experiences of collegial inquiry into effective on-the-ground leadership practices that support growth in diverse contexts.

Creating Structures and Protocols for Inquiry Into Dilemmas of Practice. Many leaders (about one-third of the participants) in this study described how they promote collegial inquiry and reflection among their colleagues by talking, inquiring, and learning together in safe, structured learning environments. In this section, we share examples of how these LTL leaders are using concrete structures and protocols to constructively address problems of practice through collegial inquiry.

For example, as the head of a large, urban charter school (composed of three divisions), Jed tries to create safe spaces to initiate dialogue around teachers' dilemmas of practice. He views dialogue among teachers as opportunities to discuss and unpack complex problems with each other's help. As you read in the opening quote, Jed does not believe that there are "quick-fix solutions to complex problems." Rather, he emphasizes the importance and power of "managing dilemmas" and often takes a collaborative approach to building capacity in this way. With this in mind, he transformed the format and focus of the academic leadership team meetings at his school to welcome and support collegial inquiry. As he shared with us, he attempted to "reframe" that time to encourage people to bring "real dilemmas to the meetings." This structure enabled the department leaders, "who seldom had any opportunities to step back" and think about the "burning issues" in their practice, to share their dilemmas and struggles in the presence of other trusted colleagues. Jed explained that, in this form, collegial inquiry constitutes a holding environment that invites articulating and sharing dilemmas with colleagues. He felt that it transformed their team into a truly "collaborative" and "democratic" group. As he further elaborated,

> [I]n some ways, that moment is a holding environment of itself. It really did transform the way that our team was working, and rather than me as principal being the driver of the group, it really became a much more collaborative and democratically governed group.

Moreover, Jed noted that these collegial conversations are modeled on the LTL practice of convening, as he invites other administrators and teachers to bring their dilemmas for sharing and discussion. Similarly, Jed uses protocols to structure these collegial conversations in order to engage individuals with different ways of knowing. He believes that these protocols, which he's picked up and modified from various sources, help create "a holding environment for those conversations to happen," rather than just "facilitating meetings with the same kind of conversation over and over and over again."

Jed described the process by explaining that he first invites his colleagues (members of the senior administration) to brainstorm the "big" and "burning" issues in his organization at the start of every semester. After developing a collective awareness of the general issues, he next encourages individuals to talk about their own particular dilemmas in these meetings. Furthermore, he selectively employs protocols to provide continuity and connection between the various issues discussed in these conversations. As he explained,

> I've probably used six to eight [protocols] really frequently in my leadership work. . . . So it might be helpful to others to incorporate the protocol into their repertoire because oftentimes the protocols do create the holding environment for those conversations to happen.

Like Jed, Brenda, a former academic dean and Spanish educator, stressed crafting structures to enact safe and collegial contexts for mutual inquiry into problems of practice. As she explained, LTL's structure "gave me a framework to think about" reflective inquiry in one's practice. Moreover, she emphasized the importance of understanding collegial inquiry from both teachers' and leaders' perspectives.

According to Brenda, from a teacher's point of view, collegial inquiry involves looking at one's practice through "the act of self-reflection" as well as with the help of other colleagues to "see it the way an outsider would see it." By providing this kind of critically supportive "mirror," Brenda shared, collegial inquiry invites partici-pants to "improve yourself professionally and personally." From a leader's perspective, on the other hand, collegial inquiry means "understanding reflective practice" and "providing the space and time for teachers to do it," in her opinion. Moreover, she believes that it is important for leaders to "reflect on yourself as a leader and how you help teachers."

In order to create robust contexts for collegial inquiry into teach-ers' practice, Brenda adapted the LTL and critical friends protocols to initiate an inquiry group at her school comprising teachers from dif-ferent disciplines (e.g., math and language). In this group, teachers brought their students' completed homework assignments and exam-ined them in terms of student learning and their curricular goals. Brenda was excited about what she and other teachers learned from each other about how to promote student learning in different sub-jects. The protocol that she used to structure collegial inquiry into practice involved allocating a particular amount of time to present student work, ask questions, and then invite comments from the group to improve their work with students. The presenters discussed their students' actual homework, how they as teachers "assigned the assignment," how they worded and explained it to students, what their "expectations" were, how they were "going to assess them," and what they thought about students' learning. Brenda further explained that initially she led the group, but later rotated moderators for each meeting who made sure that the group accomplished its goals within the prescribed time. As she explained,

> I got it [the group] started, but then we rotated the person who would lead each time. There'd be somebody who'd vol-unteer to come in and actually share the student work, and then there was somebody who would moderate and make sure we stayed in our time limits and that we're answering the questions.

While this kind of structure and facilitation helped Brenda and her colleagues most efficiently use time, a precious commodity in any busy school day, it also helped them more effectively explore and unpack questions and assumptions that were central to their work and instructional practice. This is a theme we explore in more detail in the section that follows.

Critically and Collaboratively Examining Issues of Practice. Collegial inquiry, as you know, is all about asking deep and meaningful questions in the company of dedicated colleagues. About one-half of these LTL leaders explained that they indeed employ collegial inquiry to encourage adults in their organizations to critically understand and examine central issues of practice. Below, we share two representative examples to illustrate some of the ways these leaders are employing collegial inquiry to support learning and growth in their diverse workplaces.

For example, Sarah, an education faculty member at a university, believes that understanding issues from teachers' perspectives is a crucial part of creating safe contexts for problem solving. She considers it important to involve teachers in decisions about school policies and programs, such as changes to the student discipline policy or rethinking interventions for students with behavioral problems. In her work with teachers as an educational leader, she creates opportunities for critical, collaborative reflection among teachers to help them consider particular problems, better understand their assumptions, and think through their roles in relation to key issues. Sarah noted that this practice helps leaders anticipate, understand, and learn from potentially negative reactions in workplaces, like those that can occur when teachers are casually informed about revisions to school policies that may or may not have their support. Sarah explained that collaborative discussion through collegial inquiry with her colleagues helped her "really think about where teachers might be in their thinking about what their role is" as professionals. Moreover, it enabled her to gain a better understanding of "how they see students [and] their assumptions about student behavior." A better understanding of teachers' views about their work and their students further helped Sarah to "be able to figure out where to begin the conversation in schools."

Melanie, a former middle school principal who is currently pursuing a doctorate in education, shares Sarah's view and believes that opportunities for collegial inquiry can make professional development an inspiring and meaningful experience for teachers. When Melanie first joined her school, she noticed that there was a "congenial culture" where people had strong social relationships, but she felt that it was not *collegial*, as they did not share their practices with each other. Therefore, she made efforts to move beyond friendly surface discussions by creating a space for growth where teachers were encouraged to talk about their work with each other and felt safe to "take risks" as well as to "try out new ideas by working with each other."

Explicitly aiming for this kind of authentic collaboration and having the space to discuss these deeper (and more difficult) kinds of feelings and thinking can make a big difference in schools and organizations, leaders shared. And, as you know, collegial inquiry, a developmental practice, requires the hard and honest work of looking beneath behaviors—even the comfortable ones—to examine underlying thinking, feeling, and meaning making. In this way, collegial inquiry, like all of the pillar practices, can help individuals and groups push their instructional practice to new levels and heights.

Providing Leadership Roles

> [O]ne of my moves was to create this team of teacher leaders who would function as an instructional leadership team . . . [I] use them as models of people who were willing to do something new and take some risks, and be recognized as leaders, both formally and informally, with their colleagues.

> —Melanie, Former Middle School Principal

Another way that Melanie, like many of these leaders, transferred her LTL learnings about supporting adult growth to her leadership as a principal was by providing colleagues with leadership roles. As you learned in Chapter 2, and as we offered once more in Table 5.2 to be of help, inviting colleagues to take on leadership roles contributes to their personal and professional growth. Indeed, with the appropriate supports, adults in leadership roles learn to share their work, knowledge, and expertise with other colleagues and in this process strengthen their own capacities. Engaging in leadership work serves as a professional growth opportunity for everyone as the leaders become aware of their own and others' assumptions about their work and develop new ways of sharing their professional expertise with others (Drago-Severson, 2009).

Some school leaders (4/20) talked about the importance of providing leadership roles (PLR) to teachers to create holding environments for their own as well other adults' growth. They deemed it an important practice to enhance teachers' professional growth by sharing new ideas and theory with each other. In the following sections, we discuss noteworthy features of how these leaders are using PLR as a developmental practice, including

- creating opportunities for teachers to lead professional development sessions and workshops for peers, and
- creating opportunities for teachers to lead content learning and schoolwide initiatives.

In particular, we illuminate the ways in which various leaders are adapting and incorporating PLR in their work to create safe learning environments that support their colleagues' professional growth.

Teacher-Led Professional Development Programs. In order to support teachers' growth in the areas of content and technology, Melanie (educational leader), Palia (high school assistant principal), and Adrian (secondary school principal) stressed the importance of teacher-led initiatives. Melanie, for example, attempted to create instructional leadership opportunities for teachers during her tenure as principal by inviting them to lead professional development for other teachers. To achieve this goal, as she described in the opening quote, she created a team of instructional leaders specializing in particular content areas with the task of developing and modeling new pedagogical approaches. She aimed to improve all teachers' content knowledge and pedagogical practice at her school by using experts as "models" who were willing to try out new approaches and "take some risks" in terms of creating innovative curricular and instructional strategies. Yet Melanie was simultaneously careful to offer these new teacher leaders appropriate supports as they took on and grew into their leadership roles. "I would meet with them," she explained, "to provide them with specific content areas to talk about, [and] to try to steer together directions of the school." This more collaborative and developmentally mindful approach to supporting new leaders was key to ensuring their success. Melanie also shared that she builds choice—another important kind of support and show of respect—into professional development activities for adults. For example, although she invites expert teachers at her school to "model lessons on a particular topic or content area," teachers then choose and attend the workshops that resonate with their interests.

Similarly, Palia creates teacher-led "learning groups" at her school where lead teachers share effective examples of practice from their own and other educators' work. Moreover, Palia creates opportunities for intellectual discussions led by veteran teachers who share new research, theory, and developments in the field. As she described,

> We have . . . a book group on a specific new research that's come out. That's [facilitated] more [by] veteran teachers usually, but it's less classroom based and more like discussion of new theory and application of new theory, and even just intellectually discussing the field at large.

Adrian similarly believes in the importance of providing instructional leadership roles to enhance his teachers' instructional performance, and he offers regular opportunities to teachers who are technology experts to conduct professional development for other teachers at his secondary school in Singapore. In this way, teachers design and conduct technology workshops for their colleagues to expose them to new digital/multimedia instructional technologies and develop their skills to use these applications in their instruction effectively. We will discuss this in more detail and provide additional examples of Adrian's work in Chapter 6, which focuses on rich case examples from the field.

Teacher Leadership in Developing Schoolwide Practices. Like other LTL graduates, Elizabeth, a math department head, employs PLR to make teachers' professional development meaningful for the larger community at her school. In addition to soliciting teacher feedback on a new assessment program, as we described earlier, Elizabeth initiated a teacher-led program to help design assessment tasks as part of her larger assessment work in school. In particular, she involved teachers in developing preassessments and diagnostic tools in mathematics to gather baseline data to help track students' learning trajectories over time. The baseline data helped them assess students' existing understanding of math concepts and skills. This baseline information also informed the curriculum in terms of selecting and differentiating the content and instruction in accordance with students' understanding of math concepts. As she explained, the teacher-led program made a significant contribution:

> We've been able to differentiate instruction much more strategically because of that, and yeah, it's really been, I think, a big step forward for us.

Elizabeth also noted that she is working toward achieving the goal of creating and sustaining professional learning groups led by her mathematics teachers. This, she felt, would be a strong step away from primarily administrator-led professional development. In her words,

> [T]he teachers would really be running their own groups and having their own discussions and setting their own agendas and things like that, [but] we're definitely not there yet.

Still, Elizabeth initiated the process of involving teachers in leadership activities and ultimately hopes to develop professional development opportunities that are entirely designed and implemented by teachers. As you can see from many of the examples we've already shared, however, Elizabeth's efforts remain—like those of many of her former LTL colleagues'—in transition. This is an illustration of both the complexity and the promise of employing the pillars as holding environments that support adult growth.

Mentoring

And another wonderful thing that came up [is] . . . seeing a very experienced teacher . . . pairing up with a very young teacher, and when we pair them together, the young teacher helps the senior teacher with the technology, and the senior teacher helps with the classroom management.

—Adrian, Secondary School Principal

In addition to teaming, collegial inquiry, and providing leadership roles, several leaders (about one-fourth) talked about how they are employing and adapting the pillar practice of developmental mentoring to create holding environments for mutual learning and growth in their schools and educational organizations. As we revisited in Table 5.2, mentoring, from a developmental perspective, is a relational practice that can enhance the growth and learning of adults on both sides of the mentoring relationship, as they help each other expand their knowledge, broaden their perspectives, and enhance each other's professional skills (Drago-Severson, 2004b, 2009, 2012). Unlike some of the other pillars, however, which LTL students experienced directly in the course, mentoring, in our view, is a longer-term relationship that could only be "sampled" in the fifteen-week class though relationships with instructors and fellow classmates. Nevertheless, the power and promise of mentoring remained at the forefront of LTL discussions and mini-mentoring experiences, and a number of the leaders we learned from emphasized the centrality of the practice to their own growth and to their efforts supporting colleagues. Prevalent themes that emerged from the leaders' accounts of how they are employing developmental mentoring in their current leadership work include

- reciprocal learning between novice and expert colleagues, and
- professional development through specialized coaching.

Some LTL leaders shared the specific ways in which they are adapting mentoring as a developmental practice to create holding environments for learning in their workplaces. Below, we share insightful examples from leaders' current work employing mentoring to nurture spaces for professional learning.

Reciprocal Learning Between Novice and Expert Colleagues. Dana, an English department chair and mentor in her high school, talked about the different ways in which she organizes mentoring opportunities for her teachers. Dana noted that she pairs "more experienced" teachers with novice colleagues so that they can work together individually and share specialized knowledge and pedagogical expertise. She also provides opportunities for her teachers to offer and obtain peer feedback on their instructional and assessment plans.

Through these mentoring opportunities, she encourages her teachers to learn about each other's best and most successful practices. Toward this end, she tries to share "models of successful work" to encourage and inspire colleagues to use effective curricular and instructional activities in their own practice. Her intention is to highlight and recognize the work of teachers who are "doing well" in their classrooms and provide learning opportunities for sharing their knowledge, strategies, and skills with others. Specifically, she first pairs teachers with peers in their subject areas, and then pairs them with colleagues in other departments to give teachers "opportunities to look at examples of different work and student work." Dana firmly believes that these kinds of mentoring opportunities are essential for teachers to look at as "concrete examples of things that have been successful" in their peers' instructional practice.

Dana further explained that she tries to "support the variety of learning styles that adults have" through these collaborative mentoring activities. Also, as an "informal mentor for teachers that are newer" to her staff, Dana works to bring her developmental mindfulness to bear. When mentoring teachers in her department, for instance, she specifically asks them what kinds of help they need and what kinds of support or challenge would be most helpful.

As she explained, when informally mentoring teachers, "I ask them to reflect on how well they're doing, [how] what I'm doing works for them, [and] what further supports they need." Asking these kinds of questions, as you know, can help mentors and mentees develop shared expectations and build a working relationship that feels personally and professionally meaningful. Still, as Dana acknowledged, she hopes to even further employ a developmental perspective to extend these kinds of holding environments in her school. As she explained,

> I don't know if that's [developmental principles] been as explicit in everyone's mind as we've been coplanning [for mentoring and professional development], but I know for me, it's been underlying the work that I do because adults also need to have a good learning environment. . . . [I'm] so much more cognizant of the types of learners they [teachers] are, . . . [and] I think we have to do an even more effective job of doing that for them.

Please recall from the quote that opened this larger section on leaders' sharings about mentoring in their work, Adrian likewise employs developmentally sensitive mentoring to pair novice and experienced teachers in his secondary school. In case helpful, we discuss his approach in some detail in Chapter 6, where we highlight integrated cases from leaders' work.

Professional Development Through Specialized Coaching. Increasingly described as developmental coaching as well as mentoring, this pillar, as we discuss below, is an effective strategy for sharing and building more specialized expertise and capacity in schools and other contexts. In her work as a high school assistant principal, for example, Palia is largely responsible for coaching and supporting teachers, and in this role, she often has to support both teachers' individual goals and the focus of the larger school community. To help do this, Palia shared that she works to shape coaching opportunities as holding environments for the adults she works with by providing specific supports in accordance with teachers' individual needs. She explained that she sometimes engages in "formal coaching" to work with teachers one-on-one, and that she also works with small groups of teachers to provide regular feedback on their instruction. As Palia explained,

I coach certain people more in depth, kind of over the course of the year or half the year, that sort of thing, and more in a long-term process. And then other people, I'm just observing . . . as it relates to specific things that they're working on or specific kind of things that the school is working on.

By meeting with teachers individually to "talk about their practice, their other contributions to the school, . . . their interests . . . [and] what they want to focus on . . . for the end of the year, for next year, [or] what kind of support they need," Palia is able to better understand teachers' goals and priorities for learning and can better help shape and place teachers during larger, schoolwide professional development sessions that "work for the school" as a whole. These more formalized professional development "pods," as she calls them, focus on specialized schoolwide improvement initiatives—including theory, practice, and new research. Based on a careful assessment of teachers' specific needs in relation to their work or schoolwide programs, teachers' placements grow out of the more individualized coaching relationships described above, and they reflect "where they [teachers] are in their career and interests."

While Palia acknowledges that the system could further improve in terms of "how we address every particular person's needs," these specialized mentoring and coaching activities serve as important professional development opportunities for the teachers in her school, and they illustrate some of the very real promises and tensions of mentoring teachers as a school leader.

Summary: Creating Holding Environments for Growth by Employing Pillar Practices

In this section, we learned about the various ways these leaders have transferred their LTL learnings about the pillar practices as holding environments to their own leadership, years after successfully completing the course. After learning about and experiencing the pillar practices that make up Drago-Severson's (2004b, 2009) learning-oriented model for school leadership—teaming, collegial inquiry, providing leadership roles, and mentoring—the leaders we learned from were able to employ these practices in unique and constructive ways in their own work contexts to foster individual and collective growth.

Examples from various leaders' practice showed that teaming helps in developing constructive professional relationships that foster individual and organizational growth. Teaming enables professionals to develop a common vision for personal and institutional improvement. It also helps colleagues discover and build on diverse perspectives when improving professional practice.

We also discussed how many of these leaders are using collegial inquiry as opportunities to discuss challenges and dilemmas concerning practice. Collegial engagement with other colleagues helps in collaboratively examining problems of practice and thinking about creative solutions for addressing them. The purpose of collegial inquiry, as several leaders noted, is to create safe spaces where colleagues can constructively respond to challenges that may hinder their professional growth.

Providing leadership roles also surfaced as an important practice that encourages teachers to grow professionally by contributing to other colleagues' professional practice. Many leaders said that they intentionally create opportunities for teachers to lead instructional improvement efforts by sharing their knowledge and expertise with other colleagues.

A number of leaders also employed mentoring to create holding environments for mutual learning and growth in educational contexts. They believed that pairing colleagues can foster reciprocal growth through the sharing of specialized skills and strategies. Table 5.3 showcases the pillar practices these leaders are employing to create holding environments to enhance their colleagues' professional growth.

Next, we further describe some of the developmental strategies these leaders employed to differentiate supports and challenges *within* the pillars, reflecting their understanding that adults experience collaborative practices differently depending on their ways of knowing.

Differentiating Supports and Challenges Within the Pillar Practices to Support Adult Development

In this section, we further describe the specific ways these educational leaders are differentiating supports and challenges in their current work with the pillar practices (discussed above) to make them meaningful and responsive to adults' unique developmental capacities. Notably, all of these leaders recognized that people with different developmental capacities may respond differently to learning and growth-oriented tasks—including the pillar practices—so they try to adapt and tailor different strategies to support adults

Table 5.3   Creating Learning Environments for Professional Growth Using Learning-Oriented Pillar Practices

Pillar Practice	How LTL Leaders Employed and Adjusted Pillar Practice
Teaming	• Creating teams as safe spaces for dialogue and collaborative reflection on practice • Gathering ideas and working together on focused tasks in a safe learning space • Respecting and valuing individuals' different viewpoints in the organization • Examining issues from multiple perspectives • Developing productive and rewarding professional relationships • Understanding issues from teachers' perspectives • Engaging team members in developmentally oriented supports and challenges for growth and internal capacity building • Collaboratively creating new practices and tools for instruction and assessment
Collegial inquiry	• Critically examining issues of practice (e.g., student work) through collaborative, meaningful engagement • Offering and receiving constructive feedback on practice and ideas • Creating structures and protocols for inquiry to investigate dilemmas/problems of practice • Engaging in dialogue about and uncovering tacit assumptions that guide thinking and practice • Providing developmentally appropriate supports and challenges to facilitate growth • Inviting teachers to collectively address common issues and problems and welcoming their perspectives • Viewing and *honoring* teachers as problem solvers rather than blaming them for issues
Providing leadership roles	• Creating opportunities for teachers to lead content learning and to facilitate processes • Engaging teachers in developing curricula and writing assessments • Inviting teachers to share their expertise to build other teachers' knowledge and skills • Encouraging technology experts to conduct workshops for other teachers
Mentoring	• Reciprocal learning between novice and expert colleagues through the sharing of particular skills, knowledge, and expertise • Offering and receiving feedback on colleagues' practice • Pairing adults to support each other in thinking about and addressing challenges

who make meaning in different ways. "Meeting people where they are" and supporting them to expand their potential surfaced from these leaders' accounts as a significant goal and orientation toward leadership.

For example, nearly all interview participants detailed efforts to cater to developmental diversity among adults by offering differentiated supports and challenges when employing the pillars and other LTL-inspired practices. Indeed, many years after the course, they reported using a range of learning-oriented practices to help adults acquire new ideas and skills as well as enhance their capacity to manage complexity in their professional responsibilities. Key on-the-ground practices employed by these educational leaders to differentiate supports in accordance with adults' unique ways of knowing included

- working to understand teachers' developmental orientations or ways of meaning making through informal conversations,
- offering choice to colleagues when implementing professional development,
- structuring complex tasks (like collegial inquiry) with concrete, manageable increments, and
- inviting adults to pair-share or free-write in response to prompts before larger-group discussions.

Employing these kinds of smaller-scale differentiation strategies can help adults feel comfortable and successful in any of the pillar practices. Below, we highlight a few of the ways these leaders described differentiating their practice to meet teachers "where they are" and offer a few additional strategies you might find helpful in your own work or context. We hope these examples will help illustrate what differentiating supports for adults with different developmental needs and orientations can look like in actual educational/school contexts.

Assessing Individual Needs Through Informal Conversations

The majority of LTL leaders (over two-thirds) noted that they use intentional strategies and scaffolds to differentiate professional development to suit the individual needs and learning orientations of their teachers. Most important to this process, perhaps, is developing an informal understanding of the kinds of supports and challenges that would feel most helpful to different adults through conversation.

As a principal, for example, Melanie explained that she tried to ascertain teachers' professional needs through informal conversations to understand and meet teachers "where they were." She noted that she learned about this developmental practice of identifying individual needs in relation to their ways of knowing in LTL. As she described, LTL "met me where I was" and helped her see the importance of ascertaining individual needs in light of their diverse developmental orientations.

In both LTL and leaders' practice, they shared, the simple act of *asking other adults what they need* can be both revealing and supportive in important and promising ways.

Offering Choice to Maximize "Fit" and Show Respect

Melanie also described the importance of offering adults choice when designing and implementing professional development as a principal. When, for instance, she organized professional development sessions focusing on particular content areas, she then offered teachers a choice to attend the sessions they were interested in as a show of respect and to maximize their learning. She also offered special sessions where teachers could volunteer to "model lessons" on different content topics to share best practices in content instruction. Melanie further explained that she believes in giving "free choice" to colleagues in relation to spending their learning time productively in light of their particular interests and professional goals. In large part, Melanie explained, the flexibility and invitational style of LTL helped her see and understand the importance of choice as a support for adults with different interests and ways of knowing. As she explained, that feeling of being well held was "something I wanted to replicate for others."

In describing his work as a school principal in Singapore, Adrian also stressed the promise of choice as a key tool for developmentally oriented differentiation. As he explained,

> I think adult learners, they must be given choices from a very varied menu of learning experiences, and I think if you give them a certain menu and you understand which phase of development they are in, I think that would more or less improve the match between their [teachers'] style or maybe even the readiness of our teachers in terms of the learning that we offer to them.

For both Melanie and Adrian, like a number of the other leaders in this study, the opportunity to "choose from a menu" of options was a meaningful form of differentiation that they worked to implement in their own leadership practice.

Structuring Complex Tasks in Manageable Increments

As an educational leader and university professor, Sarah also recognizes that adults are at different levels in terms of their thinking, knowledge, and capacities. As she elaborated, "at the team level, just because people are investing their time and effort around a certain initiative doesn't mean they all have the same thoughts and capacities."

Therefore, while engaging adults in teamwork, she is mindful of developmental diversity and carefully works to make tasks meaningful for everyone. While creating opportunities for collaborative and critical reflection, for instance, she is mindful of colleagues who may not yet be comfortable or "developmentally ready" to critically share their own practice and vulnerabilities in a group setting. As she explained,

> [Y]ou can't [just] start discussions about school improvement with critical reflection because you can't expect everybody to be developmentally ready to critically reflect [from the start].

"Critical reflection," in Sarah's view, "requires a certain capacity for being really able to compartmentalize things about yourself and put them as object and look at them." Nevertheless, she tries to develop ways to involve everyone in collaborative thinking and reflection around school improvement efforts to build both trust and capacity. To achieve this goal, she invites teachers to begin "self-reflection" with a focus on their own immediate "working conditions" and "social relations in their context." This more individual, manageable focus, she explained, can help establish a culture of reflection:

> So if you begin at a point that allows people to be self-reflective about their [own] working conditions and their social relations in their context, then I think you're probably going to put yourself on a better path.

In Sarah's view, engaging people in reflection about what is working well and what kinds of supports they need in their social context provides an entry point into reflection that can help adults grow into questioning, examining, and critiquing the more tacit and underlying aspects of their practice. Structuring the complex and sometimes challenging task of critical, collaborative reflection in this way can help teachers with different orientations toward teaming or collegial inquiry gradually develop the capacity to engage in critical and reflective thinking about their practice.

Inviting Adults to Free-Write or Pair-Share Before Important Conversations

Another effective practice that these leaders described using to differentiate supports and challenges within the pillars and other developmentally oriented practices was inviting adults to *free-write or pair-share before sharing out in larger groups*. As these leaders shared—and as they learned and experienced in LTL—allowing adults to think privately or with a small group of trusted colleagues *before* offering their thoughts, reactions, or opinions to larger groups can feel particularly supportive to adults with a socializing way of knowing and can also support greater participation in general.

Jackie, for instance, acknowledged this link when describing her work supporting aspiring teachers as an adjunct instructor. In her class, she explained,

> I've borrowed some of the ideas from adult development in terms of the structuring [of the class]. So we always start off with, or almost always start off with small-group discussion and it's really—it's to help those socializing [knowers]. . . . To get them to feel comfortable talking in small groups first and then to open it up to a larger group discussion I think is helpful.

Matt, a lower school division head and former director of curriculum at a private school, similarly described the importance of freewriting during large staff meetings—or chambers meetings, as he calls them—to meet people's developmental orientations, capacities, and needs. For example, Matt carefully considers how teachers with different ways of knowing may perceive and respond to questions in faculty meetings and tries to frame his questions and views in ways that would feel supportive to them. Additionally, he makes a conscious effort to create comfortable spaces for teachers to share their answers with him. As he elaborated,

> So some of the things that I do in my faculty meetings, I try to create a structure. . . . I can share information at faculty meetings where teachers will feel more supported in the way that they share their answers with me, while at the same time, I'll get a clear representation of what would be the type of information that I'm looking for as we move together as a team.

Matt shared that, to do this, he invites teachers to write down their thoughts in response to his questions before moving to whole-group discussions. Matt also carefully considers how he is going to record and make meaning of the information that he receives from his colleagues. As he explained,

> [B]efore going into a question, maybe I'll have each teacher fill out a note card for five minutes. . . . And then I would probably also think about the complexities of how I was managing that conversation. So I am going to call on people, or am I looking for volunteers? How am I recording the information?

Matt further explained that his decisions regarding the structure of these conversations with colleagues depend on where they are in the process. He tends to have less structure and offers colleagues more time to develop ideas if they are thinking about and discussing a new initiative or system. When he feels that people have thought through a particular issue and have developed their thinking and response to it, he tends structure those conversations in a "more directed" manner.

Brooke likewise emphasized the importance of differentiating the structure of meeting times with university students when describing her work as an assistant professor in a school of education. "I try to differentiate instruction" for students, she explained. For example, "If I have an hour and fifteen minute class, I will not lecture for more than twenty minutes." Brooke also expressed how her experiences in LTL provided a model of what developmental differentiation could look like in practice. As she elaborated, she remains inspired by "the way that we did things [in LTL], in terms of never doing the same thing all the time in the classroom, doing jigsaws, doing think-pair-shares, [asking] . . . where do you stand in terms of an activity."

Now, for Brooke, her intention is to create similar opportunities for the students in her own university class—and in her new role as a school principal. Doing so, Brooke believes, can help support both learning and personal growth:

> I'm constantly changing things up with them so, one, it keeps their attention, but two, they're actually doing something and it's making them think. Think about what they believe.

For Brooke, like Matt and Jackie, differentiating in terms of structure—such as providing opportunities to free-write or pair-share—is an essential feature of their developmentally oriented leadership and teaching, and it remains key when implementing the pillar practices to support adult learning and growth.

Summary: Differentiating Supports and Challenges Within Pillar Practices to Support Adult Development

Differentiating supports and challenges in light of individuals' developmental levels is key to successfully implementing the pillars, these leaders shared, and to learning-oriented leadership practice in general. Most participants in this study shared differentiation strategies they use as developmental supports and challenges to build adults' internal capacities. For example, they tend to (a) spend time with their colleagues individually to identify their professional needs and learning orientations, (b) offer colleagues choice in professional development to show respect and maximize "fit" with needs and interests, (c) offer concrete guidelines and steps to help structure complex tasks, like collegial inquiry, and (d) differentiate in terms of structure, including providing adults opportunities to free-write or pair-share before engaging in larger conversations. These strategies respond to various developmental needs and the orientations of different types of learners and can help in creating safe and nurturing holding environments to expand internal capacities, professional knowledge, and instructional skills.

In case helpful, we offer in Table 5.4 an overview of additional strategies for differentiation that can support the learning and growth of adults who have diverse ways of knowing.

Chapter Summary

To get through the hardest journey, we need take only one step at a time, but we must keep on stepping.

—Chinese Proverb

In this chapter, we explored the fundamental question of transfer to practice. In other words, we described what we learned from leaders about how, if at all, they now employ learning-oriented ideas and strategies in their own work, years after learning about and experiencing developmentally oriented leadership in LTL. You might want to consider these as their big "takeaways." As we have discussed, all of these leaders went on to implement and adapt key aspects of their LTL learnings in different ways, and we focused our discussion on a number of key themes, including

- leaders' hopes for practice immediately after completing the course,
- the importance of establish trusting, respectful relationships as *preconditions* to larger developmental initiatives,
- the ways in which leaders are using the pillar practices and adaptations of them for supporting adult growth and capacity building, and
- leaders' strategies for differentiating supports and challenges within the pillars to best meet adults with different ways of knowing.

Table 5.4   Differentiating Supports and Challenges Within Pillar Practices to Support Adult Development

Way of Knowing	*Developmentally Supportive and Challenging Practices for Internal Capacity Building*
Instrumental knowers	**Supports (Meeting Them Where They Are)** • Developing and agreeing upon concrete rules, routines, and structures • Providing technical information about the tasks and responsibilities • Using think-pair-share activities • Providing scaffolds to help navigate challenging tasks **Challenges (Developmental Stretching)** • Constructing protocols for engaging in thinking, reflection, and sharing and explaining why we are employing them • Free writing and case-based reflection with rationale for use • Creating structured problem-solving opportunities and explaining the reason behind the activities • Helping instrumental knowers develop a shared understanding of organizational vision, rules, and practices
Socializing knowers	**Supports (Meeting Them Where They Are)** • Providing ample opportunities to engage in dialogue and reflection • Encouraging socializing knowers to share their own strengths and successes • Acknowledging and appreciating their ideas and contributions **Challenges (Developmental Stretching)** • Writing about problems of practice • Engaging in collegial inquiry to explore practice and offering leadership roles in doing so • Supporting them in voicing their views when constructing and developing a common vision for organizational improvement
Self-authoring knowers	**Supports (Meeting Them Where They Are)** • Providing opportunities to address complex issues of practice and inviting self-authoring knowers to share theory competencies • Offering increased opportunities for leadership roles when engaging in dialogue about important organizational issues • Engaging them in developing new programs **Challenges (Developmental Stretching)** • Encouraging them to consider tasks and issues from multiple perspectives • Inviting them in uncovering, examining, and critiquing their *own* tacit assumptions and convictions as well as their belief systems • Providing developmentally oriented challenges for developing/ considering diametrically opposed perspectives • Inviting them to serve as facilitators in developing a common understanding of the organizational vision and seeking their insights in rethinking goals

As all of these examples we've shared show, leaders' experiences in LTL helped shape and inform *their actual practice* in meaningful and complex ways. For nearly all of these leaders, re-creating the feeling of being well held in a developmental sense was an important motivator and model for their own work supporting the growth and learning of colleagues in their schools and organizations.

Still, as you know, the picture we've painted of these leaders' practice is more of a snapshot—a still-frame representation of a leadership journey in progress—as most of these leaders described not only the effective, LTL-inspired practices they are *currently* using, but also their *intentions* for doing more still and beyond. Like all adults who approach their work with seriousness and passion, these leaders will continue to grow and learn just like their colleagues, and we can only imagine that their leadership in support of adult learning and development will continue to evolve to even better meet the mounting and complex challenges they face as educational leaders today.

In fact, in the next chapter, we offer in even greater holistic detail a portrait of three leaders' work in support of adult development in integrated cases. Whereas in this chapter we teased apart many of the themes to highlight key ideas and shine a light on particular aspects of these leaders' important and noble work, we hope that the cases that follow help illustrate how these developmentally oriented ideas and strategies can work *together* for experienced leaders in diverse contexts.

Below, we offer both reflective questions and larger takeaways from this chapter to help guide your own thinking and practice. Perhaps most important to remember, however, is to "keep on stepping," as the proverb at the opening of this section reminds us. While approaching leadership with a learning-oriented lens is inarguably an ongoing process that takes both time and deep commitment, we truly believe, as do the leaders we learned from, that it could nonetheless make a tremendous difference for learners of all ages and orientations. Below, in Table 5.5, we present the hopes that some of these leaders shared with us immediately after LTL and the actual strategies that they went on to use and adapt in their leadership practice.

Reflective Questions

We offer the following questions as an opportunity to reflect on learnings from reading this chapter as well as to consider any ideas you might have in terms of enhancing the opportunities you offer

Table 5.5   A Comparison of LTL Leaders' Post-Course Hopes and Their Real-Life Practices for Supporting Adult Growth and Learning in Their Workplaces

LTL Leaders' Hopes for Developmentally Oriented Leadership When Completing LTL Course	LTL Leaders' Actual Strategies and Practices for Supporting Adult Development **Years** After the LTL Course
Building mutually respectful and trusting relationships to support adult growth	Building respectful and trusting relationships as preconditions for supporting adult growth Listening carefully and respectfully to colleagues Critically examining assumptions Using data to guide critical conversations and collegial inquiry Seeking out and considering teachers' input on policies Building trust and respect by modeling true collaboration
Bringing adults together by creating safe opportunities for sharing, dialogue, and collegial inquiry	Bringing adults together though teaming Engaging in collegial inquiry to explore dilemmas of practice Providing leadership roles to teachers Reciprocal mentoring between expert and novice colleagues Professional development through specialized coaching/mentoring from a developmental perspective
Identifying adults' particular needs in order to help them grow Differentiating developmental supports and challenges for individuals with qualitatively different capacities and ways of knowing	Differentiating supports and challenges within the pillar practices to support adult growth Working to understand teachers' ways of meaning making Offering choice to colleagues when implementing professional development and pillar practices Structuring complex tasks (like collegial inquiry) in concrete, manageable increments Inviting adults to pair-share or free-write in response to prompts before larger-group discussions

to adults in your care—and yourself. Please take a moment to consider these questions. You might want to respond to them privately first and then engage in collegial inquiry with a partner or group of colleagues.

1. How would you create a safe holding environment for mutual inquiry into practice in your work context?

2. Please take a moment to think about a challenge, dilemma, or issue that your organization is facing. In what ways could you address it by employing the pillar practices discussed in this chapter? What particular pillar practice could you adapt for this purpose?

3. In what ways could you differentiate supports and structures to help your colleagues to grow professionally?

What This Means for You, and What Might You Do With It? Takeaways for Practice

In addition to the examples and insights from leaders that we shared in this chapter, we hope the following overarching takeaways are useful to you in your noble and important work.

- Meet colleagues "where they are" (by identifying individual capacities and needs and developing appropriate tasks with and for colleagues in relation to their interests and expertise).
- Build a safe learning community based on mutual trust and respect.
- Offer developmentally appropriate supports and challenges for people with different developmental capacities.
- Encourage teachers to share their ideas and examples/stories from their classroom practice.
- Constructively challenge teachers' thinking and ideas for practice.
- Discuss issues or dilemmas of practice with peers.
- Engage in collegial inquiry in practice by offering and obtaining constructive feedback.
- Establish ground rules, norms, expectations, and confidentiality agreements for discussion and collaborative reflection.
- Use free-writes, pair-shares, journaling, and group work/ discussions to support teachers with diverse developmental capacities.

6

Integrated Lessons From the Field

Three In-Depth Cases of Developmentally Oriented Leadership Practice

Introduction and Overview

Great things are not done by impulse, but by a series of small things brought together.

—Vincent Van Gogh

You may be wondering, after reading about leaders' representative on-the-ground experiences of enacting practices inspired by the Leadership for Transformational Learning (LTL) course in Chapter 5, how these ideas and structures *actually fit and work together* to shape schools as true learning centers that support the learning and growth of all educators. How, for example, does one nurture *preconditions* while implementing the pillar practices? How can a leader care for the details of differentiating to support adult growth while—at the same time—moving forward with the "big picture" mission of a school or organization?

To help answer these questions and to illustrate in greater depth some of the ways these leaders approached and tackled the complex challenges associated with leading in support of adult development years after successfully completing LTL, in this chapter, we present holistic portraits of three LTL-graduates' efforts to build—together with their colleagues—individual and organizational capacity in their schools. While in Chapter 5 we zoomed in on discrete examples of these leaders' work (a) establishing and nourishing the preconditions for developmentally oriented leadership, (b) implementing and adapting the four pillar practices for growth—teaming, collegial inquiry, providing leadership roles, and mentoring—and (c) differentiating supports and challenges within the pillars to support adults with diverse ways of knowing, we highlight in this chapter how, in practice, these ideas can be carefully and caringly *woven together* in different and intentional ways.

As this section's opening quote from Vincent Van Gogh reminds us, "great things" are often the result of "a series of small things brought together." As you know, and as these leaders shared, effective leadership similarly involves a totality of purposeful acts rather than a series of singular acts in isolation. We hope that this chapter helps foreground the interrelation of the big ideas we describe in this book. While we learned a great deal about this important point from *all* of the insightful and inspiring leaders in the study, we have purposefully selected the cases of three leaders—Matt, Tara, and Adrian—to illustrate the flexibility and variability of learning-oriented leadership and also to suggest the unique and different ways leaders can shape, weave, paint—and sustain this work as their own.

For example, to highlight the interrelationship between establishing *preconditions* and enacting the pillar practices, we first present an integrated example from Matt's work as the head of a private lower school. As you will see, when working to support the teachers in his school, Matt works carefully to build relationships with colleagues (i.e., establish trust and mutual respect) while simultaneously *honoring and deepening those relationships through the process of collegial inquiry*. With a developmental, inquiry-oriented approach to collecting and discussing data with teachers, Matt works to enhance teachers' performance while simultaneously demonstrating his great care and appreciation for them as individuals.

Next, we offer a portrait of Tara's work as a middle school assistant principal who employs both teaming and collegial inquiry to support adult growth. Tara's case illustrates her use of grade-level teams—which she calls "gleams"—and helps demonstrate how teaming and collegial inquiry can be employed *together over time* to help teachers and other adults grow and learn their way to improved practices and understandings. In other words, the pillar practice of collegial inquiry, which involves examining with others one's most fundamental questions, values, and assumptions, can help give *form and purpose* to teaming as an overarching structure. Moreover, as Tara's case demonstrates, adults' capacities to work together in these important ways require explicit support, and they grow and evolve over time.

Finally, we present Adrian's case to demonstrate how the practices of providing leadership roles and mentoring can be adapted meaningfully in diverse settings. In his leadership role as a secondary school principal in Singapore, Adrian intentionally invites adults to share and exchange expertise in ways that help them—and the entire school community—grow to meet the complex demands of teaching and leading. In addition, his powerful example helps illustrate how the pillar practices can support targeted learning in particular domains. More specifically, Adrian and his teachers rely on the pillars to support more effective and efficient integration of instructional technology—a key focus and goal of the school as a whole.

Ultimately, we hope that these powerful cases suggest and open possibilities for employing and exploring learning-oriented leadership in your own context, whether in K–12 schools and districts or in your work in districts and universities preparing educational leaders to support adult development in schools. As we describe in greater detail next, the ideas, theory, and practices learned in LTL continue to inform—even many years after the course—the texture of graduates' leadership vision, their thinking about how to support adult development, and the multifaceted and nuanced practices they employ *in combination* to best meet the many and mounting challenges they face today as school leaders.

Matt's Leadership Case: Nurturing the Preconditions and Collegial Inquiry Through Developmentally Oriented, Data-Driven Discussions of Practice

When describing his work as the head of a private suburban New York lower school, Matt repeatedly emphasized what he understood as the deep and profound connections between supporting the adults in his school community and "supporting kids in their independence, in their beauty, [and] in their wonder, as they go through our K–4 program." As he explained, his driving and fundamental concern for students "sort of abstracts out from there" and so involves "working with teachers, working with families, working with colleagues at an administrative level, and working with [the] board" in extended but direct ways.

Five years after successfully completing LTL, and two years into his role as head of school, Matt spoke passionately about supporting the development of the adults he works with and cares for and about the special importance of building mutually trusting, developmentally oriented relationships with teachers, in particular. When asked to describe how he conceptualized his leadership philosophy, for example, Matt explained:

> So I think a good part of it [leadership] is supporting the work of teachers and supporting these relationships to develop, particularly along the lines of adult development in the idea of supporting teachers. [T]his is how I think about it, right? . . . [W]e need to become—as teachers and as administrators and as people working with children—we need to become the most beautiful people that we can be. Not in the way of "mirror, mirror on the wall, who's the fairest of them all?" but in the way that we can only give away what we have, so we better have something. So the more complex, the more beautiful, the more interesting people we develop ourselves into, the more that we can give back to kids.

As we will share here, and as you may have gathered through examples presented earlier in this book, Matt places high value on what we described in Chapter 5 as the *preconditions* for learning-oriented leadership (i.e., pillars practices for capacity building). While in that chapter we highlighted a variety of practices several LTL leaders employed to establish, build, and sustain the respectful, trusting relationships that make possible and sustain developmentally oriented leadership practice, we present Matt's case here to illustrate his strategy of using observable data during one-on-one discussions of practice with teachers to deepen relationships, improve practice, and build capacity.

In particular, we discuss how Matt's developmental approach to working with data serves simultaneously as a show of respect for his colleagues (a precondition) and a jumping-off point for collegial inquiry (a pillar practice). As we explained above, these and the other strategies and practices described throughout this book are often woven together in careful, complex, and intentional ways, and we hope that Matt's case helps illustrate one leader's promising approach to holistically implementing and adapting some of the ideas discussed and modeled in LTL. We also hope that Matt's case serves as a powerful reminder that "data" and "data-driven leadership"—compelling imperatives in education today—can take many different forms and serve many different ends.

Data as a Demonstration of Care and Respect

As Matt explained to us, mutual trust and respect are *crucial* when discussing potentially sensitive and delicate issues of instructional practice with teachers. Since his academic leadership responsibilities involve continually assessing and reassessing the educational program, talking directly with teachers about their classroom work is a big—if not always easy or comfortable—part of his job. Without trust and respect as *preconditions*, he explained, teachers would not feel safe engaging in difficult conversations with him about their assumptions, vulnerabilities, motivations, and hopes for growth.

As he further shared, "sometimes there are things that happen, either in a classroom or the way that [a] teacher handles a certain situation . . . [that] require some type of conversation. . . . And so, I've thought a lot about the nature of those conversations." In order to shape these one-on-one meetings as "structures of trust" and "structures of sharing and open communication" that support teachers' growth and development, Matt underscored the importance of shaping professional dialogues as holding environments. As he put it,

> [R]egardless of how people are making meaning, there's some common elements of trust and of nonjudgmental responses and of really honoring and respecting what people say. You know, so that when conversations develop, they develop in a way where people are respected, regardless of where they are [developmentally]. And I think a lot about my role in that. So how I'm being, how I'm being interpreted, and how I'm interpreting myself. What things can I do that can lead us in a direction where this type of space can be developed?

One strategic way that Matt answered this significant question about how he, as a leader of teachers' learning, could best support others' professional growth, was by working to avoid *his own* assumptions and judgments when discussing questions or problems of practice with colleagues. In particular, he stressed the promise of focusing initially on "directly observable data" when engaging in these conversations—rather than *his* interpretations of events—to make his points clear and specific and also to demonstrate his deep respect for teachers' perspectives and experiences. In his words,

> So one piece of learning [from LTL] that I use a lot is . . . directly observable data . . . and I think that I'm always trying to think about how I'm observing things, and how I'm using what I'm observing.

For instance, Matt explained that he attempts to structure his conversations with teachers very openly and carefully, especially in situations where a teacher's instruction—at least on the surface—appears to conflict with his view of best classroom practices. It would be very easy, Matt explained, to simply assert his authority as the head of school and say to a teacher, "I didn't like the way you did that. I want you to do this. Thank you." But, as Matt wisely realized, using judgmental and evaluative language can jeopardize trust—a key precondition for growth and development.

Notably, and as you will see, Matt's emphasis on *what* he observes as well as *how he uses the data* expands common understandings of using hard data in education. While in today's high-stakes, accountability-driven climate, data are generally referred to in the context of measuring progress through evidence-based instruction or testing hypotheses in educational research, Matt uses directly observable data with developmental intentions to help his teachers critically look at and enhance their practice in safe and supportive ways. As explained earlier, Matt believes that developing mutually respectful and open relationships and "supporting these relationships" are key to enhancing practice, building organizational capacity, and figuring out—together with his teachers—"what best serves kids" in their lower school program and beyond.

Data as a Support to Collegial Inquiry

In addition to enhancing the trust and respect that serve as *preconditions* for supporting adult development, Matt's use of directly observable data in one-on-one conversations with teachers also serves as a springboard for collegial inquiry. As you know, the pillar practice of collegial inquiry involves reflecting critically *with at least one other adult* about deeply held beliefs, professional orientations, and the assumptions that drive our practice and our lives. Along these lines, while Matt relies on directly observable data to respectfully manage and hold back his own assumptions about colleagues' work, his observations serve simultaneously as *invitations for teachers* to examine, consider, and discuss their professional actions and intentions with supportive company. By focusing closely on a particular event, action, or inaction, Matt and his teachers can begin to explore the thinking and motivations that lie just beneath observable behaviors in order to grow and learn. In the LTL convening process (case-based learning), which we discussed previously in Chapters 2 and 4, concrete evidence can help adults realize that, as Matt explained, "there's a lot of different ways of looking at things that can add to one's understanding of what's really going on." Collaboratively unpacking events in this way, Matt continued, "puts the flashlight in a couple [of] areas" in order to help educators on both sides of the conversation better understand and grow from the exchange.

To illustrate how these private, reflective conversations work to nurture the preconditions for supporting adult growth and collegial inquiry, Matt shared a hypothetical but representative scenario. He explained, for example, that he might notice during an observation or classroom visit that a teacher did not seem to pay attention to a particular student. While seeing this would inevitably bring up certain negative feelings for Matt, he would invite the teacher to talk about the situation before jumping to any conclusions himself, and he would carefully structure the conversation in respectful and intentional ways. As he described it, he would first share with that teacher the concrete specifics of his observation and then honestly share his questions or concerns:

> So the first part of those kinds of conversations . . . is to be very clear about what I was talking about, so at the beginning, I'd say, "I noticed that seven times during your instruction, there was a child who was raising their [*sic*] hand that you didn't really call on." And then the second thing would be telling them how that made me feel. . . . So then at that point, once I feel like they know where I'm coming from and they know what exactly I'm talking about, I need to stop [to let them think and talk], right?

Matt emphasized the importance of creating this kind of space for teachers to think and respond and explained that sharing negative reactions with teachers without first listening to their points of view might jeopardize his efforts to create mutually respectful, caring, and honest relationships—an aspect of his leadership that he tries to "prize before everything else." Therefore, rather than proffer judgments or dictates, Matt consciously attempts to invite his teachers to probe their own understandings of a particular situation in order to better understand their pedagogical decisions and actions. This approach helps establish trust because the teachers in Matt's division feel that he cares about them, and it also helps the teachers critically reflect on their own teaching and work in order to more effectively serve students.

While this type of collegial inquiry can clearly serve as a developmental support for the teachers participating in the conversations, engaging in the pillar in this safe and supportive way adds to Matt's *own* "data stream" as head of school, in that it allows him to more intimately understand how his teachers are making sense of their work and experiences. In other words, supporting teachers to grow their practices and meaning making through collaborative conversations *simultaneously positions Matt as a more effective manager and supervisor* who can "make the best type of decision possible." As he explained, "if I don't check in with people and [learn more about] . . . some of the thinking that goes on behind why they're acting the way that they're acting," he won't be able to support his teachers, his students, and his school community in the ways he considers most important.

Learning From Matt's Case

Ultimately, Matt shared with us that a large part of his leadership involves "putting things in place that make sure nothing is remaining static, that there's a lot of reflection that's involved." Building trust and respect *through and for* collegial inquiry by grounding private conversations with teachers in data was one important strategy Matt employed to prioritize learning and improvement in his school and to keep adult development as a central and important focus. As Matt learned in LTL, supporting adults is one key way that educational leaders can *also* support children and youth, and as we have seen, using directly observable data when conversing with teachers about practice can help nurture and sustain the *preconditions* that make professional growth possible. In addition, it can serve as an entry point into collegial inquiry for supervisors and teachers alike. Together, Matt explained, he and his teachers are "constantly asking questions." "Is this a good program?" they ask themselves. "How can we make it better?"

Moreover, Matt realized, some of his most important leadership questions involve his own intentionality as a leader—because when he, as head of school, can effectively support teachers to grow and "make meaning in more complex ways, they'll be able to offer more to the kids." For Matt, like many of the leaders we learned from, weaving together different strategies and practices inspired by LTL became an integral and authentic part of his own leadership practice—and one that carried over years after successfully completing the course. While in this case we emphasized Matt's integration of the preconditions and collegial inquiry, we will see in the following cases that adaptations and implementations of learning-oriented leadership ideas can take many forms. For instance, Tara's case, which we will consider next, highlights the often-powerful connections between teaming and collegial inquiry.

Tara's Leadership Case: Building Teams for Collaboration and Collegial Inquiry

At the time of her interview, six years after completing LTL, Tara was beginning her fourth year as the assistant principal of a K–8 school in Arizona. After two prior years of teaching in this same school as a third- and fourth-grade teacher, Tara took on the role and responsibility of serving as the assistant principal—a position she described as both "exciting" and "busy." Tasked with caring for "the general day-to-day operational side of things," as she put it, as well as serving as an instructional leader, coordinating educational intervention services for the entire school population, and managing much of the school's discipline and half of the teacher evaluations, Tara explained that "part of my job description is 'will be willing to do anything'!" Still, even with so much on her overfull plate, Tara unequivocally and intentionally prioritized supporting the learning and growth of her colleagues.

In this case, we focus on Tara's work establishing and enhancing grade-level teaching teams, or "gleams," as opportunities for teachers to enhance their classroom practice through collaboration and collegial inquiry. As we will highlight, the evolution of these gleams demonstrates both the journey and process of leading for adult development, and the often overlapping and mutually reinforcing attributes of teaming and collegial inquiry as pillar practices.

Establishing "Gleam" Meetings: Making Space for Teachers to Be Together

One of Tara's first goals as an assistant principal, she shared with us, was creating opportunities for teachers to learn and be together. Since Tara's school employed a multigraded format—or as Tara explained it, "third and fourth graders in the same class, fifth and sixth graders in the same class, and so on"—one of her first moves as a leader in the school was to implement weekly meetings for each of the grade-level teams, or "gleams," as she calls them. Simply carving out this space was a significant challenge and goal, she shared, because it was "a real process getting those up and off the ground because we didn't have those prior to when I came."

As you know, teaming is the most commonly used practice for promoting collaborative work in educational organizations, and—as we learned from Tara and other leaders—teaming can also serve as an important jumping-off point for a more developmental, learning-oriented approach to leadership. For example, besides bringing people together to perform team tasks, teaming can serve to develop team members' reflective thinking, perspective-taking abilities, professional knowledge and skills, and internal capacities (Drago-Severson, 2004a, 2004b, 2009, 2012). As Tara shared with us, teaming in her school actually involved—and continues to involve—an unfolding journey. As teachers grew more comfortable working and learning together, teams also grew to support more complex forms of collegial inquiry and collaboration.

To better understand the potential and powerful connections between teaming and collegial inquiry as pillar practices, it might be helpful to think of teaming as a larger form or structure—like a pond—that can be filled and made even more robust with "the water" of collegial inquiry. While not all kinds of teams engage in collegial inquiry and not all collegial inquiry happens in teams, teaming can serve as a powerful context for supporting collegial inquiry when the conditions are ripe and the appropriate supports and challenges are in place. Tara's experiences with leading weekly gleam meetings help illustrate the *process* of teaming as well as the *promise* of creating and prioritizing opportunities for adults to learn and grow together.

Starting From Scratch: First Steps for Implementing Gleam Meetings

Just as we said of Matt's practice in the last case, Tara took thoughtful measures to establish a sense of trust and safety in her teams from the outset as an important first step in leading and supporting her teachers' development. Along with these essential *preconditions*, Tara valued the *invitational quality* of much of her learning in LTL, and she wanted to offer teaming opportunities as positive supports for teachers rather than as mandates or additional requirements. Therefore, in her first year as assistant principal, she invited her colleagues to come together every week for about an hour without any particular agenda for the discussions. Her rationale, as she explained, was to be mindful of teachers' workload and not add more work to their existing responsibilities. Initially, she encouraged teachers to meet at a convenient time or at lunch just to begin the process of learning and being together in safe and supportive ways. As she elaborated,

> So that was my first step. [I decided] to block out the time and the space for [teaming] to happen without having an agenda, just to . . . make sure that the teams could come together without adding to their workload. [Teachers] came together in the same room, over lunch or whatever time worked best for them, to just physically sit in the same room with each other.

As time went on, Tara also encouraged teachers to discuss various matters that were important to them. For example, conversations in early gleam meetings, she explained, began with informal topics like weekend activities or interesting and "funny" stories about things from teachers' classrooms. Teachers themselves guided the discussion, for Tara saw her role at this point as more of a facilitator of teachers' "coming together." This openness and flexibility helped create the teams as spaces in which people felt comfortable sharing what was most meaningful to them. As Tara explained,

> So [at first] I attended all of the [meetings] to make sure that they were happening and to just kind of facilitate them. . . . [Meetings were] pretty casual and just kind of oriented toward establishing trust and relationships and all that.

Eventually, these earlier meetings also became spaces for teachers to share difficult dilemmas with each other and find support "if they wanted to cry or break down." As Tara explained, "creating a space where all of this could happen [and] where people would feel comfortable talking and sharing things" was a very important step and precondition for building effective teams.

Tara also reinforced that it was an intentional (if sometimes challenging) decision not to impose her own thinking or ideas on the group during the initial stages of the gleam meetings. While not always easy, given the urgency of her hopes for growth, Tara understood from her experiences in LTL that teacher buy-in and ownership were key to making the gleam meetings productive and meaningful for all. As she explained,

> I know for me personally, I'm kind of Type A, and it's usually more my style to just jump in and say, "Okay, this is how we're going to do it . . . [and] get it done." And I think [LTL] really gives me pause [because] . . . when I think about that class, I think about making sure that I'm always building in the time for the relationship establishing and the trust to be built, and just . . . that foundation to be laid before anything else can be accomplished.

Accordingly, Tara challenged herself to sit quietly, listening attentively to her colleagues and "not trying to direct" their exchanges. In the same way, she did not enforce any set agenda during early gleam meetings or ask the teams to take up issues that *she* wanted to address as the assistant principal. Instead, she carefully crafted a space that her teachers owned, and as we will describe next, this process paved the way for even deeper and more complex teamwork and collaboration based on mutual trust and respect. It also allowed Tara to learn more about what felt most urgent, important, and pressing for her teachers during any given week and over time.

Growing and Learning Together: Gleams 2.0

After successfully carving out safe and productive time and space for teachers to work in gleams, Tara's next goal was to move beyond shared anecdotes of practice or operational issues in these meetings. In other words, while during initial phases of teaming teachers often focused on logistical details and challenges (like "when's the field trip?") or shared burning questions, feelings, and stories, Tara hoped the gleam meetings could develop a more "directed purpose" and protocol for teachers to examine problems of practice together, considering them from multiple viewpoints and sharing their expertise. Taking steps in this direction, she shared, was an important milestone because they'd "slowly been able to get at more meaty issues in those groups over the years." As Tara further noted,

And now, we're working towards establishing those meetings more as professional learning community meetings . . . [with] more of a directed purpose, as directed by the teachers . . . [N]ow they have more of a "let's look at student work, let's really delve into some big problems and issues when we can" [approach to teaming].

Tara also learned that she could bring questions to the gleam meetings that felt important to *her* and contribute as an administrator and facilitator in more active ways without undermining the safe and trusting environment they'd created together. As she explained, "Towards the end of that [first] year, I would bring in a question to pose [to the teachers], like 'What do you think about such-and-such that's going on at school?' And just kind of get them to dialogue about it." Eventually, these questions prompted larger discussions and careful inquiry. For example, Tara shared that she once asked gleam members to bring examples of how they were teaching spelling and vocabulary in their classrooms to a meeting. Some of the parents, Tara explained, had voiced concerns about the lack of consistency in spelling and vocabulary instruction in different classrooms. Tara, too, had noticed that it was taught in some classrooms and not others, so she decided to bring the issue to the gleams so they could talk about the inconsistency, understand some of the reasons behind it, and decide what to do next. Moreover, in addition to looking at the vocabulary instruction, she shared, this invitation would allow teachers to "really collaborate and dialogue with each other and understand more about each other's practice." This, she knew, would be a support for growth and learning—and could also help them shape a collaborative "solution" to the instructional challenge at hand.

Similarly, reflecting on her evolving and more active role in the gleam meetings, Tara underscored the importance of a *developmental* approach to teaming. As she learned in LTL, understanding that her teachers oriented to teaming and collaboration *differently* helped her craft gleam meetings as both developmental supports and challenges for growth. As she explained,

In my work with those meetings . . . I really am able to employ a lot of the concepts and understandings that I got from [LTL] . . . in looking at different individuals' need for differentiation in terms of leadership opportunities, what kind of learner is each teacher in the bunch, what is the group dynamic, [etc.] . . . [For example, I'm always] making sure that I'm able to provide for different roles and responsibilities among teaching teams, . . . noting each teacher's comfort zone, where they are, where they might need to go, what their learning style is. Is it somebody who enjoys being in charge? Is it somebody who enjoys communicating verbally with others? Is it somebody who enjoys communicating via e-mail? . . . [T]aking the time to really get to know each individual and where their skills and comforts are and also where their challenges are, and seeing what they might need to get out of their work with our group [is key].

As we describe next, employing this kind of developmental intentionality, as we call it, when designing, leading, and facilitating collaborative opportunities is also key when shaping teams as supportive contexts for the mutually reinforcing pillar practice of collegial inquiry.

The Evolution of Gleams as Collegial Inquiry Groups: Embracing the Process

As Tara shared with us, with time, effort, and dedication, gleam meetings have the potential to evolve into even more sophisticated learning contexts that support collegial inquiry and adult development. As she noted, "We're not where I want to be yet, but we're getting there." As you know, collegial inquiry involves reflecting on one's deeply held beliefs, values, and assumptions *with at least one other person*, and so it differs in this way from more traditional forms of reflective practice, which are often done independently (Drago-Severson, 2004b, 2009, 2012). Likewise, working collaboratively with others does not guarantee collegial inquiry, for it is only by peeling back the surface layers of professional practice—by exploring, together, the deeper motivations, assumptions, feelings, and thinking that drive and shape one's own work and the work of colleagues— that real collegial inquiry can take place.

That being said, Tara hopes that the teachers in her school will be able to bring difficult and sensitive issues to their gleam meetings in order to collaboratively examine the most fundamental questions and challenges of their classroom work. She envisions gleam meetings as spaces for teachers to not only talk about these concerns but also seek, welcome, and learn from constructive and critical feedback from colleagues about new ways of looking at and managing these issues. In her words,

[What] I'm working towards is having teachers be able to bring . . . a case that might be really sensitive to them or really tough, or a case that they feel like they maybe mishandled or they maybe would have done something different[ly], but they're not sure what. . . . I'd love to be able to have them bring something [like that] to the group and have the group give feedback on it in a constructive and positive way. That's where I'd like to head towards.

As Tara explained, "This is where I [would] really like to use the convening model," a process for case-based collegial inquiry that we described earlier in Chapter 2. For Tara, like many LTL leaders, convenings were a powerful and meaningful learning experience that helped bring into focus previously unseen motivations, assumptions, and commitments (please see Chapter 4 for leaders' sharings about convening). Accordingly, Tara shared with us that she is eager to re-create convenings in adapted form for her teachers in gleam meetings. Although teachers are already using these meetings to discuss pedagogical strategies or ways to better support struggling students, Tara's goal is to acknowledge the importance and urgency of these concrete issues while also addressing teachers' *own* challenges, dilemmas, and meaning making rather than "problem[s] that they're seeing" in others. In other words, she believes that this type of collaborative and reflective engagement would help teachers "take their own development to the next level"—that is, it could help them develop alternative perspectives on issues and ways to resolve them as well as build their capacities to understand, share, confront, and manage dilemmas of practice.

Of course, as Tara emphasized, such work is a *process*. Supporting real change requires a willingness to take risks at multiple levels, the patience to see things through, and the foresight to recognize that it will all be worth it. As Tara explained, she's learned that she needs to "just let things take longer than I wanted them to." Still, she reminded us, "We're getting there."

Moreover, even though a more encompassing focus and direction for gleam meetings requires teachers "to put themselves out there and show themselves as being vulnerable as educators," Tara let us know that the feedback she's received about her work with gleam meetings has been overwhelmingly positive. Teachers "really appreciate having the time," she shared. "They appreciate . . . having the time and space carved out [because] they know that if they don't have time to sit down with their gleam . . . during the day, they know that they'll have everybody in the same room on this one day and time every week." Even more important, she shared, the teachers "appreciate learning from each other" and learning about what goes on in different classrooms. In fact, she added, sometimes "they've been surprised to hear what's going on in different classrooms. Pleasantly surprised."

Ultimately, by combining aspects of teaming and collegial inquiry, Tara explained, the weekly gleam meetings have helped her teachers develop "more of an appreciation for other people's teaching styles"—and greater insight into their own.

Learning From Tara's Case

In sum, Tara's leadership practice helps demonstrate the promise of teaming and collegial inquiry as mutually reinforcing practices that support teacher collaboration and adult development—and her case helps confirm the lasting influence of her LTL learnings, which she referenced repeatedly throughout her interview. Likewise, by illustrating the *process* behind developmentally oriented initiatives in schools, Tara's case underscores the fact that leading for adult development requires intentional investment and foresight on the part of leaders. Without first establishing the foundational preconditions—mutually respectful, genuine, and trustworthy relationships—and without growing teacher ownership and buy-in, this work cannot be done. Moreover, like individuals, teams and groups can be stretched—in the developmental sense—to consider, address, and learn from increasingly complex and sophisticated challenges and opportunities over time.

While Tara shared one important approach to building trusting and effective team communities in this way, you might find it helpful to revisit Chapters 2, 3, and 4 for additional suggestions about how to shape safe and confidential teams and inquiry groups (e.g., using norms and protocols).

Adrian's Leadership Case: Supporting Professional Learning Through Reciprocal Mentoring and Providing Leadership Roles

When we spoke with Adrian seven years after successfully completing LTL, he was excited to share many of the developmentally oriented practices and structures he was using to support his teachers as the principal of a secondary school in Singapore. Along with his staff of eighty-one teachers, Adrian works very hard to care for the more than 1,500 students aged twelve to sixteen who learn and grow in his building—and whom he lovingly describes as "precocious teenagers." Moreover, he explained to us that, unlike school systems in the United States which are typically divided into elementary, middle, and high schools, the public school system in Singapore consists of six years of primary school followed by four years of secondary school—like Adrian's own—and then two years of a junior college experience. In addition, Adrian shared with us that students in Singapore sit for a national exam at the end of their secondary-school experience. While in many ways the leadership context presented in this case is different from many others discussed in this book—and perhaps your own—it is important to note that Adrian, like all educational leaders, faces the universal challenges of building human capacity in his school and staff and of demonstrating student proficiency and academic success.

For example, Adrian immediately emphasized that employing "theories of adult development for transformational learning" in his professional development efforts was helping him to see "a lot of results" in his teachers and students. Indeed, the "killer concepts" (as he called them) that he "picked up from [the LTL] course" have helped him put a number of developmentally oriented structures in place to help teachers learn, grow, and cooperatively improve their practice on behalf of students and each other. While, as you may have gathered from other examples we've presented throughout this book, Adrian applies his LTL learnings in a number of promising ways. In the case that follows, we highlight his mutually reinforcing use of mentoring and providing leadership roles to support his teachers in general and regarding their use of instructional technology in particular.

While, as Adrian shared with us, caring directly and purposefully for adult development can go against the grain of established conventions in education or traditional understandings of professional learning, doing this "hard work" up front can make a tremendous difference for teachers and students alike. Likening the experience of leading a school to parking a car, for example, Adrian described the benefits of carefully backing into a parking space rather than pulling in headfirst. Speaking literally and figuratively, Adrian put it this way: "We reverse our car because we believe in working hard first. You park your car carefully because when you get out it's easier." As we will explore next, employing adult developmental theories and learning-oriented leadership practices as a principal is one strategic way that Adrian makes the work of learning and growing with his teachers "easier" over the long haul, despite the initial care, effort, and hard work it takes to put these structures in place. In the sections that follow, we focus more on his use of mentoring and providing leadership roles to build technological, developmental, and organizational capacity with his teachers.

"High-Tech, High-Touch": Support and Challenge for Instructional Technology

One of the first things Adrian shared about his school was that it was designated as "a center of excellence for ICT [information and communication technologies]." Yet, as he explained, the school's strong technological focus requires an equally strong orientation on his part toward the *human* side of teaching, leading, and life. In other words, in order to help teachers "infuse and harness technology to make teaching and learning even better," Adrian shared that he takes a developmental approach to shaping learning and working contexts as holding environments. As he further explained,

> Now when you [have a strong focus on instructional technology] . . . it's really, really scary because not every teacher is going to use technology in [the same] way. . . . I have to be very cognizant of the kind of teachers I have, [and] . . . it doesn't mean that all our teachers are ready for it. . . . So when I came here in 2007, I was here as a vice-principal for about nine months, [and] I really felt the need to organize the teachers in a way that would give them that kind of holding environment, a perfect holding environment for them, to challenge them. And of course, this holding environment I'm talking about, I would say it comes with a good mix of support as well as challenge.

Paralleling his LTL learnings about different ways of knowing and the support and challenge inherent in the most effective holding environments, Adrian described his leadership approach as "high-tech, high-touch," referencing the dual focus on technological and interpersonal support. As he described this philosophy:

> High-tech, high-touch. So the touch really refers to the support that you give, the close support that you give to the teachers, really whatever they need, the care and concern

about their professional development, even their lives outside school . . . . [And] the high tech, [well] technology . . . tends to give you a very cold feeling if you're just talking about technology alone. So I think the high-tech, high-touch approach sort of sends a message or a signal to the teachers that as a principal, yes, I may ask you to develop very advanced teaching tools using technology in the classrooms, but at the same time, I'm willing to sit down with you and support you in all you need.

As we will see next, by creating safe, supportive opportunities for teachers to build capacity through mentoring and providing leadership roles, Adrian is able to care simultaneously for individual and collective growth.

Reciprocal Mentoring: Building Capacity Together Across Domains

One important practice that Adrian adapted from LTL in order to help his teachers meet new technology and proficiency demands was developmentally oriented mentoring. Adrian's practice illustrates how mentoring can be employed as a growth-oriented practice to scaffold newer as well as experienced teachers' learning and professional work in technology and beyond. By pairing teachers according to their technological "way of knowing," he attempts to create a dynamic learning context in which each member of the mentor-mentee pair benefits and shares expertise in different domains—for example, in technology and classroom management skills.

In Chapter 5 we explored how the leaders we learned from went on to implement and adapt the pillar practice of mentoring as a support to adult learning and transformation years after successfully completing LTL. Here we elaborate on Adrian's reciprocal mentoring model as a developmentally oriented context for professional growth with a technological focus. As he's structured it, Adrian pairs technology "Grand Masters" (as he calls teachers with a great deal of ICT experience) with "Rookies" (who are just learning about these tools) in mentoring pairs. "Grand Masters," he helped us understand, are generally early-career teachers who nonetheless possess a great deal of knowledge about technology tools and applications. "Rookies," on the other hand, are mostly experienced teachers with more emerging technology skills. Because of the tension or division this can cause in a staff, Adrian explained, he uses reciprocal mentoring to tap into and unite both groups' expertise in order to improve teaching and learning—and the collaborative environment—for all of his teachers and students. As he explained,

> I have teachers of different age groups. . . . There are more and more young teachers in Singapore because a lot of the teachers are retiring, so in terms of the more experienced, older teachers, there is [often] a fear in dabbling with technology, and when they see the younger teachers fly with technology, you can potentially . . . create a chasm in your school where you have two camps: the non-techies and the technology kind of thing, so you've got to be very careful of how you manage relationships. So what I'm trying to say is that you have to provide a good mix of support. I mean I go by that principle. In order to provide teachers with a holding environment, there must be a good mix of support and challenge, and support and challenge mean different things to teachers at different stages of their development.

Further unpacking this "good mix of support and challenge" for different teachers in the mentoring relationships, Adrian explained that he encourages each teacher in the pair to share his or her own expertise *and* be open to learning. For example, "younger" teachers in the mentoring pairs are often aware of and adept at using technology tools in instruction, so he supports them by giving them the space and opportunities to use and share these skills with experienced colleagues. At the same time, Adrian is mindful of the challenges that many beginning teachers face regarding classroom management. Accordingly, he pairs newer, technology-savvy teachers with veteran teachers who can support them through the inevitable bumps and bruises of starting out in the classroom. Adrian described this mutual benefit:

> [A]nother wonderful thing that came up from this is when we pair the Masters with the Rookies, usually you end up seeing a very experienced, a very senior teacher who's a [technology] Rookie pairing up with a very young teacher, and when we pair them together, the young teacher helps the senior teacher with the technology, and the senior teacher helps with the classroom management.

Ultimately, by meeting each teacher's needs and respecting the different but equally valuable contributions teachers can make to and for each other and the school, Adrian continues to see improvement and growth. As he put it,

[S]o the younger teachers pick up very good skills from the senior teachers, and the senior teachers pick up very basic, simple, good technology skills from the younger teachers. It's amazing. And with that, I managed to level everybody up in terms of their competencies, whether it is in ICT or classroom management.

Growing and Learning Through Leadership Roles

In a similar and reinforcing way, Adrian also provides his teachers with leadership roles to help them grow, flourish, and learn. For example, he encourages teachers with advanced technological skills to attend conferences and professional development seminars to share and enhance their work and to bring back innovative tools for the school community. Supporting this kind of initiative and teachers' shared leadership in the school is key to developing a nurturing holding environment and to fueling passion and excitement about one's work, in Adrian's view. As he explained,

> You need to talk about the work that you're doing and get excited about it, and that's why I send a lot of my teachers for conferences to talk about their work because when you talk about your work, you usually fire a certain passion in them.

Inviting teachers to share their expertise back at school, too, promotes buy-in, excitement, and capacity building, as Adrian explained. In fact, he very directly stressed the power of inviting and supporting his colleagues to help shape the practice and vision of their school together through different kinds of leadership opportunities. As he put it,

> Look, you know, we're in this together. And sometimes, really, I feel it [inviting adults to share and lead] promotes ownership . . . [A] lot of times I have to tell myself to hold back some of the answers and to let the teachers and even my vice-principals and heads of department surface the answers because when they surface the answers and they surface the solutions, there is greater ownership. It is not top-down; it is ground-up.

Importantly, sharing leadership in this way also helps Adrian feel more comfortable and confident with his teachers and administrative colleagues—and allows him to focus more directly on the important work of instructional leadership at the school. This kind of mutual trust, he explained, can help sustain the momentum of success over the long haul:

> I think a school must be self-sustaining, so really the principal's job is to put structures and processes in place with the community in terms of expertise so that when the principal is not around for a while, the school is . . . self-sustaining, and it can grow without that leader being there all the time.

As we have seen, implementing and adapting the pillar practices and other developmentally oriented strategies can make a big difference—and build capacity over time—in many different and very important ways.

Learning From Adrian's Case

Ultimately, just as with Matt's and Tara's examples, Adrian's case helps us understand that the pillar practices, preconditions, and other LTL-inspired strategies can be employed effectively together in diverse and sophisticated ways. Both mentoring and providing leadership roles, for instance, can help adults grow each other—and themselves—through shared expertise, mutual support, and a powerful feeling of coownership regarding professional learning and the school mission. Still, as Adrian cautiously reminded us, as a principal and leader of adult development, he always has more to do and more to learn. As he explained,

> And really I feel I have so much more to learn [about] . . . my teachers in terms of where they are, what makes them tick, and what holds them back—and that's really about where they are at the different stages of development. . . . And I think this is an ongoing thing. I don't claim that I have the silver bullet to solve that problem, . . . but I think when you realize that at the beginning, that you want to learn more, the learning never stops.

Ultimately, this case—like the rest of this chapter and the book as a whole—is all about this remarkable ability to keep on learning. Even and especially as adults, we can continue to grow, learn, and meet the mounting demands of teaching and leading when we work together in safe, supportive contexts. We hope that you found this closer look at mentoring and providing leadership roles in action helpful, and we encourage you to revisit Chapters 2 and 3 for additional strategies about how to infuse these approaches into developmental intentions.

Chapter Summary

The three cases presented in this chapter offer robust and contextualized examples of how LTL graduates, many years after the course, went on to support teachers' development through different combinations of the preconditions and the pillar practices. While in their diverse school settings Matt, Tara, and Adrian used their LTL learnings in different ways, they also explained to us that their leadership work continues to evolve and grow as they gain experience and expertise as leaders. Nevertheless, we've learned from all of them that striving to build meaningful, trusting, and caring contexts for reflective and collaborative practice in schools drives their work and success, even though their school contexts and personal philosophies influence the shape and feel of the developmental practices they employ. While Matt, for instance, builds and sustains trust through private, data-driven collegial inquiry meetings, Tara carved out the time and space for her teachers to meet in increasingly sophisticated and focused grade level teams. Through his use of reciprocal mentoring and providing leadership roles, Adrian too reminds us that the pillars and preconditions are often woven together in complex patterns and arrangements—but the big idea across all three cases is that these LTL leaders are employing a number of learning-oriented strategies *in concert* to realize their visions and goals for individual and collective growth. Of course, all three also use other kinds of learning-oriented practices in their leadership, as we've described throughout this book, but we thought it might be helpful in this chapter to zoom in closely on how some of these ideas can intertwine and overlap in actual practice.

In this spirit, and taken together, Matt, Tara, and Adrian's leadership work paints a holistic portrait of how some LTL-inspired ideas can take shape and form in real-life leadership. Below we summarize some of the salient tips and takeaways from their cases:

- Suspend assumptions and respectfully listen to colleagues.
- Pay attention to concrete and observable data while observing teachers' classroom practice to avoid acting on your own assumptions.

- Avoid evaluative and judgmental language while looking at teachers' practice and invite colleagues, instead, to reflect on key thoughts and actions.
- Use observable data as a jumping-off point for collegial inquiry into dilemmas of practice.
- Strive to better understand the intentions behind teachers' instructional decisions and actions through conversation.
- Develop supportive structures—including time and space—to bring teachers together in teams.
- Value teachers' ideas, work, and input on instructional programs and interventions.
- Allow teams to evolve into collegial inquiry groups over time by inviting teachers to delve into deeper issues of practice through critical and alternative viewpoints.
- Encourage experienced and novice teachers to share their special expertise, knowledge, and skills through reciprocal mentoring.
- Invite adults to assume leadership roles both in and out of school in order to grow themselves and support their colleagues collaboratively.

Of course, supporting adult learning and development is a complex, challenging, courageous, and worthy feat, even for the dedicated and well seasoned. Accordingly, in Chapter 7, we explore some of the major obstacles the twenty leaders we learned from faced in this important work—as well the promising strategies they've developed to work their way through and beyond them.

Reflective Questions

We offer the following questions as an opportunity for you to reflect on your learnings from this chapter as well as to connect any new insights you are having with practices you currently employ in your school and/or workplace. We also invite you to consider any ideas you might have in terms of enhancing the opportunities that you offer to adults in your care and, of course, for yourself. Please take a moment to consider these questions. You might want to respond to them privately first and then engage in collegial inquiry with a partner or group of colleagues. We hope you find these reflective moments helpful.

1. What are two insights you are having after reading about the leaders' cases and/or other ideas offered in this chapter?

2. What are one or two of the more important ways you will enhance a practice that *you currently employ* in your leadership in support of adult development to make the practice even more developmentally appropriate for adults who have different ways of knowing and/or learning needs?

3. What, if anything, is a new practice that you would like to employ after reading about leaders' practices in this chapter? What is one small step you might take toward implementing this new practice with developmental intentions? What kinds of supports would enable you to best implement this practice? What questions about implementation do you have at this time?

4. Please take a few moments to consider one of the more important challenges, dilemmas, or issues that you face in your practice of supporting adult learning and/or growth. In what ways, if any, do you think you could address it even more effectively by employing one or more of the pillar practices discussed in this chapter? What particular pillar practice do you think would be helpful? How so? How might this practice work synergistically with other practices or initiatives? What kinds of supports would help you implement it/them most effectively? What do you think would be a good next step for you?

7

Growing From, Through, and Beyond Obstacles

Leaders' Big Challenges and Their Strategies for Overcoming Them

Opportunities to find deeper powers within ourselves come when life seems most challenging.

—Joseph Campbell

Introduction and Overview

It has been said in many ways and by many people—from the ancient Romans to President Theodore Roosevelt—that nothing worth doing comes easily. As you might suspect, this maxim holds true for supporting adult development and learning-oriented leadership as well. While the educational leaders we learned from shared that they implemented, adapted, and invented many meaningful developmental practices drawn from and inspired by the Leadership for Transformational Learning (LTL) course, which we highlighted in Chapters 5 and 6, they also shared that leading for adult development does not always come without challenges. While they explained that it was *always* worthwhile, they also shared that shaping truly collaborative cultures that meet the evolving needs of all educators (and hence students) requires dedication, persistence, and a willingness to celebrate small successes. From our point of view, doing this important work also requires deep courage. In this chapter, we share the obstacles and challenges most frequently named by these courageous leaders as well as the promising strategies they are using today to overcome these difficulties in their unique and diverse contexts. We hope these are useful to you as you pioneer pathways for supporting the adults with whom you work in your important roles.

In particular, we offer leaders' encounters with

- changing and challenging norms in their schools and organizations,
- understanding and managing the resistance of colleagues,
- "managing up," or working with supervisors who are reluctant to adopt or appreciate developmental ideas,
- the hectic pace of and limited time in a busy school day,
- professional isolation, and
- the very real and important responsibility to grow *oneself* as a leader.

For each of these complex challenges, we present leaders' on-the-ground strategies for growing through and beyond these obstacles, as well as additional tips and takeaways for addressing these important issues in your schools and school systems. Importantly, while a few of the leaders named additional obstacles relating more broadly to professional development in general (e.g., challenges with financial resources and staffing), we focus here on the issues raised by these leaders that most directly relate to supporting adult development in schools and organizations.

A Note About Obstacles . . . and Overcoming Them

To accomplish great things, we must not only act but also dream, not only plan but also believe.

—Anatole France

Before diving more deeply into the organizational, cultural, technical, interpersonal, and intrapersonal challenges that can complicate the work of leading for adult development, we thought it worthwhile to share our reasons and hopes for illuminating these issues. First, of course, there is the practical value of understanding potential obstacles and some strategies for overcoming them in the field. As we learned from the former LTL learners now serving in various educational leadership roles, successfully supporting the growth of other adults—and themselves—requires a certain degree of tenacity and perseverance, and a faith that the vision is not only worthwhile but essential to meeting the adaptive challenges we face as educators today and to making schools and organizations true learning centers for all.

We know that a setback can stop us only if we let it, as French poet, novelist, and Nobel laureate Anatole France suggested in the passage above. However, as this quote also implies, we must be ready to push beyond our carefully tailored plans—even our best and most cherished ones—to adapt, grow, redefine, and believe in something even bigger and better. Based on the leaders' experiences we've shared with you throughout this book, we believe that pushing through challenges by helping others and ourselves grow is a promising path.

In this same spirit, we opened this chapter with a powerful quote from mythologist and author Joseph Campbell to highlight his wise assertion that challenge is ultimately an *opportunity* to grow and learn. Echoing a similar idea, developmental psychologist Erik Erikson (1968, 1980) asserted that crisis is a necessary and important part of identity development, and transformative/transformational learning theorists (e.g., Kegan, 1994, 2000; Mezirow, 2000) likewise emphasized that disequilibrium helps us grow to new understandings and insights.

Along these same lines, teachers, motivational speakers, and leaders of all kinds often point out that the Chinese word for "crisis" doubles as the word for "opportunity," and we find these related ideas compelling and undoubtedly applicable to the work of supporting adult development. As the LTL leaders repeatedly shared, it is the balance of *both support and challenge* that drives learning and growth, so it's no surprise that the challenges these leaders faced in the field have ultimately helped them become even more effective leaders. Put another way, as Gina explained of her work as a counselor and leader in schools, leaders need to recognize "that level of discomfort where you begin to internalize . . . the skills that you need, yet at the same time challenge yourself to live in that discomfort." This, we believe, is a leader's gift and journey.

Challenging Norms: Confronting "The Way It's Always Been"

We learned that, for these LTL leaders, the most prevalent challenge to leading for adult development was the fundamental and often painful difficulty of running up against "the way it's always been"— or what they described as the ingrained expectations, routines, and traditions of their schools and organizations. For more than half of these leaders (12/20), confronting the status quo and organizational norms that did not prioritize adult learning and development was an early but unavoidable obstacle to implementing their learning-oriented goals.

More particularly, these leaders shared the following common threads:

- with the focus first and foremost on children and youth, little attention is paid to adult development in schools,
- in general, professional learning opportunities for educators and other adults often reflect a one-size-fits-all model and prioritize informational rather than transformational capacity building, and
- despite the growing urgency of adjusting these approaches, given the connection between supporting adult development and improved student outcomes, change remains difficult or uncomfortable for many.

Still, as we share below, a number of these leaders developed promising strategies for pushing past limiting norms and expectations and working *ad astra per aspera*—or "to the stars through adversity," as we like to think of it.

Struggles With "Ingrained Traditions"

We know, for instance, that the building blocks of the classroom and schoolhouse have remained relatively stable throughout the history of public schooling in the United States (Tyack & Cuban, 1995) and that, despite many changes and reforms, the fundamental traditions of schooling are notoriously difficult to change. As Matt shared of his work as a lower school division head, sometimes the common traditions or expectations of what a school is and does can get in the way of new ideas:

[A big] obstacle that I face as [a principal] . . . is consistently trying to bring a focus to what's best for children, when that focus sometimes faces the status quo or it faces an ingrained tradition that either is not functioning as it used to function at some point, or is not aligned to the outcome. . . . And sometimes around these traditions in schools, I feel like there's a tremendous amount of resistance in terms of changing them.

Change, after all, is *very* hard. Or as Matt put it, people tend to resist change when things feel "comfortable and safe, regardless of whether or not they're [actually] comfortable and safe."

One such norm these leaders were working to change was the limited attention paid to supporting adult growth and learning in schools. Without shifting the focus away from children and youth, these leaders understood the powerful and promising connection between supporting adult development and positive student outcomes (Guskey, 2000). Adrian, for instance, lamented the initial inattention to adult development that he encountered in his work as a school principal in Singapore. Reflecting on this disconnect, he shared,

[W]e learn from Piaget, we learn Vygotsky's theory, and we tell ourselves our kids have different learning styles, different qualities, and we know all that as teachers because that's our craft. And we learn that in school, we learn that doing our work. But I feel there is little attention paid to developing adults, teachers, so to speak . . . and I think that caps our teachers' development. That . . . holds them back, [so] you're unable to unleash what a lot of teachers have to offer.

Moreover, according to Adrian and other leaders we learned from, the attention we do pay to teachers and their learning often fails to take into account their different developmental needs and preferences. With a "one-size-fits-all kind of model," as Adrian termed it, many professional learning initiatives miss the opportunity to help teachers and other adults grow toward their biggest, best selves. As he and other LTL leaders understood after learning about and experiencing developmental ideas in the course, differentiating supports and challenges within professional learning opportunities and structures is key when working to build individual and organizational capacity.

Similarly, by focusing largely on skill-based learning, traditional professional development sessions may miss out on the transformational potential of more developmental approaches. While, of course, increasing our skills and knowledge is essential in today's complex educational world, it is not enough. Recollecting his own initial assumptions about this issue, Adrian bravely shared,

> I still remember sending teachers for workshops and asking them to come back and do certain things and expecting teachers to be wonderful just because of that one workshop that we sent them out to attend, you know? Those kinds of things are still happening, and to me, some people still see that as professional development.

While, as you know (please see Adrian's case in Chapter 6), Adrian now runs his school in Singapore as a rich, developmentalized holding environment for growth, his concern was shared by many of the LTL graduates—in the United States and abroad. Today, successful teaching and leading all over the world require the internal capacities to manage many complex demands and tasks, and—just as a developmentalized curriculum (like the one experienced in LTL) can help leaders grow and learn—so too can a learning-oriented approach to leadership (Drago-Severson, 2004a, 2004b, 2009) help build human capacity in schools and school systems. Indeed, rather than simply mandating teachers to perform "smarter," "more efficiently," or "better," a leader needs to consider the developmental fit between expectations and capacities and help teachers grow into more complex ways of knowing and working. Or, as Diane put it, "if you want people to work better for you, perform better, you're going to have to teach them instead of just demanding it."

Strategies and Solutions for Challenging Ingrained Norms

So, how did the LTL leaders approach the very complex and at times daunting job of confronting the status quo and changing norms and expectations? In general, they explained that they did this in two ways, by

- recognizing and accepting that establishing and nurturing a learning-oriented culture is an ongoing and complex process, rather than a quick fix, and by
- starting with smaller, more manageable goals with an eye toward cumulative effects.

By keeping their eyes on positive possibilities and the promise of the future—rather than potentially discouraging initial results—the majority of these leaders were able to offer promising practices for initiating learning-oriented structures and experiences in schools and school systems.

Recognizing and Accepting Change as a Process

Perhaps the most important in-practice learning—and surprise—for many of these leaders was the time and dedication required to effectively lead for adult development. For example, in her work as a middle school principal, Tara, like other LTL graduates, lamented that her learning-oriented work in supporting collegial inquiry in teacher "gleams" took "so much longer than I thought it would take" (please see Chapter 6 for a more detailed account of Tara's powerful leadership practices). Reimagining and recrafting the "established culture" of her school was and remains an ongoing effort, yet accepting change as a process was key to both her leadership and her peace of mind. As she explained,

> I've had to be a lot more patient and just take a lot more deep breaths and let things, just let things take longer than I wanted them to with this [establishing collegial inquiry in grade-level teacher teams], but you know, we're getting there. It's a process.

Gina, too, in describing her work as a school counselor and adult educator who provided professional development for others around building capacity, underscored the importance of recognizing that learning-oriented leadership is never a quick fix or an easy stopgap. Indeed, we agree that it requires the hardest work—within ourselves, our schools, and our organizations—and these important struggles are part of what pushes us further. Rather than signs of personal or professional failure, these leaders explained, challenges are simply a part of doing this work, and recognizing them as such can make a big difference. As Gina shared of her own experience, which resonates with what we and others have learned,

> It's always comforting to know that these things [challenges] are sort of universal and that everyone is struggling with them, because I think that knowing that helps us understand, . . . it sort of alleviates some of that frustration.

Starting Small, Starting With You

Similarly, a number of these leaders shared that one of the most powerful ways to confront ingrained norms was to lead and live according to one's beliefs and aspirations. The feeling that one's school, organization, or society has not *yet* embraced a developmental perspective does not prevent a leader from embodying and sharing this promising message himself or herself, they felt.

Concerned, for instance, about how she felt constructive-developmental theory and related principles of learning-oriented leadership were undervalued in the South American educational context in which she worked, Marisa, a therapist and adult educator, began to consider the fit between developmental theory and "the spectrum of society." Hypothesizing that the governmental context of her country—which included at different times a dictatorship, military rule, and now an emerging democracy—may have influenced and perhaps limited the ways people conceptualize and embrace new ideas, she began to ask herself important questions about her work and her approach:

> I began to think about society because I understand that we develop our ways of knowing based on our experiences. But I think that society has tremendous influence on our experiences, and therefore on how far we're going to go in developing our ways of knowing. . . . I'm a great believer in creating holding environments, but I realize that if I have this resistance to change [from the larger society], how am I going to be able to go out there and create a holding environment?

Given her concern and her deeply held beliefs about the power of a developmental perspective, Marisa approached her work in the best way that she could: through her own heart and contributions. Describing her home-based therapy practice, for instance, she talked about taking small but courageous and hopeful steps:

> Well, maybe it's because I know it can happen here within this small environment of my house, which I call a small school. So then I'm thinking, well, maybe out there, it's not kicking in yet, but if it can start here in this small environment as a holding environment, then maybe the people that pass through here can take it out there too, you know? So there's a bit of a hope, I would say, in that regard. And also I never give up in any circumstances. I'm one that keeps trying, no matter what.

I'm like that. And I think . . . that once you believe in something with your heart, and you know it's true, then you never give up, you know?

For many of these LTL leaders, like Marisa, the challenge of introducing learning-oriented ideas required the determination to push beyond the way it's always been, and to begin the very hard but rewarding work of leading in support of adult development. We hope that these leaders' experiences and strategies will be of help to you as you engage in your own noble and important leadership practices.

Adding to These Leaders' Wisdom: Additional Strategies for Reshaping Norms

Below is a list of additional strategies and suggestions we offer to complement these leaders' wise sharings about how to begin to alter established norms that need modification in order to lead and learn together in today's complex educational climate. For example, we have often found deep value in

- Starting with small changes in norms
- Being patient with one's efforts to create change
- Celebrating small achievements publicly
- Reminding those participating in the work—including oneself— of the importance of honoring the process and the time it takes to achieve results
- Finding ways to acknowledge and recognize hard work (e.g., giving journals, sending appreciation notes), as little things mean a lot
- Providing food/snacks during meetings
- Prioritizing time for conversation

Facing Resistance: Pushing Forward Despite "Pushback" From Colleagues and/or Supervisors

A second and related challenge these leaders described in relation to supporting adult development (i.e., capacity building) in their schools and educational organizations was a degree of *reluctance* or *resistance* from the other adults they worked with.

While recognizing that all adults—like all human beings—have both the potential and desire to grow, more than half of these leaders

(12/20) nonetheless described a kind of hesitance or skepticism on the part of colleagues that complicated their initial efforts to encourage, model, and support developmentally oriented practice and collaboration. When characterizing the nature of this pushback, these leaders attributed this painful and challenging resistance to a number of factors, including

- the many complex demands that educators face as part of their daily work,
- the challenge of convincing others of the value of a developmental approach before they've experienced it, and
- adults' reluctance to engage in work that feels unfamiliar or beyond comfortable competencies.

While, as we describe in greater detail next, LTL leaders recognized that resistance can often be developmental in nature, we present leaders' encounters with these challenges, as well as the promising strategies they identified and employed as they've worked to address and overcome resistance in their schools and organizations in the following sections.

"One More Thing": Fitting in a Focus on Development

As we emphasized in Chapter 1, today's complex educational environment places more demands on educators and leaders—both individually and collectively—than ever before. With the pressures of high-stakes accountability systems, new standards and performance review procedures, and the challenges of meeting the needs of an increasingly diverse student body, teachers and other educators may feel already "filled up"—meaning maxed out or overwhelmed—by the seemingly countless tasks and responsibilities that pepper and at times define their over-full days.

Despite teachers' heroic efforts and leaders' best intentions of support, the call for teachers to do something different, something more, may feel at first like too much to even consider, these leaders explained. As Jane, an educational consultant, described of the many courageous educators she works with in her role as data consultant,

> [D]oing this [developmental] work is different for people, it's hard. They don't know how to do it. They don't feel like they have time to do it. These schools that I'm working at have above average dropout rates and gun violence. These are tough urban schools. They're the lowest-performing school districts and the

teachers are . . . working at capacity in every sense of the word. And so when they're asked to be doing something different, of course there's going to be a [challenging] response to that.

Additionally, LTL leaders explained that they had to acknowledge that, while they brought from their LTL experiences a faith in the lived promise of developmental leadership and collegial holding environments for growth, many of the adults they worked with were encountering these ideas and practices for the first time. They needed opportunities to see and feel for themselves the power of feeling "well held" (Drago-Severson, 2012), but with so much else on their very full plates, not all teachers were competing to get to the front of the line when such opportunities arose. As Brenda explained, recalling her work organizing a teacher reflection group as the academic dean at her school,

> I guess a challenge would just be convincing other people of the value of it—that it's worth giving up their time to do. . . . [T]hey [many other teachers] weren't intrinsically motivated to do this [the reflection group] for themselves, but I think anybody who would've participated would've seen the value, but you had to get them there.

Recognizing the Developmental Underpinnings of Resistance

In addition to this general unfamiliarity, the LTL leaders we learned from explained that new practices and ideas sometimes called competencies into question for adults. In other words, they explained that they understood that resistance might be developmental in nature. Rather than a refusal to "do things," resistance may very well be related to not having the internal capacities to demonstrate requested actions (e.g., sharing views with colleagues who may not agree).

For example, describing her work as a middle school principal, Melanie wisely explained that "resistance to improved practices or new ideas or high expectations"—while painful and frustrating at first—was ultimately a reflection of what teachers really needed from her as a leader, of what they both hoped for and felt uncomfortable with, *even if they couldn't explain that out loud*. In fact, rather than an "intentional slowing-down of the pace of progress," Melanie came to understand that teacher resistance itself was frequently developmental in nature. And with so much on the line for her personally as a principal, and for the teachers as individual professionals, she came "to recognize resistance as an expression of emotional need or fear or anxiety over [job] performance." Still, she admitted, facing the sting of resistance was "hard."

Managing Up: Helping Supervisors Understand the Importance of Developmental Intentionality

For more than one-third of these leaders (7/20), working with supervisors who were reluctant to adopt or appreciate developmental ideas was a particularly challenging aspect of resistance. Indeed, working to "manage up," as a number of these leaders called working in contexts in which they had to introduce LTL ideas "up" the chain of command, involved negotiating the complex nuances of power and authority in their schools and organizations—and stretching the boundaries and expectations of their own roles. As Lucy described from her vantage point as a Foreign Service officer, when an organization is "very hierarchical" and supervisors expect that decisions and ideas are "not to be discussed or questioned," it can at times be daunting to introduce a promising new practice or perspective.

Similarly, Jane recognized that many of the educators (e.g., teachers, principals, assistant principals, district officers, superintendents) she works with in her data-consulting role in districts face this very challenge when they bring new ideas back to their schools. As she explained, after the educator-analysts return from the data workshops, they have to

> bring their principals on board because their principals haven't been trained . . . and they're just hitting people that aren't helping them—I mean that don't want to do it or that aren't clear how to lead the work. . . . And so the analysts are in this position of managing up even though they're not the "leaders," and that has been a huge challenge.

Working, then, to equip her leadership colleagues with the tools to "manage up" was a significant but unanticipated aspect of Jane's important work in schools and districts.

Jenai described a similar predicament that occurred when, as an assistant principal, she was paired with a principal who approached the work from a very different angle, as he had spent significantly less time directly in classrooms. While, as she acknowledged during her interview, this principal brought many strengths to the administrative team despite his different approach, "actually living" the partnership was difficult for Jenai because she felt that she had a lot to offer but "wasn't really in the position to make a lot of the decisions."

In fact, she described managing up as "one of the more major challenges" she faced in her leadership work for adult development, and—despite her best efforts to remain "humble" and "supportive" in this context—she realized she needed to seek a better professional fit when she began to lose sleep over the challenges of the collaboration. As she explained, given what she knew after LTL and her other professional learning experiences, it was difficult *not* to implement certain practices and to have less say than she would have liked, for she knew her developmental ideas and perspectives could ultimately benefit both the staff and the students. "I feel so urgently about the work," she told us, "and it's so hard looking at students" when more could be done. As she sadly explained further,

> I did not know how to manage up, and I tried my best to provide solutions in as best a way as I could. But eventually it just didn't work. I think he [the principal] felt pressured by me, I'm sure. It became a tense environment.

On a more hopeful note, Brenda identified one key root to supervisor resistance in her reflections on managing up as an academic dean in her independent school.

Sometimes, Brenda realized—and emphasized to us—that resistance stems simply from a lack of exposure to new ideas—or from supervisors' unfamiliarity with new concepts rather than their lack of willingness to do the work. In her own context, for example, she found that the principles and practices she learned in LTL were quite foreign to the team of administrators she was working with. While the realization didn't erase the resistance, it did give her a starting point or a foothold from which to begin. As Brenda described it, the problem she needed to address was "convincing older administrators that giving teachers time to collaborate is not putting the teachers before the kids. That in the end, you're not doing it [just] for the teachers, you're doing it because it's going to benefit student learning." As she elaborated,

> [I]t was often taken as I was always on the side of the teacher. . . . So I was coming from this very different framework. I think I was working with some people who saw it more traditionally. . . . [And so] I had trouble getting time for teachers because of administrative issues, and [trouble] supporting teachers and showing others the value of that—of giving teachers time to reflect.

For Brenda, then, as for many of these leaders, addressing resistance from colleagues and supervisors was key to their success in pushing forward their learning-oriented goals and visions. That is not always easy, but we describe below a number of strategies these leaders employed to combat pushback and make a difference in support of adult development.

Strategies and Solutions for Combating Resistance

Despite the many forms and layers of resistance these leaders experienced, they shared with us a wide variety of promising strategies for helping allay colleagues' and supervisors' initial fears and apprehensions. These strategies enabled them to lead this important work in ways that were meaningful to all stakeholders. In particular, their lived experiences serve as helpful examples from which we can learn, as they highlight the power of

- maintaining "objectivity" as a leader, and not taking complaints or pushback personally,
- inviting "resistant" adults to share their thinking and feelings, rather than demanding compliance,
- investing the "time" to stay in place as a leader, or to consistently and patiently persevere,
- building "trust" in all through authenticity, and
- remaining "open to learning" from other adults' different perspectives.

We hope you find these strategies helpful as you lead in support of adult development in your own schools and contexts.

Maintaining Developmental Balance: Keeping the Personal in Perspective

Given the dedication and heart educational leaders bring to their work with children, youth, and adults in their schools and organizations, few things feel more personal, more intimately tied with identity, than the success of their efforts. Resistance, then, can indeed be a difficult and painful obstacle to overcome, especially when a leader is dedicating his or her heart and soul to improving conditions for all. Yet as we learned from many of these leaders, a developmental perspective can help make clear that resistance is often less about an individual leader than about the developmental capacities others bring to the work. As we described earlier in the section about recognizing the developmental roots of resistance, colleagues' discomfort with new initiatives can often stem from their developmental orientations toward change and new expectations, and keeping this truth in mind was an important strategy many leaders used to keep resistance in perspective. This, they shared, took the personal "sting" out of colleagues' or supervisors' initial hesitations. Jenai, for instance, keeps LTL ideas in the back of her mind whenever resistance crops up. As she explained, reflecting on her various roles as a school administrator and consultant,

> I think a lot about the concept of complaints [as] signs of passion in teachers, and I felt that that was a huge paradigm shift in me. And it was so helpful because I really—when I work in schools, I'm never overwhelmed by the amount of feedback that teachers have about the program or about leadership style or anything. I just take it in and really—it's almost like my respect level grows . . . and that's just so helpful because it could be such a demotivator if I didn't have that paradigm in my head.

Of course, resistance (while it always signals *something*) can have many roots. Acknowledging the multiple possibilities of resistance and asking developmental questions is one important way these leaders began to address adults' resistance. As Jane describes below, working to understand the *reasons* behind a colleague's pushback is often more effective and meaningful for all involved than demanding compliance.

Inviting Others to Share Feelings and Concerns: "Inquiry vs. Advocacy"

In describing a difficult encounter with a skeptical teacher in a professional development session she was leading, Jane shared another promising strategy for overcoming resistance that she found helpful as a data consultant working with district level leaders and teachers: inviting reluctant adults to share their concerns and points of view. Indeed, when, during one of Jane's sessions, a veteran teacher stood up—in front of the seventy other participants in attendance—and said, "that she thought it [the workshop] was [nonsense], and that she didn't understand, that she thought it was a waste of time," Jane was deeply shocked. As she described it, "my jaw was (in my mind) hitting the floor." Fortunately for Jane, however, her developmental understanding of resistance allowed her to take a step back and handle the potentially disastrous situation with clarity, wisdom, and patience. By inviting this initially resistant teacher to share her frustrations privately—rather than confront her in front of the group or demand compliance—Jane was able to diffuse some of the tension. As she described,

> So I had a couple of side [private] conversations with her, and I mean that's fine. I was really taken aback that she said it, but I think deep enough inside of me, that's really okay that she feels that way. . . . [So,] I was able to kind of cover it pretty well, and I . . . invited her to share why she felt that way and what her frustrations were and really just left it at that.

Even more encouraging was the teacher's eventual adoption of some of Jane's ideas, including a strategy for careful observation and description that they worked on together in the context of data analysis. Now a "real convert," according to Jane's district contacts, this teacher was able to find meaning in her work with Jane on her own terms and at her own pace, and Jane's invitational quality seems to have made a big difference. As Jane described it, because of her low-pressure approach, "there was some part" of the workshop that the teacher "was able to sort of connect with."

Perhaps even more important than this inspiring result was Jane's developmental rationale for handling the situation in this way. As she explained, inviting the teacher to share her frustrations and concerns

> was a good example of meeting people where they're at [developmentally] and hanging in there. I think it's really easy in leadership positions or . . . as a facilitator when you get . . . pushback or resistance, to really get into defensive or advocacy mode. . . . [I]t would have been easy for me at that moment in time to really just advocate my position about why she should have done [the activity], but—and I'm so grateful for this— somehow I was able to shift into inquiry mode and, like I said, just invite her to share her experience about why she felt that way and leave it at that . . . but it's really hard . . . when you're standing up in front of that many people and they're paying you the big bucks and you're trying to be impressive.

As Jane learned in LTL, people truly value the opportunity to be *heard*, and genuinely *listening* to what adults have to say—even when it's very hard to hear—can go a long way when working to build collaborative and cooperative cultures that support growth.

Staying in Place: The Gift of Time and Presence

Just as Jane worked to "hang in there" to better connect with and truly understand the teacher in the above example, Rachel described the importance of consistently staying in place when working to support adults who may be struggling to meet complex demands. In her work as the vice president of a charter management organization, for instance, Rachel mentors regional directors who oversee principals, and she recounted one painful experience of a working relationship that did not begin smoothly. Despite her initial efforts to help one director grow to feel less "apprehensive about making decisions or taking responsibility" and to rely less on "a lot of other people's approval"—classic characteristics of a socializing way of knowing, as we described in Chapter 3—she realized that his hesitance and approval seeking might in fact signal a need for growth in these areas and that this capacity would have to develop over time. Her solution, then, involved just that. By remaining in place—by investing the time to model and scaffold the types of developmental capacities she hoped the director would learn—Rachel was able to find an inroad into an otherwise unnavigable relationship. As Rachel described,

> I think part of it was just time. Part of it was working . . . with him as opposed to making it seem like I was working against him. . . . So really trying to [ask], "Okay, what do you need help with on this?" . . . So as I continued to do those things . . . I think he started to see my competence and saw me as somebody more trustworthy.

While, arguably, there are times when an adult's role seems too much of a stretch—developmentally speaking—for a position to be a good match, gently guiding and structuring supports for promising individuals can help schools and other organizations build capacity from *within* and harness the potential of the dedicated and hardworking adults who already work and learn together every day to serve their students and the greater good.

Building Trust Through Authenticity

Additionally, a number of these leaders emphasized another very important strategy for overcoming resistance: building trust through authenticity. By demonstrating, for example, that they *truly* wanted to support teachers' development and cared deeply about colleagues as professionals and human beings, these leaders worked to overcome resistance by "walking the walk" that accompanied the developmental "talk," so to speak.

Adrian, for instance, when describing his work as a secondary school principal in Singapore, explained that it was important that his teachers knew he was "for real" about supporting their growth and development. By caring for the preconditions for learning-oriented leadership that we described in Chapter 5 (i.e., the importance of building mutually trusting and respectful relationships) and the ongoing work he does structuring reciprocal mentoring and learning opportunities (please see Adrian's case in Chapter 6), Adrian works to continuously communicate to teachers that he's not punitive or "out to get" them. By consistently embodying his beliefs in ways both big and small, Adrian explained that he was able to break through some of the skepticism and resistance that he faced at the outset.

Moreover, Adrian explained that he worked hard to build trust and relationships *before* launching bigger initiatives:

> I didn't do this [larger-scale, developmentally oriented reforms] on the first day I took over the school. I was very blessed because when I came into the school, I had nine months . . . to be in the school [before the former principal left]. . . . So in the nine months, I just rolled up my sleeves and I worked—I worked together with all my heads of departments and I got myself involved in every single project . . . and when I say getting involved, it's not just giving direction but doing the work. And so I really got to know my teachers and my heads of department really, really well, and I really got to know what makes them tick and their concerns. And when I took over and could make the [big] decisions . . . I felt like I had a lot more for teachers. Knowing that I was a teacher once . . . helps a lot, you know?

While Adrian's on-the-ground experiences helped him better recognize and appreciate his colleagues' perspectives, his willingness to work hard and be "one of the team" likewise helped his staff understand and trust Adrian's authentic vision for the school—and paved the way for their successful implementation of growth-enhancing practices.

Similarly, when Brenda first began her work as an academic dean in an independent school, she was troubled by the "tension" that existed between the administration and the faculty. Sensing, however, a "hopefulness" from the teachers that things could change for the better,

Brenda worked carefully and intentionally to show them her best and truest intentions. "I want to listen to you, and I recognize you as a professional, and I want to use your feedback," she would tell them again and again, and her honesty—and willingness to follow up on her words with actions when implementing new ideas—eventually helped her establish "a great rapport with the teachers." She hoped that teachers would think, "Maybe this administrator's going to listen to us," if they recognized her dedication and care as authentic. As Brenda explained,

> I'm still in touch with a lot of them [the teachers]. . . . I just had a good rapport with them. In a way that made it easier for me to make certain changes because there was a trust there, so even if they didn't necessarily like something we [the administrative team] were doing, it was helpful . . . to be coming from a place of trust. . . . That trust was so important to how effective I could be.

For both Brenda and Adrian, like other LTL leaders, building relationships by caring for the preconditions and then maintaining and deepening trust through authentic follow-through helped teachers and other colleagues buy in to their developmental ideas and leadership practices and ultimately lessened the amount of resistance they needed to overcome.

Learning From Others: Remaining Open to Different Perspectives

Perhaps most simply, these leaders shared one last strategy for handling resistance: openness to learning from it. While it is inarguably a leader's task and challenge to bring to fruition the best of what he or she has learned and hoped for, it is also true that a static vision can lack luster and life. After all, even the best principles and ideas do little to effect change without the human leaders who live them into being. While LTL, then, provided these leaders with a very useful framework and toolkit for their work, their willingness to adapt, grow, stretch, and fit LTL ideas to meet the needs of their particular schools and organizations was key to managing resistance and to their success.

For instance, like other LTL graduates, Brenda explained that even the administrators who she felt to be "resisters" helped her refine and improve her own leadership as dean:

> I have a lot of respect for everybody that I worked with, and they helped me in some ways. Sometimes I think I had a habit of too much freedom—of let's just let the teachers decide

this . . . [and] some teachers can't handle that; they don't want to handle that. They want to be told a structure, so you can't use that across the board. . . . I also did have a habit of—to a fault—wanting to make teachers happy, and so it would be hard for me . . . [and] other administrators helped me in that way, I think.

As this example shows, remaining open and flexible to learning from diverse and even contrary perspectives can help leaders grow to broaden and strengthen their leadership in support of adult development and can also help include and incorporate the ideas of adults who may not otherwise have been "on board" with new initiatives or opportunities.

Adding to Leaders' Wisdom: Additional Strategies and Suggestions for Overcoming Resistance

What follows is a list of additional suggestions for complementing these leaders' strategies for how to begin to overcome and address resistance.

- Share short articles about developmental theory and learning-oriented leadership to help others understand where you are coming from, and explain why this is important to you.
- Explain the relationship and direct links between supporting adult learning and increasing student achievement.
- Meet adults where they are—by being present to them with developmental understandings.
- Scaffold adults' understanding as they strive to grow by offering developmentally appropriate supports and challenges (please see Chapter 3).
- Help them understand that you are with them—that you know change is hard and that it takes time.
- Ask questions to learn more about what they are resisting and why.
- Ask how you can help. What supports might be useful? What, in particular, are they finding challenging?

The Urgency of Time: A Common Challenge

Another very important obstacle named by more than half of these leaders (11/20) was "time." Time—as both pressure and limitation—was a common cause of resistance and a challenge to these leaders' developmental work in terms of

- the hectic pace of the workday in most schools,
- the many competing and multiple demands placed on educators, and
- the lack of common planning or meeting time for teachers and other adults in most educational organizations.

With all that is increasingly expected and demanded of educators of all kinds—especially in light of new reform initiatives such as the Common Core State Standards, new models for professional evaluation, and a strong focus on student outcomes—and with the relatively limited time of each school day, term, and year, these leaders underscored the importance of deliberately "fitting" developmental structures and opportunities into their very busy schedules. Without this kind of intentionality it was *all too easy* to let this important work take a backseat to everyday exigencies, they emphasized.

For example, as Dana recognized, describing on her own experiences as a high school English teacher leader, finding the time to commit to the work of growing and learning was difficult in the high-pressure, high-stakes context of her school:

> I think it's really hard to find time to reflect as a teacher, especially because you're in a profession where . . . your attention is constantly in demand from all sorts, like colleagues, your administrators, your kids, parents. I mean, it's so consuming that I think it's often difficult to even make the time to reflect.

While painful, this reality was echoed by many and often stood in sharp contrast to leaders' strong *desire* to approach their leading, teaching, and learning with a more critically reflective approach.

Matt, too, emphasized the challenge of navigating the many time-sensitive demands he manages as a principal. With so much resting on his actions and decisions, Matt truly felt the weight and responsibility of resolving issues "in a very quick way, but also in a way . . . that is supportive to the individuals involved." As he described,

> [T]he nature of the position, the nature of working in schools, and the nature of working with people . . . [is that sometimes] if I don't do something, then a child is going to be waiting after school not knowing where their mom is. Or a teacher's going to be hung out to dry with the lesson. Or . . . a family would suffer because we didn't schedule a team meeting as soon as we were supposed to.

With all of these competing demands and commitments, it is little wonder that these leaders identified time as a significant obstacle to implementing their collaborative, developmental, and personal goals. And the urgency only seemed to increase as leaders took on wider responsibilities. Rachel, for instance, similarly found the pressures of time a major obstacle in her work at the district level. As the vice president of her charter management organization, she shared with us a deep wish for more opportunities to step back, reflect, and consider the nature of her work and progress. Speaking of her own practice and the role of time in her organization, Rachel shared,

> I think we need to get out of the hubbub of the school day [when] everything's flying at rocket speed and things need to get done quickly and rapidly and things are popping up and flying up that need to be acted upon immediately and weren't anticipated, and just take some more time . . . to reflect about how things are going.

Finding the time, as Rachel suggests, to step out of the fast-paced world of caring for students, teachers, parents, other administrators, *and external demands* can be difficult, of course. She, like other LTL leaders, emphasized that it is often the case that by making time to intentionally care for oneself and others that we begin to make real headway toward these urgent goals and responsibilities.

Similarly, leaders explained that carving out specific time and space for meaningful collaboration and reciprocal learning with colleagues was often a challenge. For example, Brenda, like other LTL leaders, highlighted the fact that educators and leaders often have little time to meet together or interact. As she described of her administrative work as dean in her high school,

> I did the schedule for middle and upper school, and one of the biggest issues was just that—no time for teachers to meet. There was no common time for departments to get together or for teachers to share.

This more structural limitation of time was a common concern shared by LTL leaders and one that Brenda recognized as linked to building trust and authentically filling one's leadership role. As she explained,

> In an actual leadership role, I think the logistics are sometimes just as important [as a leader's beliefs]. . . . [Y]ou can value it [collegial inquiry and adult development], but if you don't give teachers the time and support they need and the space—then

you're not really showing that you value it. You can say you value it, but I think the act of giving the time and space—the logistics of that—are just as important, because you're putting your money where your mouth is.

As Brenda shared, failing to merge intention and action—even in the seemingly small but nonetheless *big* logistical details of scheduling—can significantly hinder one's work and can inadvertently send mixed messages to the adults in your care.

Adrian, too, recognized that teacher growth and collaboration require *explicit* administrative and logistical support in terms of allocating—and holding sacred—common time and space in the workday for teachers to work and learn together. As a principal, Adrian, like other LTL leaders, emphasized his understanding that teachers "are required to do many, many things," and that adding new expectations requires adjustments on the part of administrative structures and procedures. Without these accommodations, he warned, "you keep adding to the system, you strain the system, [and] it's going to blow."

Strategies and Solutions for Managing Time

Despite the many demands placed on educators and educational leaders and the quick pace of a typical school day, we learned from these LTL leaders that support for adult development cannot happen unless *time* is prioritized and room is made for this important work. In terms of managing the multiple and urgent demands of time, these leaders shared two key strategies—and also helped demonstrate that prioritizing time for adult development can in turn help alleviate demands by enhancing individual and organizational capacity. In particular, leaders shared the promise of

- carving out and protecting time for collaborative work and reflection within the school day, and
- carefully budgeting and structuring their own time as leaders to meet multiple demands.

Below, we outline some of their experiences with both.

Allocating Time for Collaboration: Prioritizing Adult Development During the Day

Despite the hectic pace and multiple demands of teaching and leading today, these leaders worked to build meaningful opportunities for supporting adult growth and collaboration into the structure of the school day.

Sharing one powerful strategy for bringing adults together for collegial inquiry, for instance, Adrian described his approach as a principal when carving out time and space for teachers' collaborative professional reflection at his school in Singapore:

> [O]nce every week, we start our school an hour later, so I don't allow the students to come to school. [Typically], my school starts at 7:50 in the morning, but every Wednesday, I ask my students to report to school only at 8:50, so I give my teachers about an hour in the morning where . . . their focus is on the convening, the learning. . . . I mean, it's just teachers learning together early in the morning, and they are fresh. When we go for professional learning, usually we go at the end of a teaching day, [and] we're all so tired. Really you're not in the right frame of mind to learn. When you're fresh in the morning and you're coming to school with a lot of energy [there's so much more potential for learning]—and of course, I don't hold it on a Monday . . . nobody learns on Monday (laughs). . . . [S]o on Wednesday, my teachers do get a lot of time to learn together.

While, of course, educational leaders at different levels and in different contexts have different amounts of control over and input into their school schedules, Adrian's willingness to foreground teacher collegial inquiry in such an intentional and creative way speaks of his passion for and commitment to learning-oriented leadership and helps demonstrate the importance of finding and making time for collaboration, however one can.

Organizing Time, Organizing Oneself

These LTL leaders also shared the importance of structuring one's own busy days and life to best manage the complex and competing demands of educational leadership. In other words, they explained, one key approach to organizing time as a school leader was to actually organize *oneself*.

While many of the LTL leaders voiced this, Matt's use of a detailed calendar and daily planner—which outlined and prioritized his many obligations and commitments as a lower school head—perhaps illustrated this strategy most explicitly. Describing the various components of his organizational approach, for instance, Matt explained,

> [S]o I have these lists where it's broken up into To Do Right Away, To Do Soon, To Do Later, My Personal Life, things that I've done but I need to make sure they've gotten done, and

then all the different meetings that I have. . . . I get better at prioritizing what goes in the To Do Right Away box or [the] To Do Soon box, but sometimes it is thirty things (laughs), and then I've got to do these right away.

Despite the complexity of his days and the occasionally overwhelming amount of urgent tasks in his *To Do Right Away* box, Matt emphatically underscored that attending to the learning and growth of his teachers was always more than worth his time. This was a common theme among LTL leaders, who prioritized their deep regard for colleagues and teachers by consistently making time to care for adults' learning and growth.

For example, while it might have seemed more expedient—in the short term—to put the developmental components of his work on hold on particularly busy days, supporting teacher practice through reflective meetings was a nonnegotiable for Matt. Despite the heavy pressures of running a school, he often held private meetings with teachers to discuss their teaching and progress. As he explained,

In my schedule, it would have been easier not to meet with them, right? But at the same time that's a false truth, I think . . . because in doing this proactive work with teachers, supporting them not to be static with their teaching, they're actually going to be doing much higher-quality work. . . . It actually saves time to meet with them; that's my point of saying it. And not only does it save time, but like I said, I think it's a real central theme to our work.

By building time into his *own* calendar for engaging in these conversations with teachers, Matt was able to clearly communicate his value for collegial inquiry—and also to create an invitational time and space for teachers to reflect on their practice with caring feedback and support.

Adding to Leaders' Wisdom: Additional Strategies for Addressing the Challenge of Time

Below is a list of additional suggestions that we offer to complement these leaders' ideas and practices about how to secure time for supporting adult development in their work contexts.

- Invite adults to meet before or after school and provide food.
- Create lunch clubs where educators discuss practice, articles, initiatives, or problems of practice.

- Once a month, host a two- or three-hour dinner meeting during which mentors, grade-level, or discipline-focused teachers meet to share experiences, reflect on practice, discuss challenges, and engage in collegial inquiry.

Professional Isolation: The Loneliness of Leadership

It is a well-documented truth that leadership today can be lonely (Ackerman & Maslin-Ostrowski, 2004; Barth, 1980, 1990; Donaldson, 2008; Evans, 1996). Leading in schools and other educational organizations is no exception, and for nearly all of these leaders (14/20), the loneliness of leading stood out as a significant obstacle to supporting adult development. While at times difficult to talk about—and always painful to experience—the isolating nature of the principalship and other leadership roles made these leaders' work and developmental efforts even more difficult, they shared.

As Adrian explained, "it's a very lonely job as a principal, and you have so many things that are confidential [so] you can't share with anybody." Marisa, too, lamented the loneliness of her work as a counselor and adult educator in South America—especially since she was doing this work abroad in a context different from that in which she learned about developmental theory and leadership:

> I really feel I need to have someone else or other colleagues that I can brainstorm with and have a little bit of a back-and-forth dialogue regarding this. I'm kind of alone in this. I feel alone right now.

This kind of professional isolation seemed particularly problematic for leaders working in university contexts. Brooke, for instance, described the double-edged independence of life as an assistant professor:

> People are very independent. You don't—it's strange. At times I interact more with my colleagues outside of the university than I do with the people right down the hall from me. . . . I don't know if it's the nature of the division I work within—I haven't figured that out yet—but it can be very isolated. I love the independence, but I could use a little more intellectual stimulation from my colleagues and peers.

Jackie likewise underscored the solitary nature of her many roles and responsibilities:

> [A]ll the work I do is really isolating. I'm a poet, so I'm sitting in front of my computer. I tutor, so I'm sitting with one student. Or I'm a teacher, an adjunct professor, and I'm there for a few hours at school and then I leave. So I really don't have the opportunity to talk to many adults, people in education . . . [and] just as I don't really have the opportunity to talk to my colleagues, they don't have the opportunity necessarily to get to know me.

For Jackie, like many of these leaders, this feeling of separateness was a considerable challenge—and the yearning for deeper connection with other like-minded adults a powerful need. Yet as Jackie explained, this hope extended beyond the professional realm, and mirrored a larger, more holistic need for community and interrelation in one's life. As she insightfully explained,

> [W]hat would help me in my life, and not just being a leader . . . [but] in terms of feeling more fulfilled in my life and feeling more hopeful is if I had more connections. . . . [T]he more we're . . . fulfilled and nurtured in our regular life, the more energy we have to bring to our professional lives, so I think it's all intertwined. Like a happy person is going to be a happy teacher.

As we share below, finding, creating, and nurturing these kinds of deep professional connections were some of these leaders' most powerful solutions for managing the complex pressures of leading in support of adult development. Yet as we report later in Chapter 8, they were also some of the hardest to find and most sought after.

Strategies and Solutions for Addressing Professional Isolation

For a number of these LTL leaders, who were fortunate enough to find and develop relational professional connections to alleviate professional isolation, the support generally took two forms:

- mentoring, and
- peer inquiry groups.

Adrian, by way of one LTL school leader's example, described his meaningful work with his mentor principal in Singapore. As a new principal, he was able to benefit from the expectation that he would seek out a mentor, and the opportunity remains a big support for him as he continues his important work leading the school. As he explained,

> I think having a mentor principal to support me is really important. . . . [I]n Singapore, we have a system where when you're a new principal, you can approach any experienced principal to be your mentor . . . and when I was a teacher, [my mentor] was the principal running the school. So I sought her out. . . . [S]he's very special because she's always a phone call away when I need help . . . and also somebody to bounce ideas [off of]. . . . And I think that she is way ahead of me in terms of experience. She has dealt with more cases in schools. When I talk about cases, I'm talking about meeting with difficult parents and dealing with very tough situations in school when it calls for it. Even dealing with difficult teachers. I do consult her and I do talk to her, so it's not a very lonely journey for me, so to speak.

Like Adrian, who deeply values the support he receives from his mentor around the difficult or challenging situations he faces as a principal, Sarah described trusted peers as an invaluable support of her work at the university level. By building on the relationships she formed with fellow students in graduate school, Sarah was able to maintain important connections that support her work as an assistant professor in a school of education. As she describes,

> I have a research group that was started when I was a student [in graduate school]. We just kind of naturally came together, and . . . one person has been particularly helpful for me in debriefing things that I bump up against. Makes me really kind of process them and understand—she helps me understand what the issue is and why I'm feeling the way I'm feeling. . . . I think that's probably the only support that, right now, feels . . . meaningful.

While, as we describe in Chapter 8, the desire for community and authentic connection was voiced as an important hope by a great majority of the leaders we learned from, for those lucky enough to already have such supports in place, opportunities to deeply engage with trusted others around issues central to their work and leadership made a tremendous difference—both practically and psychologically. In Chapter 8 we offer some additional ideas about how to reduce isolation.

Growing Oneself: A Fundamental Need and Responsibility of Leadership

> *Leaders are more powerful role models when they learn than when they teach.*

> —Rosabeth Moss Kantor

Nearly one-third of these LTL leaders (7/20) deeply emphasized the importance of growing one's own internal capacities as leaders and how this was an additional challenge—and fundamental responsibility—of leadership in general and of leading for adult development in particular. While growing oneself is a complex challenge that takes many forms, these leaders described two main issues related to self-development that stood out as key imperatives:

- a mindfulness of one's own developmental capacities and preferences, and
- a willingness to step out, at times, of the role of expert and assume a learning stance.

Below, we describe leaders' reflections on these challenges, as well as strategies employed by a number of them to address these important considerations.

Awareness of One's Own Way of Knowing as Leader

A number of these leaders shared that an awareness of one's own way of knowing—and all of its strengths and weaknesses—was key to maximizing and growing one's leadership and to modeling a commitment to lifelong learning. As Brenda explained of her work as an academic dean in an independent school, "Meeting teachers where they are and helping to support them" in a developmental sense requires "recognizing where *you* are on that [developmental] spectrum as well" and understanding how "those two things intersect"—meaning the ways your own capacities, expectations, and ways of seeing things as a leader accord with your teachers'. As Brenda wisely understood, leaders' developmental preferences do indeed often color the types of supports and challenges they tend to offer, as well as their expectations of the adults in their care. Like teachers, who sometimes (at least at first) tend to teach in ways that reflect how they learn best (Bennett, 1991; Dunn & Dunn, 1979; Weinsten, 1989), leaders—like all human beings—orient to leadership differently depending on their ways of knowing and their prior experiences with authority. Without a critically reflective approach, these tendencies can limit our effectiveness as leaders, LTL leaders shared, and so it is important to consider and understand one's leadership stance when working to learn, grow, and improve.

Jed effectively captured this challenge when describing his early work as a principal:

> One of my biggest challenges as a self-authoring knower is that I—and I'll acknowledge my bias—I do better with other people who are self-authoring than I do with people who are certainly in the instrumental stage and even people who are in a socializing stage. And so [as a] . . . young principal, I often . . . made the mistake of thinking that everybody would want to hear feedback the way that I would want to hear it. . . . And it's just not true.

In the end, though, unless we have the courage to reflect and build on our own ways of making sense of the world, leadership, and life, we may, as Matt wisely described of his work as a principal and of leadership in general, be our own "biggest obstacle in achieving . . . whatever goal it is that we are trying to achieve."

Contrast With Expectations of the "Expert Leader"

For many leaders, however, like those we learned from in this study, such a learning stance ran contrary to conventional understandings of leaders as "fully cooked" and "done" human beings, so to speak. Indeed, we often expect our leaders to *already* know the right answers, the best information, or a wise course of action when faced with daunting and challenging experiences and scenarios. Perhaps not surprisingly, then, acknowledging one's own continuing learning journey was not always comfortable for leaders hoping to establish authority and maintain respect. What would others think, some wondered, if they knew their leaders didn't always know exactly what to do next? Yet, on the other hand, what would happen if a leader began truly to believe that he or she "had all the answers" and stopped listening to or learning from others?

Maintaining a commitment to one's own learning and growing, while challenging and sometimes uncomfortable, was all the more important for these LTL leaders when supporting the growth and learning of adults, these leaders shared, because it modeled the type of *openness and vulnerability necessary for growth*. Still, as Melanie shared of her leadership as a middle school principal, the pressure to fill a more conventional role as a leader was always there:

> I think the challenge is the sense [that], as a heroic leader, you can't ask for . . . supports, and you can't admit that you're developing. [A]nd, . . . as much as we don't want to feel trapped in that role, I think it's still a very powerful social model for those of us who lead.

As she bravely continued, "It can be very difficult to say, 'I don't have the answers and I'm learning,'" because "when you're in a leadership role . . . you're supposed to have all the answers because that's the way society views it." For Melanie and many other LTL leaders, moving past this pressure was a challenge, a gift, an opportunity, and an imperative.

Strategies and Solutions for Addressing Self-Development as a Leader

While, as we will discuss in Chapter 8, the leaders we learned from in this work—and many other contexts since then—shared important and needed requests for supports that would help them build their own capacities in order to better support the growth of other adults. They also offered a number of important strategies that they are currently using to grow themselves and their leadership. For instance, in addition to reading, keeping abreast of current ideas, spending time with loved ones, and even working out, these leaders identified the powerful benefits of

- reflecting deeply and carefully about their own practice,
- seeking advice and guidance from trusted others, and
- soliciting feedback from key stakeholders.

Below, we outline some of these leaders' reflections on these practices and their impact on their work.

Private Reflection: The Simple Power of Journaling

Marisa, for instance, described the deep meaning she found in reflecting through writing. "At the individual level," she explained, she valued opportunities to step back from her practice as a therapist and adult educator and

> take time to . . . write in my journal and reflect about some of the things that I'm encountering and maybe question some of the things, some of my thinking, maybe even things that I'm assuming or the way I'm looking at things. . . . [I]t helps me to question myself and say, "Well, is there any other way that I can look at this, maybe from a different perspective?"

As she further shared, journaling involves "trying to open up my way of looking" at things, "so that perhaps I can find solutions and other ways of solving the situation"—and this process was intimately connected to expanding her understandings of her work and leadership. Oftentimes however, as Marisa pointed out, and as Jed further details below, "it gets better when you have someone else to do that with."

Thinking and Reflecting With Trusted Others

Indeed, as we described above in the section on addressing professional isolation, thinking and reflecting with trusted others is a powerful strategy for improving practice and growth. While many of the leaders we learned from still yearned for opportunities to connect professionally with other leaders, as we discuss further in Chapter 8, a number of them were already benefiting from structured and informal connections. Jed, for instance, spoke movingly about his Critical Friends Group with other school leaders, which he described as his "lifeline." Moreover, he shared, being with these other leaders was "the one space I can go to be completely vulnerable" as a professional. Being a part of this group was and continues to be of great value to Jed as he grows as a person and a leader. As he explained,

> [T]hey've [the group] helped me through a lot of things in this work. And some very deeply personal things around the

intersection between my personal life and my professional life that I couldn't really go to anyone else about.

As he explained, just the opportunity to see his work through others' eyes was deeply meaningful and helpful—and essential to his own continued development as a leader. "Perspective," as he explained, "is helpful"—especially since "it's very easy to become insular in terms of the purview that you have" when you are immersed in the very demanding and fast-paced work of educational leadership.

Requesting Feedback From Stakeholders

In addition to perspective, insights, and confidential advice, feedback from others can take other helpful forms, we learned from these leaders. Remaining open to—and even seeking out—feedback from key stakeholders in their schools and organizations, for example, was another way a number of these leaders sought to grow their own capacities and leadership. Perhaps most illustrative of this strategy, Matt's efforts to gather feedback on his work as principal from his teachers and students' families were central to his efforts to grow his own leadership. As he explained,

> I send surveys to my families on what kind of job [they] . . . think I'm doing. I send surveys to my faculty . . . particularly because I've come to an understanding that it's more about me doing a good job . . . than it is about my ego. . . . And so I want to make sure that I'm doing the best job that I can in the best way possible—because the better job I do, the better experience the kids will have here. And so I open myself up to a lot of critique, and I open myself up to . . . learning in front of faculty. So . . . I'm very open about that process, and . . . hopefully they learn from me [too].

While not always easy or comfortable, keeping "as open a mind as possible," as Matt describes it, helps keep him open to hearing and learning from what he "might not expect to hear." This type of openness is key to growth, Matt believes, for it allows him to know what he's doing well—and also to see possibility in areas for improvement. "I put myself on the line a lot," he admitted, but "I know that it's supportive to me." In Chapter 8, we offer some additional ideas and strategies related to supporting one's own development.

Chapter Summary

In the middle of every difficulty lies an opportunity.

—Albert Einstein

For all of the leaders we learned from, leading in support of adult development was not a simple or straightforward solution to the many demands, pressures, and exigencies of real-life teaching and leading today. On the contrary, these leaders learned that they at times needed to adapt, revise, adjust, and reimagine their developmental goals and visions in order to confront inhospitable norms, challenge resistance, build time for collaboration and reflection, overcome isolation, and further grow their own leadership in service to others. Despite these many important challenges, these leaders shared that finding their way through to success with a developmental approach was both possible and well worth it—and a rewarding experience in and of itself.

As wise scientist, theoretician, and inventor Albert Einstein noted above, "In the middle of every difficulty lies an opportunity." And, as poetic Marisa shared with us about her difficult but fulfilling work as a therapist and adult educator in South America, the urgent desire to grow beyond restrictive confines and lead with developmental intentionality is "in itself exciting" and continues to give her "a little bit of fuel to keep going."

We hope that these leaders' experiences and their promising strategies for overcoming challenges help illustrate the power of engaging in learning-oriented leadership as a *process* and help also to illuminate the deep possibility resting at the heart of every obstacle. We also hope that you, like us, are inspired by these leaders' courage and commitments to building a better world for all.

Reflective Questions

We offer the following questions as an opportunity for you to reflect on your learnings from this chapter as well as to connect any new insights you are having with practices you currently employ in your school and/or workplace. We also invite you to consider any ideas you might have in terms of enhancing the opportunities that you offer to adults in your care and, of course, for yourself. Please take a moment to consider these questions. You might want to respond to them privately first and then engage in collegial inquiry with a partner or group of colleagues. We hope you find these reflective moments helpful.

1. What are two insights you are having after reading about the challenges and/or strategies presented in this chapter?

2. What do you feel are one or two of the more important challenges you face in your current work and leadership? How, if at all, might a developmental approach and/or outlook help you reframe or address this challenge?

3. What, if anything, is a new strategy that you would like to employ after reading this chapter? What is one small step you might take toward implementing this new strategy or practice with developmental intentions? What kinds of supports would enable you to best implement this practice? What questions about implementation do you have at this time?

4. In light of what you shared in response to question #3, what do you think would be a good next step for you?

PART III

Implications for Practice and Policy

8

In the Spirit
of Closing Well

Implications for Leaders,
Schools, Districts, and Systems

A dream you dream alone is only a dream. A dream you dream together is reality.

—John Lennon

Looking Back and Ahead: Reflecting on Our Journey Together

Throughout this book, we have explored *together* the great promise and power of learning and leading in support of individuals' adult growth and development in our schools, districts, universities, and professional learning environments. After considering in the first chapter the vital importance of building internal capacity—or growth— in order to meet the mounting challenges we face as educators today, we set the context for the rest of the book in Chapters 2 and 3 with an overview of the Leadership for Transformational Learning (LTL) course as well as key principles of constructive-developmental theory (Kegan, 1982, 1994, 2000) and the learning-oriented model for school leadership, composed of four pillar practices for growth: teaming, providing adults with leadership roles, collegial inquiry, and mentoring (Drago-Severson, 2004, 2009, 2012).

Next, in Chapter 4, we focused on how the educational leaders described and understood the ways in which LTL made a difference in their leadership, especially in terms of how they *thought* about leading for adult development immediately following and years after successfully completing the course. As discussed, LTL graduates attributed many conceptual changes to their LTL learnings and experiences. In Chapters 5 and 6, we closely examined the ideas and strategies that they translated to their own practice of supporting adult growth in their work contexts. More specifically, please recall that we described these leaders' LTL-inspired efforts to nurture the *preconditions* that support adults in formal learning structures like the pillar practices, as well as their work differentiating within these structures to effectively serve and support growth in adults with diverse ways of knowing.

In Chapter 7, we offered leaders' reports about some of the most pressing challenges they face in terms of enacting their leadership in support of adult development in order to build capacity. These challenges, as they explained them, included institutional and collegial resistance and more. We also highlighted the creative strategies they are currently employing to work through and beyond these obstacles in order to serve all in more effective ways.

Next, in the spirit of ending this part of our shared journey well, we will consider the kinds of supports these leaders feel would help them *even more effectively* support adult growth in their unique contexts. We also offer implications for schools, districts, school systems, educational organizations, and policymakers that can help put learning and development at the top of the list for teachers, leaders, and learners of all ages. In the end, we have found—and these leaders have shared—that learning, leading, and growing *together* can make a tremendous and positive difference for the adults and youth in schools today, and they can help make, as John Lennon suggests in the quote above, the dream of brighter and more supportive working and learning contexts a reality.

Leaders' Requested Supports: Making Space for Renewal, Deep Connection, and Authentic Learning

Never, never rest contented with any circle of ideas, but always be certain that a wider one is still possible.

—Pearl Bailey

While the leaders we learned from shared *many* inspiring reflections about their experiences in LTL and their work shaping, re-creating, and adapting developmentally oriented leadership ideas in real-life practice, one important thing that we learned was that these LTL graduates emphasized that they yearn for ongoing support as they carve out spaces for growth that can sustain themselves and others. In light of this crucial truth, and the vital supports LTL leaders *specifically asked for* years after successfully completing the course, we explore below the importance of

- prioritizing time for personal renewal and self-development,
- finding and creating opportunities to collaborate with other developmentally minded leaders, and
- exploring successful, on-the-ground examples of developmental leadership in schools and educational systems.

We hope that considering these requested supports can help broaden our collective understandings of what it means to support the learning of principals, assistant principals, teachers, district leaders, coaches, and other educational leaders. We also hope that it can help pave the way for an *even wider circle of ideas and practices* when it comes to educational administration, policy, and professional learning.

Know Thyself: The Importance of Asking for Help When It's Needed

One of the most powerful insights LTL leaders shared was the importance of asking for help when you need it. Moreover, they explained that their LTL experience invited them to understand the ancient Greek aphorism "know thyself" in new ways, for it helped them see that they—like all adults—need *different* kinds of help and support, depending on their ways of knowing.

Matt, for instance, described the benefit of developmental self-knowledge. It has helped him understand what he needs to thrive and succeed when supporting others as a lower school head. As he explained,

> One thing that's really helpful about [LTL] is that it helped me figure out . . . new ways of identifying what things are supportive to *me* [emphasis his]. And then the second piece of that is it gave me systems to be able to communicate—it gave me systems and language to be able to communicate [my needs] back to others.

As you will see, like Matt, many of the leaders we had the privilege of learning from had the courage to recognize and voice the supports they need in this work. Below we share three of the most commonly voiced hopes for support that these leaders requested. These are (1) the importance of carving out time and space for self-renewal, (2) collaborating deeply with others, and (3) learning from successful and practical examples.

The Importance of Supporting Oneself: Finding Time for Renewal and Self-Development

One of the most important requests—and pieces of advice—that these leaders shared was the critical importance of supporting oneself when working to support others. We know, after all, that it can be difficult or even impossible to sustain the hard and important work of leading, caring for, and supporting others if we do not also care for ourselves (Drago-Severson, 2012). Still, making space for this essential kind of self-care can be difficult in the fast-paced and demanding world of educational leadership. Many of the leaders in this study emphasized the vital importance of maintaining a comfortable work-life balance, connecting with others as a source of replenishment, and finding private space for renewal and reflection.

Jed, for instance, wisely explained that successfully leading a charter school in this complex and demanding educational environment "doesn't fit within a forty-hour work week; it just doesn't." Still, with experience, he shared that he came to understand that an important part of his job as a leader involved figuring out "ways to contain it [the job] so that it doesn't become eighty hours or ninety hours a week, like it used to be [earlier in his leadership]." Stressing the essential importance of nourishing *oneself* as a part of effective leadership, Jed elaborated on the critical importance of maintaining a healthy work-life balance:

> I've sort of come to realize that our work [as leaders] is incredibly complex, incredibly urgent, incredibly important, and at the same time, I do really believe in the notion that there has to be work-life balance in order for people to be their best selves in the work. And what I've learned in my own life— and this might sound funny, but it's true—is that the best way to have work-life balance is to have a life outside of work that is just as important as work.

Other leaders described this balance in terms of connecting with others *and finding private time* for rest and reflection. Brooke, for example, who was an assistant professor at the time of our interview and is now serving as a school principal in an urban district, described the palpable need to surround herself with friends and family *and to make quiet space for her own thinking and renewal.* "I definitely always make time for my friends and my partner and, you know, I definitely like to have fun," she shared. However, she simultaneously emphasized that part of replenishing herself also involved carving out private time and space. "[P]hysically, I like to work out," she explained, and "mentally, I like to read a good book."

Matt likewise described the value of stepping back from more interpersonal supports to nurture himself *by himself.* A sharp contrast to his very "social" work as a lower school head, time away helped him gather his thoughts and spirits. As he explained,

> I'll spend a week or two generally with a very packed schedule here at school, which is really social, and then events on the weekends with friends or other professional responsibilities, which are very social. And then I'll reach a point with it where it will be, "You know what? Like, this Saturday I'm not making any plans. In fact, my plan is that I'm going to go do something by myself." So that might be going to see an art exhibit I'd wanted to see or whatnot. But I need an opportunity to just reconnect all the new learning that I've had from being with people to *me* [emphasis his], to grounding it with kind of how I experience myself.

For many of the leaders whom we learned from, this kind of private time took many forms—like journaling, dictating thoughts to a recorder, exercising, or reading—but the space itself remained a sacred and important part of sustaining oneself and enhancing the work. In all cases, however, making room in one's schedule for renewal required intentional and ongoing effort and the strength to put on hold—if even for a moment—the innumerable pressures and demands of leadership and life.

Searching for Deep Connections: Hopes for Meaningful Collaborative Opportunities

In addition to finding more time for personal growth and renewal, the support that these leaders most frequently requested was the opportunity to collaborate with other leaders engaged in the important work of supporting adult development. Bravely, these leaders shared that finding, creating, or being given more opportunities to genuinely think, talk, and collaborate with other learning-oriented leaders would be tremendously helpful and valuable to their work, lives, and leadership. In fact, this was a support requested in different forms by *nearly all* of these leaders (16/20), who together expressed a strong desire for expanded

- collegial inquiry opportunities,
- mentoring relationships, and
- networking/communication opportunities with like-minded colleagues.

Below we elaborate on each of these and the meaning that this kind of deep collaboration held for most of these LTL leaders.

Requests for Collegial Inquiry and Connection. Perhaps most poignantly, a number of these leaders lamented the "loneliness" of leadership. As we described in Chapter 7, they expressed a profound need to connect in meaningful ways with others in order to sustain themselves and to grow in this work. For many, this request took the form of wanting to engage critically and reflectively with "people who have similar jobs," as Melanie described it. In her work as a middle school principal, for instance, Melanie longed for opportunities to engage in collegial inquiry with other administrators so that they could bring their similar but different experiences to bear in the discussion.

Requests for Mentoring. Other leaders specifically requested the support and guidance of a mentor to help them grow and navigate the complexities of leading for adult development. "I would love to have a mentor!" Diane shared when describing her hopes for her future work as an educational leader in her state's Department of Education. "I think that would be helpful. Someone I could bounce off ideas in trying to develop, or grow a staff."

Dana, whose growing leadership roles in her school included chairing the English department and leading professional learning for colleagues, explained that she had a similar hope. "I think one of the things that I wish I had more of was a mentor, somebody who taught teachers how to be leaders," she shared. That teachers are often expected to take on leadership roles without direct support or instruction is a challenge that many of these educational leaders voiced.

Hopes for Networking. Finally, in terms of these leaders' hopes for connecting deeply and in meaningful ways with others, most LTL leaders also expressed interest in creating a network of like-minded educators. As Jane put it, describing what would be helpful to her in her role as a data consultant, the ability to connect with others who really understand the promise of a developmental approach—or those who "have the language," so to speak—would be a great personal and professional support.

Many others, for instance, recommended implementing a central online portal that would enable communication between learning-oriented leaders, or regular newsletters to share within the community. Putting this general sentiment concisely into words, Tara, who currently serves as a middle school assistant principal, explained it this way:

> I would love to have just more of a connection to the other people, for example, who have taken [LTL and] who have the same background and same knowledge set ... [so I could] find out about how they're implementing these types of professional development opportunities for their staff and ... [learn more about] the nitty-gritty of helping their teachers become more reflective about their practice and work together more collaboratively. I think that being able to dialogue with them [would mean a lot]. One thing that was so helpful to me was being in [LTL] and hearing about other teachers' experiences in working with groups of adults, adult learners, and hearing about different strategies—whether it was an operational strategy or an instructional strategy— really, what exactly are they doing? What challenges are they facing? I mean, really hearing about those and being able to use some of that in terms of my own work [would be of help].

Interestingly, Tara's request parallels the third big hope for support requested by these leaders: the desire to learn about practical and successful examples from the field. We discuss this next.

Seeing Real-Life Success: Requests for On-the-Ground Examples

For half of these leaders (10/20), greater opportunities to learn from others about what *really works* for them in practice was named as a critical hope for support. Learning, as math department chair Elizabeth described it, from "somebody who's had success with [supporting adult development] in the past" would be a key way to improve practice, many of these leaders felt, and also an important support to guiding the growth of school communities as a whole.

Palia, too, conveyed a hope for more visible and effective models, for such on-the-ground examples could help leaders bring their work to the next level. As she explained, describing what would help her in her work as a high school assistant principal, "I like to really see models of good leaders, you know." While not all models, she bravely confided, are always "particularly inspiring," seeing or learning about effective leadership in action could make a big difference for leaders at all stages of their journeys.

It is our great hope that, in some small way, the examples and strategies that leaders shared in this book can help begin to address this very important need and request for support. Indeed, in sharing their successes as well as their challenges, their creative solutions to problems as well as their hopes for improvement, these leaders have helped paint a richer portrait of what learning-oriented leadership looks and feels like at different points of implementation. This can help all of us understand how to effectively prepare and support educational leaders to take on the important and critical responsibility of supporting adult development in our schools.

Moreover, while—because of the timing of LTL and our interviews, as well as the fact that we had not published other works relating to this request until after these leaders completed LTL—the leaders in this study had not yet read the cases from the field presented in other works (please see, for example, Drago-Severson, 2009, 2012). Since then, we have learned from educational leaders of all kinds from all around the globe that such practical examples hold great value. We hope that they—and you—find the stories and examples presented here useful.

In the next sections, we share a bit more about what these leaders' hopes and requests might mean for you, as an educational leader of any kind, or as a professional developer, university professor, policymaker, coach, teacher, principal, assistant principal, district leader, supervisor, or manager of leaders. We hope that you find these suggestions useful, and we look forward to a continued dialogue with the educational community about how best to do—and support—this important developmental and educative work together.

Implications: What Schools, Districts, and Systems Can Do . . . and What You Can, Too

One thing that's vitally important and might be comforting to know is that time and time again after district leaders, principals, assistant principals, superintendents, coaches, and other educators learn about the ideas we've shared in this book, they pause and reflect aloud about how developmental concepts and practices are essential to all in leadership roles in schools, districts, systems, and other decision-making organizations.

Recently, after facilitating a series of workshops for district and school leaders in which we focused on many of the ideas presented in this book, and especially those in Chapter 3 (for example, how our different ways of knowing influence how we lead, teach, coach, give and experience feedback, and what we are able to give to others; how pillar practices can be implemented to support adults with different ways of knowing; and how we can structure them to be supportive of internal capacity building), we invited them to consider how they might apply some of their learnings from the sessions in their practice.

At the end of our time together, a superintendent raised her hand and shared a summary of what leaders at her table were discussing. While she offered many important insights, she began by explaining, "We've realized that what we've been learning about today has so many important implications for who we hire, for how we support principals, assistant principals, and coaches, and for how they will be able to support others." She continued, "We need to revamp professional learning opportunities and re-envision teams, mentoring, and coaching so that they can become structures—relationships—that can support internal capacity building and authentic growth."

In the next sections, we elaborate—as did this brave superintendent—on what we see as some of the most important

Reflective Moment: What implications might this work have for you and for your leadership?

implications of this work. Before we do though, we invite you to take a moment to consider the following question (see sidebar).

Suggestions for Schools, Districts, and Systems

The leaders in this study and many of the other educational leaders of all kinds whom we have had the honor and privilege of learning with and from in research, university courses, professional learning workshops, and seminars around the world have confirmed the great promise and importance of shaping ongoing holding environments in our schools, universities, learning teams, districts, and personal relationships that invite leaders to think deeply about their work in the company of others. In light of the complex challenges you and other educational leaders face today—including but not limited to mounting accountability demands, the implementation of the Common Core State Standards, new approaches to principal and teacher evaluation, and an increasingly diverse (in all ways) student population—we have outlined a number of suggestions and systemic implications for practice and policy that could help better support the noble work of leaders in the field. While certainly not exhaustive or all-inclusive, we hope that these ideas can help us step forward bravely and together toward shaping our schools and learning environments as places that truly embrace growth as both a promise and a principle. As you will see, these suggestions involve two big ideas:

- teaching educators of all kinds about ways of knowing and the importance of adult development, and
- helping educators understand and employ the pillar practices to support growth and internal capacity building.

Below, in relation to each pillar practice, we also discuss the importance and promise of

- building teams and structuring teamwork from a developmental perspective;
- prioritizing, implementing, and sustaining collegial inquiry groups across the system;
- providing educators with different kinds of leadership roles—as well as developmental supports and challenges to help them thrive and grow in these roles;

- supporting principals, assistant principals, mentors, and coaches in the system as they work to support capacity building in those they coach and mentor; and
- designing goal-setting opportunities that focus on improving instruction and instructional leadership *and* developing supports and challenges for self-growth.

Suggestion 1: Teach About Ways of Knowing

As we've shared throughout this book, learning about adult developmental theory and experiencing the conditions that support growth can assist internal capacity building, organizational development, and leadership development. Creating opportunities for educators within schools and school systems to learn about our differing ways of knowing and the pillar practices can, as we have seen over and over again, enhance on-the-ground practice, improve instructional leadership, and build capacity in our schools, districts, and universities.

Accordingly, teaching about the ideas and strategies discussed and employed in LTL—and creating the conditions that invite adults to experience the benefits of a developmental approach firsthand *while they are learning about this*—can help educators grow and learn—and can ignite the spark that helps leaders even more effectively support others and their growth. This kind of "chain effect" (Drago-Severson, 2012), we have learned, involves paying forward the lessons and benefits of meaningful learning and true collaboration. And, in our current high-stakes, accountability-driven educational environment, it also means refocusing our attention on the inherent beauty and worth of the individual human beings who care for our children and our future as an important complement and counterweight to more technical, compliance-driven measures.

In fact, in the end, learning about and caring for adult development is one promising way to enhance the experience of students, teachers, and leaders, to improve student achievement, and to make a real and permanent difference in the lives of all who grow and learn in schools.

In case helpful, as mentioned in Chapter 7, we have learned that reading and then discussing short articles and chapters that highlight adult developmental theory with colleagues is one promising way to begin building a collective developmental language. In this spirit, we hope that this book will similarly provide a welcomed opportunity to begin exploring these important ideas together.

Suggestion 2: Help Educators Understand and Employ the Pillar Practices

Similarly, helping adults both understand and implement the pillar practices (i.e., teaming, engaging adults in leadership roles, participating in collegial inquiry, and mentoring) as developmental initiatives can be a powerful support for individual capacity building and organizational growth. Below, we detail a number of key strategies and implications for employing and supporting the pillar practices in schools, districts, and systems.

Build Teams That Support Adult Development. While teaming is one of the most popular forms of collaboration in education today, reframing the practice with developmental intentions—and remaining mindful of the developmental diversity that exists on any team—remains a crucial step when employing teaming in ways that nurture adult development. As outlined in Drago-Severson (2009), there are a number of key strategies and considerations that educational leaders of all kinds—principals, assistant principals, teacher leaders, university faculty, professional developers, coaches, district level leaders, policymakers, etc.—can keep in mind when working to structure teams in ways that support both personal, schoolwide, and system-wide growth. These strategies include the following:

- Providing appropriate resources (e.g., allocating time, space, and necessary materials) to facilitate collaboration in teams
- Considering the developmental composition of teams when forming groups and allocating roles (including opportunities for team members to self-select when appropriate)
- Structuring teams with ground rules, norms, and/or protocols to support adults with different ways of knowing—and periodically revisiting agreed upon norms to carefully consider how they are working

Similarly, as discussed in greater detail in Drago-Severson (2012), allocating time at the beginning and end of team meetings for each member to *check in and out* about his or her experiences (both personal and professional) can help build and strengthen interpersonal relationships that provide the foundation for effective and meaningful teamwork.

Implement and Support Collegial Inquiry Groups. District, school, university, and policy leaders can support the creation of collegial inquiry groups that enable educators of all kinds to purposefully, collaboratively, and *regularly* engage in meaningful dialogue, especially in relation to assumptions, beliefs, values, and hopes for their teaching, learning, and leadership. These groups can be composed of educators in the same or similar roles, or they can be mixed groups that invite safe and confidential dialogue about the beliefs, values, and assumptions that guide practice. Over time and with colleagues, these groups can help educators renew themselves, understand themselves and others better, improve their practice, and grow to better meet the complex demands and adaptive challenges of leading and teaching today.

Additionally, developmentally oriented collegial inquiry groups—groups that both support and challenge members to grow regardless of their ways of knowing—could be incorporated into leadership preparation programs at universities and other district- and school-based professional learning venues to help support educators who serve in different roles within schools and across the system as they strive to build their own and others' internal capacities. Similarly, we believe that forming partnerships between universities and districts, schools, and other educational organizations that support collegial inquiry is another powerful and promising path to support teaching in learning across contexts and domains.

Of course, and as we discuss later, policies will need to be developed in order to support collegial inquiry groups across the system, and resources would also need to be allocated to support such an initiative.

Provide Developmental Leadership Roles With Appropriate Supports and Challenges. Remaining mindful of the important distinction between allocating tasks (to simply get jobs done) and providing adults with leadership roles (to meet goals *and help educators grow and learn from the experience*) is perhaps the most crucial component of successfully implementing this pillar practice. Carefully considering the match between the demands of a leadership role and a person's skill set and way of knowing is key when working to offer appropriate supports and challenges to an adult taking on a new opportunity. As a leader, then, it may be helpful to remember that

- Not everyone sees himself or herself as a leader or feels comfortable volunteering for leadership roles. Sometimes privately inviting teachers to take on a role—in addition to offering a larger pool of candidates opportunities when appropriate—can help teachers grow and learn in ways that stretch their talents and capacities, help build confidence and competency, and support the organization as a whole.

- In this same way, asking adults how you could be of support to them as they take on their new leadership roles can help you meet them where they are in a developmental sense.
- Leadership roles can be both short-term and long-term, formal and informal, and within or outside the school context. In case helpful, some successful examples of teacher leadership roles include leading faculty meetings, mentoring aspiring or new teachers, modeling new curricular tools or instructional technology, and delivering presentations at workshops or professional development sessions (both in and out of school) (for more examples, please see Drago-Severson, 2009).

Facilitate Developmental Mentoring/Coaching. In addition to creating multiple opportunities and structures that support mentoring—perhaps the most intimate, relational form of professional and personal support—school leaders, mentors, developmental coaches, superintendents, district leaders, and policymakers would be wise to remember that the internal capacities of the adults on both sides of a mentoring relationship influence what they bring to the partnership. Considering the developmental match of mentors and mentees—in addition to the pairing of relevant skills, expertise, and personalities (e.g., classroom management experience, technological prowess, content, and/or pedagogical knowledge)—when pairing adults in this way will remain key to successful mentoring programs and initiatives.

With this in mind, building in opportunities for adults to self-assess their ways of knowing (perhaps by introducing short articles/chapters or vignettes) can help create awareness of this important and often overlooked form of diversity, and encouraging and making space for adults to ask their mentoring partners for specific supports and challenges can likewise help to keep the relationship productive and transparent. In addition, as with the other pillar practices discussed above, checking in periodically within the mentoring relationship to discuss needs and expectations as well as progress and growth can help both the mentor and mentee consider and shape the holding environment as both parties grow and learn.

Set Goals to Improve Instruction, Leadership, and Self-Development. Finally, related to all four of the pillar practices, approaching the increasingly ubiquitous process of goal setting in schools from a developmental perspective could help superintendents, principals, assistant principals, teachers, and other educational leaders better support groups and individuals as they work to meet personal and organizational goals. Because all adults—both supervisors and supervisees—will orient to goal setting differently depending on their ways of knowing, employing a one-size-fits-all model for goal setting will likely leave some educators without the developmental supports and challenges needed to succeed and thrive. Allowing, then, for differentiation during this process will better help *more* adults set, evaluate, and ultimately meet meaningful goals. Below we offer a few suggestions to help differentiate goal setting from a developmental perspective (for more about this, please see Drago-Severson, 2009):

- Offering concrete suggestions for goals, acknowledgment of an individual's ideas, or the autonomy and freedom to shape and define one's own goals may feel supportive (or challenging) to different adults. Accordingly, *asking* teachers and other educators what would be most helpful to them during goal setting could help leaders of all kinds better meet supervisees where they are—and eventually help stretch and grow different knowers' internal capacities.
- Likewise, recognizing how one's own way of knowing—as a leader—shapes one's expectations for and about goal setting can help leaders remain mindful of the fact that adults experience goal setting, suggestions, supervision, and authority in different ways. Some teachers and other adults may require support during goal setting meetings in order to self-evaluate or honestly offer ideas. In light of this, considering how one is "holding" (in the psychological sense) teachers and other adults during goal setting can help leaders avoid labeling supervisees based on behaviors, and also help them better support adults with different ways of knowing.

We hope you have found these larger, systemwide implications helpful. Next, we present a few concrete suggestions for individual educators looking to implement ideas from this book and the principles of learning-oriented leadership.

Suggestions for Educators: Getting Started and Next Steps

Given the importance and promise of these implications for supporting adult development, we realize that you might be wondering

1. What can I do to help support meaningful growth *right away* in my own school or unique context?

2. How, for example, might I put a "toe" into this important work in ways that feel both manageable and transformative?

3. What can I do tomorrow morning (or on Monday after reading this book over the weekend)?

Based on what we have learned from these and other leaders, below we outline a few key *action steps* for you and others interested in learning-oriented leadership. These are steps (and suggestions) that leaders and educators of all kinds have used in their schools, districts, and coaching practices that have worked for them. And, we offer them here in case helpful to you:

- Perhaps the biggest lesson we have learned involves *starting small* in terms of both practice and theory. As mentioned earlier, providing colleagues with short articles or chapters about constructive-developmental theory and/or the pillar practices can provide adults with a manageable jumping-off point for building common understandings, language, and goals.
- Likewise, recognizing and celebrating small successes (for example, starting an after-school inquiry group with interested teachers and other kinds of leaders in your school, district, and/or organization) can help build a foundation for future collaboration and collegial learning.
- We have also learned that *inviting* (rather than compelling or requiring) adults to participate in developmental activities is key when working to launch new initiatives. You likely know this already. Yet, in the spirit of being helpful, we want to underscore that providing choices and offering up ideas for "rent" (i.e., explaining that you are sharing to see if they are interested) allows adults to try out new strategies and ways of thinking and also demonstrates deep respect for individuals' time, preferences, and autonomy.
- Likewise, as many leaders have shared throughout this book, and as discussed in other works (e.g., Drago-Severson, 2004, 2009, 2012), *using developmental tools* such as protocols, check-ins and self-assessments can help individuals and groups build capacity—and can also nurture the preconditions that help lay the foundation for meaningful collaboration.
- Finally, if you have found the ideas and strategies presented throughout this book meaningful, we suggest *sharing these ideas with your leadership team and asking for support*. Inviting supervisors into the process—rather than trying to change or subvert current policies—can establish a more trusting, cooperative approach to school improvement and capacity building.

While, of course, there are other things you may consider as action steps based on your unique context (and we would love to learn about these!), we next discuss key policy implications of these ideas before reviewing some of the book's big themes in our closing reflection.

Implications for Policy

We began this book by sharing the important need to help all of us—educators, leaders of all kinds in school and districts, and those who teach in leadership preparation programs—to grow to be even better able to help others—and ourselves—to meet, manage, and thrive in today's varied and increasingly adaptive context (Heifetz, 1994) as we serve children, youth, and each other. In this section, we highlight some important implications for policymaking as well, for, as a good friend and colleague recently shared with us, "When policies are made that highlight important educational needs, then people start to pay attention, and essential changes are made in practice."

Indeed, in addition to informing and better understanding developmentally oriented educational leadership *practice*, the experiences and lessons that the LTL leaders shared throughout this book have important *policy* implications. With a commitment to promoting ongoing dialogue between policymakers and practitioners (for we feel that it is only through sustained, respectful, and bidirectional communication that we can truly make a difference for students, teachers, and leaders—together), we discuss key suggestions for policy below.

Understanding Competency as a Developmental Continuum and Connecting Policy to Demands of Work: Helping Educators and Leaders Grow in the Innovation Economy

> *It has never been any secret that we change as we age. The only question is how.*
>
> —Daloz (1986, p. 43)

We are at a critical moment in time. The *innovation economy*, for example, is an ongoing conversation about the essential role of innovation in nourishing and building U.S. competitiveness in the global market. In order to meet this challenge and opportunity, we must join together in collective action to support each other's growth and capacity building. The "new normal" and the adaptive challenges of education today require that educators and leaders in schools, districts, and university leadership preparation programs have the internal capacity to handle tremendous amounts of ambiguity and complexity.

For example, experts and new standards now demand that students in K–12 schools and districts need to become better problem solvers, better learners, increase their capacities to solve complex problems, develop their skills in these and other domains, and demonstrate advanced behaviors. However, to teach these skills, behaviors, and competencies, we—as adults—need to possess them as well. To support this kind of growth in our schools—for all participants— we need policies that connect to educators' and leaders' current realities and the challenges they encounter—such as this one. In other words, policies need to link directly to building educators' and leaders' *internal* capacities—rather than simply mandating behaviors or outcomes. Accordingly, we argue that policies designed to help adults learn about the skills they are expected to cultivate in children and youth as well as to participate effectively in teams, engage in collegial inquiry, assume greater leadership, and help each other grow could lay the foundation for essential changes in our schools, districts, and systems.

Throughout this book, we have discussed the value of infusing adult developmental theory into the design of professional development and learning opportunities for adults in schools and other workplaces. We have emphasized the importance of employing components of a developmental leadership model to inform adult learning in schools, districts, and leadership preparation programs. We have also shared some of the ways real-life leaders are using these practices and ideas in their daily work. In addition, here, we would like to emphasize the great importance of acknowledging that adults demonstrate competencies and skills differently depending on how they make meaning of their experiences. Understanding—at the policy level—that competency development is a *continuum* can enable us to better support adult growth and also *set the conditions* for designing professional development initiatives as opportunities to build internal capacity.

As we've learned throughout this book, because adult learners understand and demonstrate competencies in developmentally different ways, it is critical that professional development and professional learning opportunities be shaped in ways that recognize this diversity. This has important implications for what we *do* in professional development opportunities, *practices* we employ to support adult growth, and *content and theory introduced in these programs* (curricula). In other words, a developmental perspective suggests that the *who, how,* and *what* of professional learning are of equal importance to questions about *when* and *how often.* Given the *process* of effective leadership and leadership preparation, we need more than mandated time allotments in schools for collaboration and/or reflection and an outcome-oriented focus in order to best serve both children and adults. In light of this, below we offer a few specific suggestions for policy that might help make a difference.

Policies Supporting Developmentally Informed Professional Learning in Schools and Districts

All of the rubrics associated with new forms of teacher and principal evaluation systems (e.g., annual professional performance reviews, or APPR) rely profoundly on the importance of offering effective—and we argue developmentally oriented—professional learning opportunities in schools, teams, districts, and district and university leadership preparation programs. Policies need to be in place that will support educators and leaders in learning about developmental models, adult developmental theory, and related pillar practices so that they can implement these in their schools and districts. Teacher leaders, principals, assistant principals, coaches, and district leaders need to understand developmental diversity and shape professional learning opportunities and professional development that support capacity building.

Policies Supporting Reflection (Collegial Inquiry) and Ongoing Professional Development

Additionally, policies need to be created that allocate time during the school year for teachers, principals, assistant principals, and district leaders to reflect on their practice and engage in collegial inquiry in order to improve instructional practice and instructional leadership. We suggest four release days over the course of an academic year plus additional time each week for this. One thing we know for sure—as LTL leaders have voiced in this book and as leaders in the field emphasize—there is not enough time for reflection, *and educators today need that time.* As one district leader recently shared with us when commenting on the demands of the new evaluation systems and the need for time to reflect and engage in collegial inquiry, "Such little time is provided for this [reflecting on practice], and administrators are not trained well, in my opinion, to lead for professional growth and reflection at different developmental levels." She continued, "PD [professional development] still tends to be content-driven one-size-fits-all. Even the discussion around lengthening the school day or year omits the idea that PD and time for reflection is a necessary part of that school day." This sentiment is one that we have heard from *many* leaders and educators at all levels, and this district leader's words capture their needs and experiences well. As she continued,

> The [evaluation] rubrics imply that [reflecting on practice] is something a "highly effective" teacher just does on his/her own time. I think policy has moved too far away from the idea of collective as well as individual growth and more toward rating, and weeding out, individual teachers. Yet even the student growth research—value added and all that—suggests that a bad teacher in an effective school is more effective than a good teacher in a dysfunctional or low achieving school, sort of a peer effect, which points—to me— toward the need for more policy measures that encourage well thought out, school-based, collective PD in addition to individual reflection—and for much more training for those leading the PD, especially training in understanding the model of the pillar practices and leading for adult learning!

Indeed, to make lasting changes in instructional and leadership practices, it is crucial that educators and leaders have opportunities to engage in collegial inquiry and to examine their own assumptions. While both informational and transformational learning opportunities are important, incorporating these kinds of opportunities into teamwork, the daily schedule, and professional development initiatives can assist all of us in developing a heightened awareness of the influence of our assumptions on our performance and leadership.

Policies Supporting Mentoring/Developmental Coaching for Educational Leaders

We all know that policies cannot mandate balance in a person's life. Still, given the complexity of leaders' roles, we suggest exploring policies designed to provide school and district leaders with a mentor or developmental coach. As many of the LTL leaders explained, having an experienced and trusted partner with whom to think through dilemmas of practice and important decisions would help education leaders of all kinds build both confidence and capacity and could help leaders share the often lonely load of leading an educational

community. Moreover, engaging in this pillar practice holds benefits for individuals on both sides of the mentoring relationship and
can therefore help schools and districts build capacity at both the
individual and collective levels. While we realize that long-term
mentoring programs might not be immediately feasible, providing—as a start—first- and second-year principals with a developmentally knowledgeable mentor at the beginning of their tenure
could help support principal growth and leadership at a critical time.
Just as policies exist for teachers (in many induction programs, for
instance), supporting principal and district leaders in this way
could have far-reaching effects.

Policies Supporting Adult Learning and Development Curricula in Education Leadership Preparation Programs

As we have suggested throughout this book—and as many LTL
leaders likewise shared—a developmental perspective can help educational leaders of all kinds build others' capacities—and their own.
While we would not suggest requiring aspiring and practicing
school and/or district level leaders to take any particular course in
relation to certification, we do feel that highlighting the importance
of certain skills, competencies, knowledge bases, and behaviors—at
the state level—would help shine a light on the promise of employing a developmental framework in our schools. In other words,
while states cannot mandate any particular course, having standards
connected to adult development and practices that support it would
encourage education leadership faculty to prioritize these important
ideas and also build curriculum in support of them. This could help
education leadership faculty even more effectively prepare leaders to
meet the many adaptive challenges that they will and do face in
schools today and in the years to come.

Implications for Policy: A Summary

In summary, we believe that developing policies informed by
developmental theory and practice is one key step toward improving
schools and systems. Still, from our perspective, strong policies are
those that stem from a *reciprocal exchange of ideas and expertise* between
researchers, lawmakers, and practitioners and that offer a balance of
both guidance and autonomy. Toward these ends, a developmental
perspective can provide policymakers with knowledge about how
adults make sense of the complexity of their work, the changes they
encounter every day, and the kinds of professional development and

learning opportunities they need in order to grow. This knowledge and these insights are vital to improving education today, and they can help us to develop and grow stronger—together.

New Beginnings

The future belongs to those who believe in the beauty of their dreams.

—Eleanor Roosevelt

Throughout this book, we have argued that intentionally and caringly supporting adult development in schools, school systems, university leadership preparation programs, and other organizations can help educators and leaders of all kinds build the internal and organizational capacity needed to manage the mounting adaptive challenges (Heifetz, 1994; Wagner et al., 2006) faced today. While all kinds of learning and growth are important to successful teaching, leading, and learning, we have emphasized that the complex challenges associated with serving all students well in our high-stakes, accountability-driven climate require something more than informational knowledge or expertise (Donaldson, 2008; Drago-Severson, 2004, 2009, 2012; Kegan & Lahey 2009; Lugg & Shoho, 2006; Murnane & Willett, 2010). This is a perspective shared by many LTL leaders in this study and others we have learned from in workshops, university courses, and professional development opportunities around the globe. Indeed, in order to fully support *all* students in their journeys of becoming, we too—as adults—need to nurture and bring forth our most capable selves—and a developmental focus can help with this.

In terms of educational leadership, the twenty voices we have shared in this book point to the promise and power of a developmental approach to helping leaders grow. By learning about and experiencing a developmental curriculum, aspiring and practicing educational leaders are better able to internalize and appreciate what it means to be "well held" in a psychological sense and can therefore go on to employ and adapt developmental ideas and practices as they take up different leadership roles.

Moreover, at this particular moment in time—when educators of all kinds are working to care for the Common Core State Standards and are finding their evaluations increasingly linked to student performance scores and other compliance-driven mandates—the leaders in this study helped us learn even more about the crucial importance of supporting adult growth and learning while *simultaneously* holding high and rigorous expectations. In fact, and as you know, the two are intertwined, as supporting adult growth has also been positively and directly linked with improved student performance scores and school experiences for all participants (Donaldson, 2008; Guskey, 1999, 2000; Kegan, & Lahey, 2009; Murnane & Willett, 2010). Ultimately, we truly feel that recognizing, honoring, and unlocking the potential that teachers and other educators in schools can bring to the table individually and collectively—rather than immediately labeling, blaming, or denigrating educators for "inadequate" performance—stand as a hopeful contrast to more sanctions-oriented approaches to leadership and school improvement. This, we have found, brings us back to the heart of the matter and the heart of our collective work as teachers and leaders of all kinds.

Before leaving you with a final question and an opportunity to apply the ideas presented in this book to your own noble and important practice, we want to take a moment to add our own three voices—as authors who care deeply about this work—to the oh-so-powerful voices of the LTL leaders we learned from in this research.

In the end, the deep truth is that we ourselves firmly value the promise and potential of developmental principles and the collaborative possibilities of the pillar practices. In our lives, in our work, and in this book, we—the three of us—continually seek out opportunities to challenge and grow ourselves, to support one another and those we care for and about in ways that both soothe and stretch, and to learn from the diverse gifts and struggles that we all bring to our roles, responsibilities, and revelries. It is not always easy, as we trust you know. *But it is always worthwhile and a gift we give to each other—* like the gracious gifts you give to all in your care.

Learning and growth, for us—and we trust for you—are so much more than simple words or goals. They comprise, ultimately, the painful and beautiful journey of living and loving and becoming what and who we are, as well as what and how we can give, and are intimately tied to the relationships, contexts, and experiences we encounter along the way. We feel and *are very fortunate* to have learned from the inspiring leaders who shared their courageous and dedicated experiences with us so that we could share with you here, in this book.

We are also very grateful for the holding environment that we created with and for each other in our research and writing team as we worked to present the LTL leaders' experiences. We hope that you, too, find similar holding environments as you work to support adult development. And we also hope, with all our hearts, that the ideas and practices offered herein prove meaningful for your own professional and personal growth, and that you may feel inspired to one day add your voice to the twenty-three above and speak to the promise of a developmental approach to leading, learning, and life.

In closing, then, we wanted to offer you an opportunity to think once more—before turning this final page and going back to your "real" life and your many important responsibilities—about how you might implement something you have learned about in this book in your own context.

For example, what if anything feels most meaningful or compelling to you as you think back over all that you've read? What might be one or two longer-term goals that you would like to set? What might be something you feel ready to implement as you step back more immediately into your work and leadership?

Please feel free to take a moment to pause and to brainstorm any ideas, action steps, or goals you would like to think more carefully about. Please know, too, that we are here to be of help—and that we are cheering for you! Thank you from all of us for all that you do and are. We have faith in YOU. You are HOPE.

Resource A

Research Appendix

To help you understand the larger study and how we came to learn the insights and lessons from leaders that we've presented in this book, we share in this appendix an overview of the various research projects we conducted. We hope this sheds light on lessons we've learned and how we learned them.

In this book, we have offered insights from one part of the longitudinal research we've been conducting for almost ten years. The learning presented stems largely from our latest work—interviews and surveys with three different cohorts of leaders who successfully completed the Leadership for Transformational Learning (LTL) course in 2003, 2004, and 2005. This work extends our prior work, which was also aimed at learning from and with school leaders who dedicate themselves to leading in support of adult development. In this appendix, we offer a brief summary of the different phases of this research with special attention to our most recent research with leaders, as it most directly informs the learnings presented in this book.

Origins and Trajectory of Research Informing This Book: An Overview

The research presented in this book is part of a larger nine-year mixed-methods study devoted to exploring LTL participants' understandings of their learning experiences in LTL and their conceptions of learning-oriented leadership practice in relation to their current work as leaders supporting adult growth. This longitudinal study, which informs this book, consists of surveys and in-depth interviews, and it took place during two distinct phases. In Phase 1, we collected data from LTL students before, during, and immediately after they completed the LTL course in 2003, 2004, or 2005. In Phase 2, we contacted the LTL graduates a few years after course completion to learn, through surveys and interviews, about their current leadership practice in support of their own and others' adult development. This work grew from three prior research efforts (conducted by the first author). We discuss these studies, as well as the current study, below.

Supporting Adult Development in Schools: Foundational Inquiries Into What It Means to Support Adults in Schools and Districts

This research is an extension of earlier research that began in 1991 when the first author of this book, Ellie, received the gift of learning from one school principal, who was explicitly devoted to supporting adult development in her school. This was an ethnographic study (1991–1996) of how one principal, Dr. Sarah Levine, supported and nurtured teacher growth in her school.

After this, Ellie conducted a study with twenty-five school principals from public, Catholic, and independent schools to learn how they supported teacher growth in their schools, the practices they found effective in doing so, as well as why they thought their practices worked well in supporting growth. This work was published in *Helping Teachers Learn* (Drago-Severson, 2004), and it included in-depth qualitative interviews (eighty-six hours of initial and subsequent interviews) exploring (a) the effective practices the principals employed to facilitate teacher development and learning; (b) the ways in which they felt those practices worked in their schools; (c) the influence of these practices on teacher development and learning; (d) the challenges they confronted in supporting teacher development and learning; and (e) the strategies they used to support their own self-renewal.

Later, Ellie extended this work by learning from other educators and leaders (i.e., principals, assistant principals, superintendents, coaches, professional learning specialist, and district leaders) about how they worked to support educators' growth in their work. In addition, Ellie extended the developmental framework to include more about how to support adults who are growing toward the next way of knowing—the self-transforming way of knowing—by engaging them in pillar practices. Thus, this work also offers practices and protocols that are developmental in nature and aimed at helping educators to enhance the four pillar practices to support adults with different ways of knowing.

Learnings from this study were presented in *Leading Adult Learning: Supporting Adult Development in Our Schools* (2009). This book details practical ideas and strategies for shaping professional learning contexts of all kinds as environments that support leaders' growth. It, like Ellie's most recent book, *Helping Educators Grow: Strategies and Practices for Supporting Leadership Development* (2012), highlights how creating these developmentally oriented learning environments can help leaders build internal capacities so that they are better equipped to meet the complex challenges of teaching, leading, learning, and living today. Learning Forward awarded *Leading Adult Learning's* contributions by recognizing it as one of their books of the Fall 2009. All of this work has also informed a model for leadership and adult development that is presented in *Helping Educators Grow: Strategies and Practices for Leadership Development* (2012).

These works focus on learning with leaders and draw from mixed-methods research with principals, assistant principals, teachers, coaches, district leaders *in their schools and districts*, and practicing and aspiring school leaders in the workshops, institutes, and long-term professional learning engagements in schools and districts that Ellie facilitates. Furthermore, they focus on learning with and from practicing and aspiring leaders of all kinds in university education leadership and adult development classes in which Ellie teaches about leadership for adult development, the pillar practices for growth, and a new learning-oriented model for leadership development.

The Current Study, Which Informs This Book: Exploring Transformational Learning and Transfer to Practice

Our main goal in sharing what we learned from leaders in the research presented in this book was to extend prior research to understand how, if at all, leaders who were enrolled in three different fifteen-week LTL courses transformed how they thought about leading in support of adult growth and how, if at all, they employed learnings from LTL in their *actual practice* years after completing the course. More specifically, we wanted to understand their thinking about how to support adult growth in real-life practice, how they employed practices informed by their learning in LTL, and what developmental principles, theories, and practices they are using and finding meaningful *years after successfully completing the LTL course.*

It is important to note here that our intention in this study was *not to prove or disprove the effectiveness of any particular course.* Rather, our goal was to illustrate how (if at all) developmental ideas and practices are currently being used in the field, to understand what is still hard about this work for leaders, and to illuminate the local and systemic supports that would help make things even better in terms of supporting other adults development and their own. In the sections that follow, we offer the research questions that guided each phase of this learning project as well as participant characteristics, data collection, and analytic strategies.

Phase 1: LTL Graduates' Emerging Conceptions of Leadership for Supporting Adult Development (2003–2005)

In this phase our research focused on learning from aspiring and practicing school leaders who participated in LTL in 2003, 2004, and 2005. We examined how LTL students experienced LTL-classroom structures, course content, and teaching strategies as supportive of their learning and development as leaders. We also wanted to learn how, if at all, these aspiring and practicing leaders' developing concepts of leadership were grounded in adult development principles, the pillar practices, and their aspirations and plans for using learning-oriented approaches to support other adults' learning and professional growth as leaders.

Research Questions: What Were We Hoping to Learn?

1. What course structures and content support students' leadership development, and why?

2. What kinds of pedagogical practices and exercises facilitated student learning?

3. What do these aspiring leaders name as valuable in supporting their learning from adult development theories, and how do they experience practices aimed at supporting their learning and leadership development?

4. How did LTL support changes in students' conceptions of what it means to support adult development?

5. How, if at all, might their experience in LTL influence how they think about supporting adult growth?

6. How might LTL help students translate theories and practices for adult growth to their future leadership?

Data Collection

During this phase, we administered pre-/post-course surveys and interviews for our research—conducted after course completion and after grades were submitted—with volunteer LTL students, as detailed below. In addition, course documents, such as course syllabus, e-mail correspondence from students, and midterm and end-of-course evaluations provided important contextual data (see Table A.1).

Surveys. Pre- and post-surveys were administered to all of the LTL students (all volunteered). All who were invited to participate voluntarily agreed to do so (before and at the completion of the course in 2003, 2004, and 2005). Survey questions focused on exploring students' initial and emergent understandings of leadership before and after the course. Pre-survey (before LTL) centered on these themes: (a) students' initial conceptions of adult development; (b) students' prior experiences related to adult development in their professional settings; and (c) their expectations from the course.

Post-survey (after LTL course was completed) focused on the following themes: (a) changes in students' conceptions of supporting

Table A.1   LTL Participants

LTL Year	Number of Students	Data Collection Instruments
2003	22/22 in class for surveys	a. Pre- and post-surveys b. Midterm and end-of-course evaluations c. Interviews after course completion (n = 15)
2004	22/22 in class	a. Pre- and post-surveys b. Midterm and end-of-course evaluations c. Electronic communication with students d. Interviews after course completion (n = 12)
2005	22/22 in class	a. Pre- and post-surveys b. Midterm and end-of-course evaluations c. Electronic communication with students d. Interviews after course completion (n = 14)

adult learning and development; (b) their reflections about the course activities and experiences; (c) the course structures and practices that they thought were instrumental in transforming their notions of supporting adult development; and (d) hopes for their future leadership roles and work.

The pre- and post-surveys were kept in sealed envelopes that were opened after students' final grades were submitted. Students knew that we would not look at their pre- and post-course surveys until after course grades were submitted.

The post-surveys, in particular, served as an important source of information for participant selection to engage in qualitative interviews after the LTL course. These provided valuable information about students' conceptual development related to supporting transformational learning and adult development after the course. At the end of the survey, we asked if each student would be interested in volunteering to be interviewed after course completion and after final grades were submitted. Survey responses from selected participants represented a range of perspectives, which illuminated diverse experiences in LTL as described in Chapters 4 and 5.

Interviews. In 2003, fifteen students volunteered to be interviewed after course completion. In 2004, fifteen students voluntarily agreed to participate in interviews immediately after completing LTL, and twelve of them (seven masters and five doctoral students) were purposefully selected to participate in the interviews. In 2005, sixteen students volunteered for interviews. Due to scheduling issues, we interviewed fourteen of them.

Selection criteria for all interviews included students' voluntary acceptance for participation; their responses to the pre- and post-surveys (we invited them to volunteer for interviews, and if they did, we asked them to enter their best contact information after graduation); prior leadership position (e.g., teachers, aspiring principals, and leaders in ministry); and previous work contexts (e.g., K–12 schools, universities, nonprofits, and churches). Each year, we were able to interview a larger number of females (ten to twelve) and a smaller number of males (three to five). Since females constituted the majority in this class, we felt the interview samples were generally representative of the course as a whole.

The interview sample each year was diverse in terms of prior number of years in their current role, gender, ethnicity, and prior educational background and leadership roles (e.g., teachers, aspiring principals, curriculum coordinators, leaders in ministry, and consultants) and in their work contexts (e.g., K–12 schools, universities, nonprofit organizations, and churches). We offered participants the option of using a pseudonym or their real names; all such requests were honored.

Data Analysis: How Did We Make Sense of Data?

We followed very similar analytic strategies when analyzing interview data from all three groups of students after course completion in 2003, 2004, and 2005. In total (for all three groups of students) we analyzed approximately seventy-eight hours of semi-structured, in-depth, qualitative interviews with forty-four students. All interviews were tape-recorded and transcribed verbatim. Participants were asked similar questions over the three years about various topics including (a) their experiences in LTL; (b) how, if at all, LTL served to support their learning and growth; (c) the course components that were particularly helpful to them to foster a deeper understanding of transformational learning; (d) the teaching practices that supported and challenged their development as leaders; and (e) how they planned to employ practices supportive of adult development in their future leadership work, and why.

Analytic strategies included coding of interviews and field notes for salient concepts (e.g., safe spaces, holding environment, safety and trust, dialogue, reflection, connecting theory to practice, transfer to future practice, and supports and challenges for facilitating adult development); grouping related codes into broader categories and themes; organizing codes into thematic matrices (Geertz, 1974); creating narrative summaries (Coffey & Atkinson, 1996; Maxwell, 2005); and building profiles of individual participants (Seidman, 1998). Patterns across categories (e.g., the value of collective reflection in convenings; conceptual shifts in leadership orientation) were explored by writing analytic memos (Maxwell & Miller, 1998) and by creating matrices and visual displays (Miles & Huberman, 1994).

Additionally, we, the team of researchers, crosschecked codes and discussed our interpretations with each other to incorporate alternative views and perspectives in analysis (Miles & Huberman, 1994). We also developed specific analytic questions to discover and illuminate the relationships between important concepts emerging from our analysis (Seidman, 1998). Examples of analytic questions included: (a) What kinds of classroom structures and pedagogical practices help in supporting participants' learning and why? (b) What were participants' initial conceptions of adult growth and development? (c) How did participants' ideas about supporting adult learning and development change during time in LTL? (d) How did they plan to use practices supportive of adult development in their future leadership work? These analytic questions helped in tracking and comparing participants' ideas and responses across the surveys and interviews. Because this was a qualitative study, the findings are generalized to the participants only. As Maxwell (2005) notes though, findings may have implications for other like cases.

Primary Data Informing This Book: Phase 2 Study With LTL Leaders in the Field (2009–2012)

In the second phase of this research, we were keen to learn from LTL graduates about the developmental practices that they were employing in their work contexts to support adult growth *many years after completing LTL*. We also hoped to gain insights into the particular challenges that they are facing in their efforts to lead with developmental intentions. This study explored the questions below.

Research Questions: What Were We Hoping to Learn?

1. What course structures and content supported students' leadership development?

2. In what ways did LTL shape their current work as leaders and their practices for supporting adult growth and development in their work settings? How, if at all, are participants applying adult developmental theories and pillar practices to their leadership practice?

3. What obstacles do they encounter in their efforts to support adult development in their workplaces? How are they dealing with these challenges?

4. What kind of supports would help them do this work even better and in ways that would feel more satisfying? From whom would they like to receive these supports?

Data Collection

Data were collected from practicing LTL leaders through an online survey and in-depth interviews as described below. While we do share some key findings from the survey portion of this study, our primary focus throughout this book is on learnings from interviews.

Survey. Of the forty-four possible participants from 2004 and 2005, we located e-mail addresses for forty, and all were invited to complete the survey. The response rate was 55%; twenty-two leaders completed the online survey. Later on, we decided to invite leaders from the 2003 cohort to engage in interviews in order to build the sample size for interviews.

At the time of the study, survey participants were working in diverse educational contexts as principals, assistant principals, teacher-leaders, educational consultants, and university professors. Females constituted a significant majority in LTL as well as the survey respondents (over 80%). Most were in their thirties, and 66% had one to three years of experience in their current leadership position, with over 50% in K–12 schools. The survey was confidential and voluntary and was made available to the LTL graduates in an online format (i.e., Survey Monkey).

The survey focused on learning about participants' understanding of leadership for adult development and their current practices to support adult development. Survey questions asked how and why, if at all, LTL influenced their conceptions of supporting adult growth, the practices they employ to support adult development in their leadership work, and which components of the course were most meaningful. Furthermore, participants were also invited to share the challenges and obstacles they have encountered while implementing practices to support other adults' learning in their particular work contexts. In addition to LTL, they were also asked to rate the influence of other academic, professional, and personal experiences on their personal growth and development, such as other coursework, professional development seminars before and after LTL, work experience before and after LTL, conferences, books, articles/journals, mentors, peers, and family and friends. Another set of survey questions explored participants' notions about their current and prior leadership experiences.

Interviews. Initially, as noted above, we invited LTL leaders from 2004 and 2005 to participate in the survey and interview portion of this research. However, given response rate for volunteering for interviews from leaders in 2004 and 2005, we decided to also invite LTL leaders from 2003 to participate in interviews in order to increase the sample size. All who were invited to complete the survey from the 2004 and 2005 cohorts were also invited to volunteer for interviews in an e-mail we sent to them. We asked that they let us know if they would be willing to participate in a qualitative interview. However, because we do not know who completed the survey (we did not ask for their names), we cannot tell if leaders who provided interviews also completed the survey. Nevertheless, survey responses informed our questions and probes for in-depth interviews with individual participants, and leaders from LTL 2003 (for whom we could access e-mail addresses) were then invited to volunteer for interviews as well.

In total, twenty leaders agreed to in-depth, one-to-two-hour follow-up interviews (three males and seventeen females from 2003, 2004, and 2005). Currently, these leaders are working in various leadership positions as principals of charter schools, public school principals, assistant principals, department chairs, teacher leaders, guidance counselors, educational consultants, tutors, university professors, and there is one Foreign Service officer (please see Table A.2). As mentioned earlier, the learnings presented in this book mainly draw from interviews with these LTL leaders. In case helpful, other LTL graduates also expressed interest in volunteering for interviews, but given the hectic and often unpredictable pace of their work lives, time conflicts prevented their participation in the interview part of this study.

Table A.2 Characteristics of Education Leaders: Roles and Work Context

Name[1]	Leadership Position	Work Context
Adrian	Secondary school principal	Singapore
Brenda	Graduate student; former academic dean and Spanish teacher	New York
Brooke	Assistant professor at a university, teaches educational psychology. In 2011, Brooke accepted a principalship in an urban high school.	Georgia
Dana	High school English teacher; department chair; member of the instructional leadership team; conducts professional development, supports, mentors, and evaluates teachers	California
Diane	Worked as special education intern/consultant for the State Education Resource Center and Pennsylvania Department of Education; completed a doctorate in education; working as special education consultant for the Connecticut State Resource Center	Connecticut
Elizabeth	High school math teacher; math department leader; lead teacher for data; designs and facilitates professional development	California
Gina	Guidance adjustment counselor; provides training in counseling; member of a professional learning community team; works with administrators	Massachusetts

Name[1]	Leadership Position	Work Context
Jackie	Adjunct professor at a local college; doctoral candidate; English tutor for school and university students	New York
Jane	Education consultant; works with schools and districts on data-driven improvement; former department head and teacher	Large Northeast Districts in the United States
Jed	Head of charter school (K–12); works with principals from elementary, middle, and secondary sections	Massachusetts
Jenai	Independent consultant/education consultant for school districts and consulting firms; conducts special projects in school evaluation	New Mexico
Lauren	Conducting research in cognitive science; former teacher at a private school; ESL (English as a Second Language) teacher for adults	Massachusetts
Lucy	Foreign Service officer working in U.S. embassies abroad	U.S. embassies in foreign countries
Marisa	Self-employed, entrepreneur, part-time English instructor at a postsecondary school; English tutor for adults	Argentina/ South America
Matt	Lower school division head, works with other administrators, head teachers, and families; former director of curriculum at a private school	New York
Melanie	Currently pursuing a doctorate in educational leadership; former middle school principal and instructional leader	Massachusetts
Palia	High school assistant principal; conducts professional development; observes, coaches, and supervises teachers; works with students and families on achievement opportunities	New York
Rachel	Vice president of a charter management organization, manages the regional directors who work with principals; former literacy coach at a school	Maryland/ Oversees three to four schools on the East Coast (New York and Washington, DC)
Sarah	Assistant professor at a graduate school of education in a university	Massachusetts
Tara	Middle school assistant principal; instructional leader; intervention planning team coordinator; conducts teacher evaluations; former elementary teacher	Arizona

[1]We are using pseudonyms for most of the participants in accordance with their wish to protect their privacy.

To collect comparable data, we asked similar questions about specific interview topics that related to the broader research questions guiding this study. Interviews helped in developing a deeper understanding of participants' enduring understandings and context-specific applications of learning-oriented leadership practice. Consequently, our interview questions centered on the following themes: (a) LTL course learnings; (b) applications of developmentally oriented leadership theory and practice; (c) challenges and hopes for supporting adult development; and (d) how to support their own development as leaders (see Table A.3).

Table A.3   Interview Themes and Interview Questions (Phase 2)

LTL Course Learnings	What do you see as a few of the more important learnings you took away from your experience in LTL, in general?
	Which learnings were most important to you regarding how you support other adults' growth?
	Which specific parts of the course, if any, are most helpful to you now in terms of how you work to support other people's growth, and why?
	How, if at all, were specific components/parts of LTL helpful to you—e.g., lectures, readings, case writing, papers, guest speakers, films, convenings, in-class exercises, and feedback?
Application/ Adaptation of LTL Learning-Oriented Practices	Given what you've learned from LTL, in what ways if any, have you been able to implement these ideas and practices in your work?
	Please provide specific examples from your work to help us understand the learning-oriented strategies you are employing in your workplace.
	How do you think they are working? What's going well? What is difficult?
Challenges and Hopes for Supports and Development	What, if any, challenges, barriers, or obstacles have you encountered in your efforts to support adult development in your work?
	How have you addressed them?
	If you could have some kind of support to help you in this work, what would it be? From whom?
	How do you think it would help? In what ways, if any, would you like to continue to develop your own practice of leadership in support to adult learning?
Supporting Your Own Development	How do you go about supporting your own development? What kinds of practices do you use? How are they working?
	What are some of the barriers or challenges that make it hard to support your own development or renewal? What do you think works well for you when someone else is trying to support your development?
	Given your position and responsibilities, is this—supporting your own development—important to you? How is that working for you? What, if anything, do you see as the barriers or challenges that make it hard for other people to do this—help you with this?

Data Analysis: How Did We Make Sense of Data?

We employed various analytic strategies to address our questions. Analysis included coding interview transcripts for central concepts (Strauss & Corbin, 1998), organizing salient themes into categories and then matrices (Geertz, 1974; Coffey & Atkinson, 1996), constructing individual participant profiles around each theme (Seidman, 1998), and creating in-depth narrative summaries (Maxwell, 2005). All three researchers conducted open coding. We carefully read all the survey responses and interview transcripts line by line to identify important and recurring concepts from participants' descriptions of supporting adult development and the issues confronting their practice in relation to all research questions.

After coding (both emic—in vivo—codes and theoretical codes), we clustered related codes into broader categories and themes. Examples of themes included developmental needs of leaders; change in leadership orientation; important learning/concept from LTL; important practice/activity from LTL; implemented LTL concept; implemented LTL practice; identified challenge to learning-oriented leadership; requested support for learning-oriented leadership; current strategies for continued growth and development; barriers to external support; hopes/pans for continued professional learning. These themes helped us to develop a set of analytic questions for even more focused analysis, such as the following: (a) What are participants' leadership roles and responsibilities? (b) How do they understand and describe developmental leadership? (c) In what ways, if any, did the adult developmental theories discussed in LTL change their conceptions of leadership? (d) How, if at all, did LTL practices inform their actions as leaders to support adult learning and development and the practices they employed in support of that? (e) What challenges and barriers do they face while trying to support other adults in their work contexts? (f) What strategies did they employ to overcome these? and (g) What would help them to better support adult growth in their workplaces?

Thematic matrices and analytic memos (Miles & Huberman, 1994) enabled us to search for and identify patterns in the data. Creating narrative summaries (Maxwell, 2005), participant profiles (Seidman, 1998, 2006), visual displays (Miles & Huberman, 1994), and concept maps helped in uncovering connections among salient themes and concepts, and comparing patterns of similarities and differences within and across cases (Maxwell & Miller, 1998). Responses to the demographics questions and the 7-point Likert scale statements on the survey were analyzed to compute the frequencies and means.

Our analysis progressed through an iterative process where we examined data independently to perform open and theoretical coding initially. Regular interpretive meetings helped us to conduct an in-depth cross-comparative analysis of the data. Codes, categories, and themes were regularly shared, compared, and refined. We employed a grounded theory approach (Strauss & Corbin, 1998) while incorporating various literatures into analysis. We conferred on coding and interpretations to incorporate alternative understandings and attend to interpretive validity. We attended to theoretical validity by examining data for both "confirming" and "disconfirming" instances of themes (Miles & Huberman, 1994, p. 216). For example, as we present in the book, there is no single "right" way to employ developmental practices and ideas in leadership, and it is clear that leaders are currently using LTL strategies in different ways and to different degrees. Toward this end, while we offer examples and cases from our research that we hope will be helpful to others looking to employ developmentally informed leadership practices, we often include "counts" when presenting findings to acknowledge discrepant data. We hope that these findings offer a useful framework to look at leadership practice in similar contexts, but because the sample size is limited, we generalize findings only to participants.

Resource B

Leadership for Transformational Learning (LTL) Course Topics

Readings and interactive exercises in LTL centered on the following global topics:

Topic	Citation
Theoretical conceptions related to leadership	(Boyatzis & McKee, 2005a, 2005b, 2005c, 2005d; Elmore, 2002, 2003, 2005b; Fullan, 2005; Heifetz, 1994a, 1994b).
Various theories of adult learning	(Levinson & Levinson, 1996; Levinson, Darrow, Klein, Levinson, & McKee, 1978; Marsick & Sauquet, 2000; Meier, 2002; Mezirow, 1991; Moller & Pancake, 2006; National Staff Development Council, 2005; O'Neil & Marsick, 2007; Osterman & Kottkamp, 1993a, 1993b, 1993c, 2004; Parks, 2005; Rogers, 2002; Rooke & Torbert, 2005; Rossiter, 2002; Schön, 1983; Schwarz, 2002; Sheehy, 1995a, 1995b; Wagner et al., 2006; Yorks & Marsick, 2000; York-Barr, Sommers, Ghere, & Montie, 2006a, 2006b).
Constructive-developmental theory	(Belenky, Clinchy, Goldberg, & Tarule, 1986; Berger, 2002; Daloz, 2000; Drago-Severson, 1994, 2004a, 2004b, 2006; Kegan, 1982, 1994, 2000; Kegan & Lahey, 1984; Kegan et al., 2001; Levine, 1989; Santos & Drago-Severson, 2005).

(Continued)

(Continued)

Topic	Citation
Essential elements for creating positive learning environments for adults—providing appropriate supports and challenges	(Arnold, 2005; Drago-Severson, 2004a, 2004b; Elmore, 2005a; Isaacs, 1999; Kegan & Lahey, 2001a, 2001b; Senge et al., 2000).
Practices that support adults' transformational learning (e.g., teaming, assuming leadership roles, collegial inquiry, and mentoring) and the developmental principles informing them	(Daloz, 1999a, 1999b; Drago-Severson, 2004a, 2004b, 2006, 2007, 2008, 2009; Drago-Severson, Roloff-Welch, & Jones, 2007; Donaldson, 1998; Donaldson, 1999; Heifetz, 1994a, 1994b; Kemmler-Ernst, 2000; Maister, Green, & Galford, 2000; Schwarz, 2002; Schön, 1983; Weingarter, 2009; York-Barr et al., 2006; Zachary, 2000, 2005).
The importance of caring for one's own development and learning while caring for the learning of others	(Ackerman, Donaldson, & Van Der Bogert, 1996a, 1996b; Ackerman & Maslin-Ostrowski, 2002a, 2002b, 2002c, 2002d, 2004; Boyatzis & McKee, 2005b; Donaldson, 2008; Drago-Severson, 2004b).

Source: Adapted from Drago-Severson (2003, 2004, 2005); Drago-Severson, Asghar, Blum-DeStefano, & Roloff Welch (2011).

Resource C

Leadership for Transformational Learning (LTL) Citations for Course Readings

Ackerman, R. H., Donaldson, G. A., & Van Der Bogert, R. (1996a). Leadership as quest. In R. H. Ackerman, G. A. Donaldson, & R. Van Der Bogert (Eds.), *Making sense as a school leader: Persisting questions, creative opportunities* (pp. 1–12). San Francisco, CA: Jossey-Bass.

Ackerman, R. H., Donaldson, G. A., & Van Der Bogert, R. (1996b). Trusting yourself. In R. H. Ackerman, G. A. Donaldson, & R. Van Der Bogert (Eds.), *Making sense as a school leader: Persisting questions, creative opportunities* (pp. 153–162). San Francisco, CA: Jossey-Bass.

Ackerman, R. H., & Maslin-Ostrowski, P. (2002a). Anatomy of a wound: Where does it hurt? In R. H. Ackerman & P. Maslin-Ostrowski (Eds.), *The wounded leader: How leadership emerges in times of crisis* (pp. 15–34). San Francisco, CA: Jossey-Bass/Wiley.

Ackerman, R. H., & Maslin-Ostrowski, P. (2002b). Narrative healing: Once upon a time. In R. H. Ackerman & P. Maslin-Ostrowski (Eds.), *The wounded leader: How leadership emerges in times of crisis* (pp. 95–106). San Francisco, CA: Jossey-Bass/Wiley.

Ackerman, R. H., & Maslin-Ostrowski, P. (2002c). To the stars through adversity. In R. H. Ackerman & P. Maslin-Ostrowski (Eds.), *The wounded leader: How leadership emerges in times of crisis* (pp. 3–14). San Francisco, CA: Jossey-Bass/Wiley.

Ackerman, R. H., & Maslin-Ostrowski, P. (2002d). What wounding teaches. In R. H. Ackerman & P. Maslin-Ostrowski (Eds.), *The wounded leader: How leadership emerges in times of crisis* (pp. 107–126). San Francisco, CA: Jossey-Bass/Wiley.

Ackerman, R. H., & Maslin-Ostrowski, P. (2004, Summer). The wounded leader. In *The best of educational leadership 2003–2004*. Alexandria, VA: ASCD. Retrieved from http://www.ascd.org/publications/educational-leadership/summer04/vol61/num09/toc.aspx

Arnold, R. (2005). Creating empathically intelligent organizations. In R. Arnold (Ed.), *Empathic intelligence* (pp. 191–222). Sydney, Australia: University of New South Whales.

Belenky, M. F., Clinchy, B. M., Goldberger, N. R., & Tarule, J. M. (1986). *Women's ways of knowing.* New York, NY: Basic Books.

Berger, J. (2002). Viewing the puzzle through a new lens: Understanding the perspective of alumni (Doctoral dissertation). In J. Berger (Ed.), *Exploring the connection between teacher education and adult development theory* (pp. 99–140). Cambridge, MA: Harvard Graduate School of Education.

Boyatzis, R., & McKee, A. (2005a). Be the change you want to see in the world. In R. Boyatzis & A. McKee (Eds.), *Resonant leadership: Renewing yourself and connecting with others through mindfulness, hope, and compassion* (pp. 201–204). Boston, MA: Harvard Business School.

Boyatzis, R., & McKee, A. (2005b). Compassion. In R. Boyatzis & A. McKee (Eds.), *Resonant leadership: Renewing yourself and connecting with others through mindfulness, hope, and compassion* (pp. 175–200). Boston, MA: Harvard Business School Press.

Boyatzis, R., & McKee, A. (2005c). Great leaders move us. In R. Boyatzis & A. McKee (Eds.), *Resonant leadership: Renewing yourself and connecting with others through mindfulness, hope, and compassion* (pp. 1–12). Boston, MA: Harvard Business School Press.

Boyatzis, R., & McKee, A. (2005d). The leader's challenge. In R. Boyatzis & A. McKee (Eds.), *Resonant leadership: Renewing yourself and connecting with others through mindfulness, hope, and compassion* (pp. 13–33). Boston, MA: Harvard Business School.

Daloz, L. A. (1999a). The dynamic of transformation: How learning changes the learner. In *Mentor: Guiding the journey of adult learners* (pp. 125–146). San Francisco, CA: Jossey-Bass.

Daloz, L. A. (1999b). The Yoda factor: Guiding adults through difficult transitions. In *Mentor: Guiding the journey of adult learners* (pp. 203–229). San Francisco, CA: Jossey-Bass.

Daloz, L. A. P. (2000). Transformative learning for the common good. In J. Mezirow & Associates (Eds.), *Learning as transformation: Critical perspectives on a theory in progress* (pp. 103–123). San Francisco, CA: Jossey-Bass/Wiley.

Drago-Severson, E. (1994). *What does staff development develop? How the staff development literature conceives adult growth* (qualifying paper). Cambridge, MA: Harvard Graduate School of Education.

Drago-Severson, E. (2004a). *Becoming adult learners: Principles and practices for effective development.* New York, NY: Teachers College Press.

Drago-Severson, E. (2004b). *Helping teachers learn: Principal leadership for adult growth and development.* Thousand Oaks, CA: Corwin.

Drago-Severson, E. (2006). Learning-oriented leadership: Transforming a school through a program of adult learning. *Independent School Journal, 65,* 58–61, 64.

Drago-Severson, E. (2007). Helping teachers learn: Principals as professional development leaders. *Teachers College Record, 109*(1), 70–125.

Drago-Severson, E. (2008). 4 practices serve as pillars for adult learning: Learning-oriented leadership offers a promising way to support growth. *The Journal of Staff Development, 29*(4), 60–63.

Drago-Severson, E. (2009). *Leading adult learning: Supporting adult development in our schools.* Thousand Oaks, CA: Corwin and The National Staff Development Council.

Drago-Severson, E., Asghar, A., Blum-DeStefano, J., & Roloff Welch, J. (2011). Conceptual changes in aspiring school leaders: Lessons from a university classroom. *Journal of Research on Leadership Education, 6*(4), 83–132.

Drago-Severson, E., Roloff-Welch, J., & Jones, A. (2007). Learning and growing from convening. In R. Ackerman & S. McKenzie (Eds.), *Uncovering teacher leadership: Essays and voices from the field* (pp. 333–350). Thousand Oaks, CA: Corwin.

Donaldson, G. A. (1998). Sharing the challenges: Critic-colleague teams and leadership development. In R. Van Der Bogert (Ed.), *Making learning communities work: The critical role of leader as learner* (pp. 21–27). San Francisco, CA: Jossey-Bass.

Donaldson, M. (1999). Teaching and traditionalism: Encounters with "the way it's always been." In M. Donaldson & B. Poon (Eds.), *Reflections of first-year teachers on school culture: Questions, hopes, and challenges* (pp. 47–57). San Francisco, CA: Jossey-Bass.

Donaldson, G. A. (2008). The learning environment for leader growth. In G. Donaldson, *How leaders learn: Cultivating capacities for school improvement* (pp. 104–126). New York, NY: Teachers College Press.

Elmore, R. F. (2002). The limits of change. *Harvard education letter,* January/ February, 1–4. Retrieved from http://www.edletter.org/past/issues/ 2002-jf/limitsofchange.shtml

Elmore, R. F. (2003). The limits of change. In M. Pierce and D. L. Stapleton (Eds.), *The 21st century principal: Current issues in leadership and policy* (pp. 9–17). Cambridge, MA: Harvard Education Press.

Elmore, R. F. (2005a). Building a new structure for school leadership. In R. F. Elmore, *School reform from the inside out* (pp. 41–88). Cambridge, MA: Harvard Education Press.

Elmore, R. F. (2005b). *School reform from the inside out: Policy, practice, and performance.* Cambridge, MA: Harvard Education Press.

Fullan, M. (2005, November). 10 do and don't assumptions about CHANGE. The learning principal: For a dynamic community of school leaders ensuring success for all students. *The Learning Principal, 1*(3), 1, 6, 7. National Staff Development Council.

Heifetz, R. A. (1994a). Assassination. In R. A. Heifetz, *Leadership without easy answers* (pp. 235–249). Cambridge, MA: Harvard University Press.

Heifetz, R. A. (1994b). The personal challenge. In R. A. Heifetz, *Leadership without easy answers* (pp. 250–276). Cambridge, MA: Harvard University Press.

Isaacs, W. (1999). What is dialogue? In W. Isaacs, *Dialogue and the art of thinking together* (pp. 17–70). New York, NY: Doubleday.

Kegan, R. (1982). *The evolving self: Problem and process in human development.* Cambridge, MA: Harvard University Press.

Kegan, R. (1994). *In over our heads: The mental demands of modern life.* Cambridge, MA: Harvard University Press.

Kegan, R. (2000). What "form" transforms? A constructive-developmental approach to transformative learning. In J. Mezirow & Associates (Eds.), *Learning as transformation: Critical perspectives on a theory in progress* (pp. 35–69). San Francisco, CA: Jossey-Bass.

Kegan, R., Broderick, M., Drago-Severson, E., Helsing, D., Popp, N., & Portnow, K. (2001). *Toward a "new pluralism" in the ABE/ESL classroom.* NCSALL Report #19. Boston, MA: World Education.

Kegan, R., & Lahey, L. L. (1984). Adult leadership and adult development: A constructivist view. In B. Kellerman (Ed.), *Leadership: Multidisciplinary perspectives* (pp. 199–230). Englewood Cliffs, NJ: Prentice-Hall.

Kegan, R., & Lahey, L. L. (2001a). *How the way we talk can change the way we work: Seven languages for transformation.* San Francisco, CA: Jossey-Bass/ Wiley.

Kegan, R., & Lahey, L. (2001b, November). The real reason people don't change. *Harvard Business Review,* 85–92.

Kemmler-Ernst, A. (2000). *Portraits of teacher researchers in Boston: Perspectives on participation in a school-based collaborative inquiry group* (Doctoral dissertation). Cambridge, MA: Harvard Graduate School of Education.

Levine, S. (1989). *Promoting adult growth in schools: The promise of professional development.* Boston, MA: Allyn and Bacon.

Levinson, D. J., & Levinson, J. D. (1996). *The seasons of a woman's life.* New York, NY: Knopf.

Levinson, D. J., Darrow, C. N., Klein, E. B., Levinson, M. H., & McKee, B. (1978). *The seasons of a man's life.* New York, NY: Ballantine Books.

Maister, D. H., Green, C. H., & Galford, R. M. (2000). *The trusted advisor.* New York, NY: Simon & Schuster.

Marsick, V. J., & Sauquet, A. (2000). Learning through reflection. In M. Deutsch and P. T. Coleman (Eds.), *The handbook of conflict resolution: Theory and practice* (pp. 382–399). San Francisco, CA: Jossey-Bass.

Meier, D. (2002). Learning in the company of adults. In D. Meier, *In schools we trust* (pp. 9–24). Boston, MA: Beacon Press.

Mezirow, J. (1991). *Transformative dimensions of adult learning.* San Francisco, CA: Jossey-Bass.

Moller, G., & Pancake, A. (2006). *Lead with me: A principal's guide to teacher leadership.* Larchmont, NY: Eye on Education.

National Staff Development Council. (2005). Beware of the generation gap! *The Learning Principal,* 1(3), 4.

O'Neil, J., & Marsick, V. J. (2007). *Understanding action learning.* New York, NY: American Academy of Management Association.

Osterman, K. F., & Kottkamp, R. B. (1993a). Developing a reflective perspective: Gathering information. In K. F. Osterman & R. B. Kottkamp, *Reflective practice for educators: Improving schools through professional development* (pp. 66–83). Thousand Oaks, CA: Corwin.

Osterman, K. F., & Kottkamp, R. B. (1993b). How to nurture reflection. In K. F. Osterman & R. B. Kottkamp, *Reflective practice for educators: Improving schools through professional development* (pp. 43–65). Thousand Oaks, CA: Corwin.

Osterman, K. F., & Kottkamp, R. B. (1993c). Reflective practice: A powerful force for educational change. In K. F. Osterman & R. B. Kottkamp, *Reflective practice for educators: Improving schools through professional development* (pp. 1–17). Thousand Oaks, CA: Corwin.

Osterman, K. F., & Kottkamp, R. B. (2004). *Reflective practice for educators: Improving schooling through professional development* (2nd ed.). Thousand Oaks, CA: Corwin.

Parks, D. S. (2005). Leadership for a changing world: A call to adaptive work. In S. D. Parks, *Leadership can be taught: A bold approach for a complex world* (pp. 1–17). Cambridge, MA: Harvard Business School Press.

Rogers, C. (2002). Voices inside schools: Seeing student learning. *Harvard Educational Review*, 2(72), 230–253.

Rooke, D., & Torbert, W. R. (2005). Seven transformations of leadership. *Harvard Business Review*, 1–13.

Rossiter, M. (2002). *Narratives and stories in adult teaching and learning.* Columbus, OH: ERIC Clearinghouse on Adult Career and Vocation Education. ERIC ID: ED473147.

Santos, M., & Drago-Severson, E. (2005). Adult learning and development today. In D. Ness (Ed.), *Encyclopedia on Education and Human Development.* Armonk, NY: M. E. Sharpe Publishers.

Senge, P., Cambron-McCabe, N., Lucas, T., Smith, B., Dutton, J., & Kleiner, A. (2000). Mental models. In P. Senge, N. Cambron-McCabe, T. Lucas, B. Smith, J. Dutton, & A. Kleiner, *Schools that learn: A fifth discipline fieldbook for educators, parents, and everyone who cares about education* (pp. 66–98). New York, NY: Currency/Doubleday.

Schön, D. A. (1983). Professional knowledge and reflection-in-action. In D. A. Schön, *The reflective practitioner: How professionals think in action* (pp. 3–69). New York, NY: Basic Books.

Schwarz, R. (2002). Understanding the theories that guide our actions. In R. Schwarz, *The skilled facilitator* (pp. 65–95). San Francisco, CA: Jossey-Bass/Wiley.

Sheehy, G. (1995a). Mapping lives across time. In G. Sheehy, *New passages: Mapping your life across time* (pp. 23–53). New York, NY: Ballantine Books.

Sheehy, G. (1995a). Prologue: Oh, pioneers! In G. Sheehy, *New passages: Mapping your life across time* (pp. 3–20). New York, NY: Ballantine Books.

Wagner, T., Kegan, R., Lahey, L., Lemons, R. W., Garnier, J, Helsing, D., . . . & Rasmussen, H. T. (2006). Introduction: Reframing the problem. In T. Wagner, L. Lahey, R. W. Lemons, J. Garnier, D. Helsing, A. Howell, & H. T. Rasmussen, *Change leadership: A practical guide to transforming our schools* (pp. 1–20). San Francisco, CA: Jossey-Bass/Wiley.

Weingarter, C. J. (2009). *Principal mentoring: A safe, simple, and supportive approach.* Thousand Oaks, CA: Corwin and The National Staff Development Council.

Yorks, L., & Marsick, V. J. (2000). Organizational learning and transformation. In J. Mezirow & Associates (Eds.), *Learning as transformation: Critical perspectives on a theory in progress* (pp. 253–281). San Francisco, CA: Jossey-Bass/Wiley.

York-Barr, J., Sommers, W. A., Ghere, G. S., & Montie, J. (2006a). Reflection in small groups and teams. In J. York-Barr, W. A. Sommers, G. S. Ghere, &

J. Montie, *Reflective practice to improve schools: An action guide for educators* (2nd ed., pp. 145–181). Thousand Oaks, CA: Corwin.

York-Barr, J., Sommers, W. A., Ghere, G. S., & Montie, J. (2006b). Schoolwide reflective practice. In J. York-Barr, W. A. Sommers, G. S. Ghere, & J. Montie, *Reflective practice to improve schools* (2nd ed., pp. 199–243). Thousand Oaks, CA: Corwin.

Zachary, L. J. (2000). Grounding the work: Focusing on learning. In *The mentor's guide: Facilitating effective learning relationships* (pp. 1–28). San Francisco, CA: Jossey-Bass.

Zachary, L. J. (2005). Connecting culture and mentoring. In *Creating a mentoring culture: The organization's guide* (pp. 15–30). San Francisco, CA: Jossey-Bass.

Source: Adapted from Drago-Severson (2003, 2004, 2005); Drago-Severson, Asghar, Blum-DeStefano, & Roloff Welch (2011).

Glossary

Adaptive challenges are problems and situations (e.g., increasing accountability, closing the achievement gap, addressing the Common Core State Standards, highly diverse populations of students and caring for their academic achievement, new teacher effect and new teacher and principal evaluation standards, and instituting standards-based reform) for which neither the problem nor the solution is clearly known or identified (Heifetz, 1994). Managing and meeting these kinds of pressing challenges and problems most often require greater cognitive, emotional, intrapersonal, and interpersonal complexity and capacities, as well as new approaches and learning since they are often solved while we are *in the process* of working on them. Such processes require ongoing support for adult growth—*internal* capacity building—and new ways of working, learning, and leading together, as opposed to specific training for discrete skill acquisition. See Chapters 1, 2, and 3.

Assumptions are the taken-for-granted beliefs that we all have. These guide our thoughts, feelings, actions, and convictions about the learning, teaching, and leadership processes—and life. We hold our assumptions as Big Truths about how the world works. Furthermore, we rarely question them unless provided with opportunities that help us see and consider them. Examining assumptions and testing them in safe contexts allow us to learn if they are, in fact, true—and if they are not, we can revise them over time. Doing so is essential for personal growth, the development of lasting change.

Collegial inquiry (CI) is related to and different from reflective practice. Collegial inquiry, in the developmental sense, is a shared dialogue with at least one other person in a reflective context that involves purposefully dedicating time to reflecting on and engaging in dialog about one's assumptions, convictions, and values as part of the learning, teaching, and leadership processes. See Chapters 1, 2, and 4.

Constructive-developmental theory is the theory informing Drago-Severson's (2004b, 2009, 2012) new learning-oriented models of leadership and leadership development. It is based on two fundamental principles: (1) we *actively make sense of* our experiences, and (2) we can *develop and grow* our internal capacities if we are provided with developmentally appropriate supports and challenges (Kegan, 1982, 1994, 2000). See Chapter 3 for further explication of this theory. *See also* **way of knowing**.

Development is a process of growing our internal capacities. In other words, this means increasing differentiation and internalization (Kegan, 1982, 1994, 2000). When development occurs, a person has a broader perspective on himself or herself and others and is better able to manage the complexities and ambiguities of leadership, teaching, and life.

Developmental capacity refers to our cognitive, affective (emotional), interpersonal (self-to-other), and intrapersonal (self-to-self) abilities to manage the complexities of our lives and work. See Chapters 1, 2, and 3, in particular. *See also* **growth** and **transformational learning**.

Developmental demands are the implicit and explicit expectations inherent in work, leadership, and life that may be beyond the developmental capacities of those expected to perform them.

Developmental diversity relates to the qualitatively different ways in which we, as adults, make sense of our experiences in *all* domains of our lives. In other words, as adults, we take in and experience our realities in qualitatively different ways. And because of this, we need different kinds of developmental supports and challenges to grow our internal capacities and ourselves. Since research suggests that in any school, team, leadership cabinet, or group adults will likely make sense of their experiences in developmentally different ways, we need to attend to this type of diversity. See Chapters 1 and 3, most specifically.

Developmental intentionality is a term we use to be mindful of the importance of imbuing any teaching and learning situation and all professional development initiatives with an understanding of how adults grow and the kinds of supports and challenges they need in order to increase their capacities (i.e., cognitive, affective, interpersonal, and interpersonal). See Chapters 1, 3, and 4, most specifically.

Goodness of fit (developmental match) concerns the match between a person's way of knowing (i.e., internal developmental capacities) and the implicit and explicit demands of an environment (e.g., school), practice, and/or role (e.g., leadership position) placed on the person. Sometimes these outpace what a person has the internal capacity to fulfill. See Chapter 3.

Growth from a developmental perspective is related to increases in cognitive, emotional (affective), interpersonal (person-to-person), and intrapersonal (self-to-self) capacities that enable a person to manage better the complexities of work (e.g., leadership, teaching, learning, adaptive challenges) and life. With the experience of growth, or transformational learning (we use these terms interchangeably), a qualitative shift occurs in how a person actively interprets, organizes, understands, and makes sense of his or her experience. See Chapters 1, 2, and 3.

Holding environment is a context or relationship that offers the gift of both high supports and challenges to support internal capacity building. Holding environments serve three functions: (1) meeting a person at his or her developmental level—where a person is without an urgent need to force them to change; (2) challenging adults, in a developmental sense (i.e., stretching by offering alternative perspectives)—when a person is ready to grow beyond his or her current level; and (3) providing continuity and stability. See Chapter 3.

Informational learning focuses on increasing the amount of knowledge and/or skills a person possesses, augmenting *what* a person knows. We refer to this as encyclopedia knowledge. This kind of knowledge is vital and helps us work to solve technical challenges. See Chapters 1 and 3, specifically.

Instrumental way of knowing is a system of meaning making. An instrumental knower understands the world and life in concrete terms. While able to control impulses, this knower does not have the developmental capacity to have a perspective on other people's needs, desires, and interests. Others are experienced as helpers or obstacles to having one's own needs met. See Chapter 3.

Ladder of Inference is a theoretical tool developed by organizational psychologist Chris Argyris (1990). The "rungs" of the ladder describe the steps we take when moving from observable data/facts to actions, which are often influenced by our beliefs and assumptions. See Chapter 5.

Leadership for Transformational Learning (LTL) is the graduate course that is at the center of this book. It is offered to educators and leaders of all kinds who attend graduate school. Furthermore, different versions of the course are offered to educators in schools, districts, and other venues. The course—or any version of it—introduces developmental theory and research-based practices and strategies for supporting adult growth in schools and school systems. In addition, the course and other versions of it were structured to intentionally model developmental practices as students were learning about them. See Chapter 2 for full description.

Learning centers are schools, school districts, and organizations where the adults and others are well supported in their learning and development.

Learning-oriented model for leadership development (Drago-Severson, 2012) is a new conceptualization of leadership preparation informed by developmental theory, Drago-Severson's learning-oriented model for school leadership (see definition), and more than twenty-five years of work and research with school leaders around the globe. These models both encompass and expand upon the pillar practices for growth.

Learning-oriented model for school leadership is informed by developmental theory and composed of four pillar practices—establishing teams, providing adults with leadership roles, engaging in collegial inquiry, and mentoring/developmental coaching. This learning-oriented model has proven to support effective, differentiated approaches to adult development in schools, school systems, and organizations. The pillar practices are developmentally robust, meaning any one of them can support growth (i.e., internal capacity building) in adults with different needs, preferences, and ways of knowing (developmental orientations). See Chapters 1 and 2 (for full description).

Meaning making is the sense we make of our lives with respect to the cognitive, affective (emotional), intrapersonal, and interpersonal aspects of life.

Mentoring is a pillar practice of the learning-oriented model. It takes myriad forms in different contexts, including (1) pairing experienced teachers with new teachers, (2) pairing teachers and university professors who have deep knowledge of the school mission and politics with other teachers, (3) pairing experienced teachers with graduate student interns from local universities, (4) pairing experienced principals with aspiring and/or newer principals, and (5) teacher team mentoring. See Chapter 2.

Mentoring communities are schools and school districts where the adults and youth are well supported in their learning and development. *See also* **learning centers.**

Object is, in developmental terms, what a person can take a perspective on, manage, be responsible for, control, and act on because the person is not run by it or identified with it (Kegan, 1982).

Preconditions are elements of mutual trust, respect, safety, and care that ITL leaders described as essential first steps toward supporting adult growth. Leaders stressed the importance of establishing the preconditions *before* and sustaining them *during* programs and practices that challenge or stretch—in a developmental sense—colleagues' thinking, feelings, and work.

Pillar practices, i.e., teaming, providing leadership roles, engaging in collegial inquiry, and mentoring, are the four developmentally oriented practices that compose the first author's *learning oriented model for school leadership* (Drago-Severson, 2004b, 2009, 2012). These practices, when employed with developmental intentions, can support internal capacity building (i.e., growth). See Chapters 2 and 3, most specifically.

Providing leadership roles is a pillar practice for growth in the learning-oriented model. It is an opportunity for adults to share power and decision-making authority and to grow from the role. As adults, we can grow and develop from being responsible for an idea's development or implementation, as well as from different kinds of opportunities to assume leadership. We use the term *providing leadership roles* rather than *distributive leadership* because of the intention behind these roles. This means that in providing leadership roles we need to offer developmental supports and challenges to the person in a leadership role so that he or she can grow from them. See Chapter 2.

Self-authoring way of knowing is a system of meaning making—a way of knowing. Self-authoring knowers have the capacity to take responsibility for internal authority and their actions. They can hold, reflect on, and prioritize different perspectives. See Chapter 3.

Self-transforming way of knowing is a system of meaning making or way of knowing. Self-transforming knowers have the internal capacity to take perspective on their own authorship, identity, and ideology, forming a meta-awareness. In other words, a person's self-system is available to the self for attention and constant judgment.

These knowers have an appreciation for and frequently question their own self-system and how it works. They are able to understand and manage tremendous amounts of complexity and ambiguity. In addition, they are substantively less invested in their own identities and are more open to others' perspectives.

Socializing way of knowing is a system of meaning making—a way of knowing. Adults with this way of knowing have a greater internal capacity for reflection and abstract thought (i.e., to think about their own thinking). They can make generalizations from one context to another and have the capacity to reflect on their actions and the actions of others. Socializing knowers orient to their own internal psychological states and cannot take a perspective on shared mutuality or societal expectations. Approval and acceptance from authorities and valued others is ultimate for them. See Chapter 3.

Subject is, in a developmental sense, what a person cannot take a perspective on because he or she is so embedded in it. It is what "runs" a person. It is so much a part of the very fabric of the self that a person cannot look at it, be responsible for it, control it, or see it (Kegan, 1982).

Teaming is a pillar practice of the learning-oriented model of school leadership. It provides adults with opportunities to question their own and other people's philosophies and assumptions about leadership, teaching, leading, and learning. Teaming in a developmental sense provides a context, a holding environment, in which adults can examine and question their assumptions and engage in collaborative decision making. See Chapters 2 and 5.

Technical challenges are problems (e.g., managing budgets, schedules, and personnel) for which we can identify the problem or offer solutions to solve the problem at hand. In other words, even if we cannot solve these challenges ourselves, we can seek out an expert who can help us resolve them. See Chapter 1.

Transformational learning or **growth**—we use these terms interchangeably—relates to the development of increased cognitive, emotional, interpersonal, and intrapersonal capacities that enable a person to manage better the complexities of work (e.g., leadership, teaching, learning, adaptive challenges) and living. With the experience of transformational learning, or growth, a qualitative shift occurs in how a person actively interprets, organizes, understands, and makes sense of his or her experience, such that he or she develops increased capacities for better managing the complexities of daily life. See Chapters 1 and 3.

Way of knowing refers to the meaning system through which all experience is filtered and understood (Drago-Severson, 2004a, 2004b, 2009, 2012). It is also known as a *developmental level*, an *order of consciousness*, and a *stage* (Kegan, 1982, 1994, 2000). It is the filter through which we interpret our experiences, and it influences our capacities for perspective taking on self, other, and the relationship between the two. It dictates how learning, teaching, leadership, and all life experiences are taken in, managed, understood, and used. See Chapter 3.

References

Chapter 1

Ackerman, R., & MacKenzie, S. (Eds.). (2007). *Uncovering teacher leadership: Voices from the field*. Thousand Oaks, CA: Corwin.

Ackerman, R. H., & Maslin-Ostrowski, P. (2004). The wounded leader and emotional learning in the schoolhouse. *School Leadership & Management*, 24(3), 309–326.

Barth, R. S. (1990). *Improving schools from within: Teachers, parents, and principals can make the difference*. San Francisco, CA: Jossey-Bass.

Bogotch, I. (2002a). Educational leadership and social justice: Practice into theory. *Journal of School Leadership*, 12(2), 138–156.

Bogotch, I. (2002b). Enmeshed in the work: The educative power of developing standards. *Journal of School Leadership*, 12(5), 503–525.

Boyatzis, R., & McKee, A. (2005). *Resonant leadership*. Boston, MA: Harvard Business School Press.

Browne-Ferrigno, T. (2007). Developing school leaders: Practitioner growth during an advanced leadership development program for principals and administrator-trained teachers. *Journal of Research on Leadership Education*, 2(3). Retrieved July 8, 2007, from http://www.ucea.org/JRLE/vol2_issue3_2007/BrowneFerrignoArticle.pdf

Byrne-Jiménez, M., & Orr, M. T. (2007). *Developing effective principals through collaborative inquiry*. New York, NY: Teachers College Press.

Capper, C. A., Theoharis, J. S., & Sebastian, C. (2006). Toward a framework for preparing leaders for social justice. *Journal of Educational Administration*, 44(3), 224–238.

Childress, S., Elmore, R. F., Grossman, A. S., & Johnson, S. M. (Eds.). (2007). *Managing school districts for high performance: Cases in public education leadership*. Cambridge, MA: Harvard Education Press.

City, E. A., Elmore, R. F., Fairman, S. E., & Teitel, L. (2009). *Instructional rounds in education: A network approach to improving teaching and learning*. Cambridge, MA: Harvard Education Press.

Donaldson, G. A. (2008). *How leaders learn: Cultivating capacities for school improvement*. New York, NY: Teachers College Press.

Drago-Severson, E. (1994). *What does "staff development" develop? How the staff development literature conceives adult growth* (Unpublished qualifying paper). Harvard University, Cambridge, MA.

Drago-Severson, E. (1996). *Head-of-school as principal adult developer: An account of one leader's efforts to support transformational learning among the adults in her school* (Unpublished doctoral dissertation). Harvard Graduate School of Education, Cambridge, MA.

Drago-Severson, E. (2000). *Helping teachers learn: A four-year ethnography of one principal's efforts to support teacher development.* Paper presented at the annual meeting of the American Educational Research Association, New Orleans, LA. ERIC #030660.

Drago-Severson, E. (2004a). *Becoming adult learners: Principles and practices for effective development.* New York, NY: Teachers College Press.

Drago-Severson, E. (2004b). *Helping teachers learn: Principal leadership for adult growth and development.* Thousand Oaks, CA: Corwin.

Drago-Severson, E. (2009). *Leading adult learning: Supporting adult development in our schools.* Thousand Oaks, CA: Corwin and The National Staff Development Council.

Drago-Severson, E. (2012). *Helping educators grow: Strategies and practices for supporting leadership development.* Cambridge, MA: Harvard Education Press.

Elmore, R. F. (2004). *School reform from the inside out: Policy, practice, and performance.* Cambridge, MA: Harvard Education Press.

Fullan, M. (2005). *Leadership and sustainability: Systems thinkers in action.* Thousand Oaks, CA/Ontario, Canada: Corwin and The Ontario Principals' Center.

Guskey, T. R. (1999). *New perspectives on evaluating professional development.* Paper presented at the annual meeting of the American Educational Research Association, Montreal, Canada.

Guskey, T. R. (2000). *Evaluating professional development* (2nd ed.). Thousand Oaks, CA: Corwin.

Hargreaves, A., & Fink, D. (2006). *Sustainable leadership.* San Francisco, CA: Jossey-Bass.

Heifetz, R. A. (1994). *Leadership without easy answers.* Cambridge, MA: Harvard University Press.

Hoff, D. L., Yoder, N., & Hoff, P. S. (2006). Preparing educational leaders to embrace the "public" in public schools. Special Edition, *Journal of Educational Administration, 44*(3), 239–249.

Howe, H., II. (1993). *Thinking about our kids: An agenda for American education.* New York, NY: Free Press.

Kegan, R. (1982). *The evolving self: Problems and process in human development.* Cambridge, MA: Harvard University Press.

Kegan, R. (1994). *In over our heads: The mental demands of modern life.* Cambridge, MA: Harvard University Press.

Kegan, R. (2000). What "form" transforms? A constructive-developmental approach to transformative learning. In J. Mezirow & Associates (Eds.), *Learning as transformation: Critical perspectives on a theory in progress* (pp. 35–70). San Francisco, CA: Jossey-Bass.

Kegan, R., & Lahey, L. L. (2001). *How the way we talk can change the way we work: Seven languages for transformation.* San Francisco, CA: Jossey-Bass/Wiley.

Kegan, R., & Lahey, L. L. (2009). *Immunity to change: How to overcome it and unlock the potential in yourself and your organization.* Boston, MA: Harvard Business School Press.

Lugg, C. A., & Shoho, A. R. (2006). Dare public school administrators build a new social order? Social justice and the possibly perilous politics of educational leadership. *Journal of Educational Administration, 44*(3), 208–223.

Mezirow, J. (2000). Learning to think like an adult: Core concepts of transformation theory. In J. Mezirow & Associates (Eds.), *Learning as transformation: Critical perspectives on a theory in progress* (pp. 3–33). San Francisco, CA: Jossey-Bass.

Mizell, H. (2006). Ability to grow teachers is a crucial skill for principals. *The Learning System, 1*(6), 2. Oxford, OH: The National Staff Development Council.

Mizell, H. (2007). Students learn when adults learn. *The Learning System, 3*(3), 2. Oxford, OH: The National Staff Development Council.

Moller, G., & Pankake, A. (2006). *Lead with me: A principal's guide to teacher leadership.* Larchmont, NY: Eye On Education.

Murphy, J. (2002). Reculturing the profession of educational leadership: New blueprints. *Educational Administration Quarterly, 38*, 176–191.

Murphy, J. (2006). Some thoughts on rethinking the pre-service education of school leaders. *Journal of Research on Leadership Education, 1*(1).

Olson, L. (2007, September 1). Getting serious about preparation. *Leading for learning.* The Wallace Foundation. S-3-S8.

Osterman, K. F., & Kottkamp, R. B. (2004). *Reflective practice for educators: Improving schooling through professional development* (2nd ed.). Thousand Oaks, CA: Corwin.

Pallas, A. M. (2001). Preparing education doctoral students for epistemological diversity. *Educational Researcher, 30*(5), 6–11.

Peterson, K. (2002). The professional development of principals: Innovations and opportunities. *Educational Administration Quarterly, 38*(2), 213–232.

Richardson, J. (2008). A fresh perspective: Network gives superintendents a safe space to learn and grow. *The Learning System, 3*(6), 1, 6–7.

Silverberg, R. P., & Kottkamp, R. B. (2006). Language matters. *Journal of Research in Leadership Education, 1*(1), 1–5. Retrieved May 19, 2009, from http://www.ucea.org/storage/JRLE/pdf/vol1_issue1_2006/Kottkamp.pdf

Stoll, L., & Seashore-Louis, K. (2007). *Professional learning communities.* Columbus, OH: Open University Press.

Wagner, T. (2007). Leading for change: Five "habits of mind" that count. *Education Week, 26*(45), 29, 32.

Wagner, T., Kegan, R., Lahey, L., Lemons, R. W., Garnier, J., Helsing, D., . . . & Rasmussen, H. T. (2006). *Change leadership: A practical guide to transforming our schools.* San Francisco, CA: Jossey-Bass/Wiley.

Young, M., Mountford, M., & Skrla, L. (2006). Infusing gender and diversity issues into educational leadership programs: Transformational learning and resistance. *Journal of Educational Administration, 44*(3), 277–280.

Chapter 2

Ackerman, R., & MacKenzie, S. (Eds.). (2007). *Uncovering teacher leadership: Voices from the field*. Thousand Oaks, CA: Corwin.

Ackerman, R. H., & Maslin-Ostrowski, P. (2002). *The wounded leader: How real leadership emerges in times of crisis*. San Francisco, CA: Jossey-Bass.

Barth, R. S. (1990). *Improving schools from within: Teachers, parents, and principals can make the difference*. San Francisco, CA: Jossey-Bass.

Barth, R. S. (2006). Improving relationships within the schoolhouse. *Educational Leadership, 63*(6), 8–13.

Brookfield, S. D. (1987). *Developing critical thinkers: Challenging adults to explore alternative ways of thinking and acting*. San Francisco, CA: Jossey-Bass.

Brookfield, S. D. (1995). *Becoming a critically reflective teacher*. San Francisco, CA: Jossey-Bass.

Byrne-Jiménez, M., & Orr, M. (2007). *Developing effective principals through collaborative inquiry*. New York, NY: Teachers College Press.

City, E. A., Elmore, R. F., Fiarman, S. E., & Teitel, L. (2009). *Instructional rounds in education: A network approach to improving teaching and learning*. Cambridge, MA: Harvard Education Press.

Cochran-Smith, M., & Lytle, S. L. (2006). Troubling images of teaching in NCLB. *Harvard Educational Review, 76*(4), 668–697.

Daloz, L. A. (1983). Mentors: Teachers who make a difference. *Change, 15*(6), 24–27.

Daloz, L. A. (1986). *Effective teaching and mentoring: Realizing the transformational power of adult learning experiences*. San Francisco, CA: Jossey-Bass.

Daresh, J. C. (2003). *Teachers mentoring teachers: A practical approach to helping new and experienced staff*. Thousand Oaks, CA: Corwin.

DeLong, T., Gabarro, J., & Lees, R. (2008). Why mentoring matters in a hyper-competitive world. *Harvard Business Review, 86*(1), 115–121.

Donaldson, G. A. (2000). *Cultivating leadership in schools: Connecting people, purpose, and practice*. New York, NY: Teachers College Press.

Donaldson, G. A. (2006). *Cultivating leadership in schools: Connecting people, purpose, and practice* (2nd ed.). New York, NY: Teachers College Press.

Donaldson, G. A. (2008). *How leaders learn: Cultivating capacities for school improvement*. New York, NY: Teachers College Press.

Dozier, T. K. (2007). Turning good teachers into great leaders. *Educational Leadership, 65*(1), 54–58.

Drago-Severson, E. (1996). *Head-of-school as principal adult developer: An account of one leader's efforts to support transformational learning among the adults in her school* (Unpublished doctoral dissertation). Harvard Graduate School of Education, Cambridge, MA.

Drago-Severson, E. (2004a). *Becoming adult learners: Principles and practices for effective development*. New York, NY: Teachers College Press.

Drago-Severson, E. (2004b). *Helping teachers learn: Principal leadership for adult growth and development*. Thousand Oaks, CA: Corwin.

Drago-Severson, E. (2009). *Leading adult learning: Supporting adult development in our schools*. Thousand Oaks, CA: Corwin and The National Staff Development Council.

Drago-Severson, E. (2012). *Helping educators grow: Strategies and practices for supporting leadership development.* Cambridge, MA: Harvard Education Press.

Drago-Severson, E., Roloff Welch, J., & Jones, A. (2007). Learning and growing from convening: A context for reflecting on teacher practice. In R. Ackerman and S. McKenzie (Eds.), *Uncovering Teacher Leadership: Essays and voices from the field* (pp. 333–350). Thousand Oaks, CA: Corwin.

DuFour, R. (2007). Professional learning communities: A bandwagon, an idea worth considering, or our best hope for high levels of learning? *Middle School Journal, 39*(1), 4–8.

Elmore, R. F. (2000). *Building a new structure for school leadership.* Washington, DC: Albert Shanker Institute.

Elmore, R. F., & Burney, D. (1999). Investing in teacher learning: Staff development and instructional improvement. In L. Darling-Hammond & G. Sykes (Eds.), *Teaching as the learning profession: Handbook of policy and practice* (pp. 263–291). San Francisco, CA: Jossey-Bass.

Farrington, J. (2007). What leadership was and what it has become. Retrieved May 19, 2009, from http://ezinearticles.com/?What-Leadership-Was-And-What-It-Has-Become&id=480082

Fullan, M. (2005). *Leadership and sustainability: Systems thinkers in action.* Thousand Oaks, CA: Corwin.

Fullan, M. (2008). School leadership's unfinished agenda: Integrating individual and organizational development. *Education Week, 27*(32), 28, 36.

Fullan, M. (2009). *Motion leadership: The skinny on becoming change savvy.* Thousand Oaks, CA: Corwin.

Guskey, T. R. (1999). *New perspectives on evaluating professional development.* Paper presented at the annual meeting of the American Educational Research Association, Montreal, Canada.

Guskey, T. R. (2000). *Evaluating professional development* (2nd ed.). Thousand Oaks, CA: Corwin.

Hall, P. (2008). Building bridges: Strengthening the principal induction process through intentional mentoring. *Phi Delta Kappan, 89*(6), 449–452.

Hashweh, M. (2004). Case writing as border-crossing: Describing, explaining and promoting teacher change. *Teachers and Teaching: Theory and Practice, 10*(3), 229–246.

Heifetz, R. (1994). *Leadership without easy answers.* Cambridge, MA: Harvard University Press.

Higgins, M. C., Chandler, D. E., & Kram, K. E. (2007). Relational engagement and developmental networks. In B. Ragins & K. Kram (Eds.), *The handbook of mentoring at work: Research, theory, and practice* (pp. 349–372). Thousand Oaks, CA: Sage.

Holloway, J. H. (2004). Mentoring new leaders. *Educational Leadership, 61*(7), 87–88.

Hord, S. M., & Sommers, W. A. (2008). *Leading professional learning communities: Voices from research and practice.* Thousand Oaks, CA: Corwin, National Staff Development, and National Association of Secondary Schools.

Jonson, K. F. (2008). *Being an effective mentor: How to help beginning teachers succeed* (2nd ed.). Thousand Oaks, CA: Corwin.

Johnson, S. M., Birkeland, S., Kardos, S. M., Kauffman, D., Liu, E., & Peske, H. G. (2004). *Finders and keepers: Helping new teachers survive and thrive in our schools.* San Francisco, CA: Jossey-Bass.

Kegan, R. (1982). *The evolving self: Problems and process in human development.* Cambridge, MA: Harvard University.

Kegan, R. (1994). *In over our heads: The mental demands of modern life.* Cambridge, MA: Harvard University.

Kegan, R. (2000). What "form" transforms? A constructive-developmental approach to transformative learning. In J. Mezirow & Associates (Eds.), *Learning as transformation: Critical perspectives on a theory in progress* (pp. 35–70). San Francisco, CA: Jossey-Bass.

Kegan, R., & Lahey, L. L. (2009). *Immunity to change: How to overcome it and unlock the potential in yourself and your organization.* Boston, MA: Harvard Business School Press.

Killion, J. (2000, December/January). Exemplary schools model quality staff development. *Results*, p. 3.

Leithwood, K., & Riehl, C. (2003). *What we know about successful school leadership.* Philadelphia, PA: Temple University Laboratory for Student Success.

McAdamis, S. (2007). A view of the future: Teamwork is daily work. *Journal of Staff Development, 28*(3), 43, 45–47.

McGowan, E. M., Stone, E. M., & Kegan, R. (2007). A constructive-developmental approach to mentoring relationships. In B. R. Ragins and K. E. Kram (Eds.), *The mentoring handbook of mentoring at work: Theory, research and practice* (pp. 401–425). Thousand Oaks, CA: Sage.

Mezirow, J. (2000). Learning to think like an adult: Core concepts of transformation theory. In J. Mezirow & Associates (Eds.), *Learning as transformation: Critical perspectives on a theory in progress* (pp. 3–33). San Francisco, CA: Jossey-Bass.

Moir, E., & Bloom, G. (2003). Fostering leadership through mentoring. *Educational Leadership, 60*(8), 58–60.

National Staff Development Council. (2008). *Coaching school results, Inc.* Retrieved May 19, 2009, from http://www.coachingschoolresults.com

Osterman, K. F., & Kottkamp, R. B. (1993). *Reflective practice for educators: Improving schooling through professional development.* Thousand Oaks, CA: Corwin.

Osterman, K. F., & Kottkamp, R. B. (2004). *Reflective practice for educators: Improving schooling through professional development* (2nd ed.). Thousand Oaks, CA: Corwin.

Saphier, J., Freedman, S., & Aschheim, B. (2001). *Beyond mentoring: How to nurture, support, and retain new teachers.* Newton, MA: Teachers21.

Schön, D. (1983). *The reflective practitioner: How professionals think in action.* New York, NY: Basic Books.

Simons, K. A., & Friedman, R. H. (2008). Seven systemwide solutions. *Educational Leadership, 65*(7), 64–68

Slater, L. (2008). Pathways to building leadership capacity. *Educational Management & Administration Leadership, 36*(1), 55–69.

Teitel, L. (2006). *Supporting school system leaders: The state of effective training programs for school superintendents.* New York, NY: The Wallace Foundation.

Wagner, T., Kegan, R., Lahey, L., Lemons, R. W., Garnier, J., Helsing, D., . . . & Rasmussen, H. T. (2006). *Change leadership: A practical guide to transforming our schools.* San Francisco, CA: Jossey-Bass.

York-Barr, J., Sommers, W. A., Ghere, G. S., & Montie, J. (2006). *Reflective practice to improve schools* (2nd ed.). Thousand Oaks, CA: Corwin.

Yost, D. S., Vogel, R., & Liang, L. L. (2009). Embedded teacher leadership: Support for a site-based model of professional development. *International Journal of Leadership in Education, 12,* 409–433.

Chapter 3

Basseches, M. (1984). *Dialectical thinking and adult development.* Norwood, NJ: Ablex.

Baxter-Magolda, M. B. (1992). *Knowing and reasoning in college: Gender-related patterns in students' intellectual development.* San Francisco, CA: Jossey-Bass.

Baxter-Magolda, M. B. (2009). *Authoring your life: Developing an internal voice to navigate life's challenges.* Sterling, VA: Stylus.

Belenky, M., Clinchy, B., Goldberger, N., & Tarule, J. (1986). *Women's ways of knowing.* New York, NY: Basic Books.

Broderick, M. A. (1996). *A certain doubleness: Reflexive thought and mindful experience as tools for transformative learning in the stress reduction clinic* (Unpublished doctoral dissertation). Harvard University Graduate School of Education, Cambridge, MA.

Dixon, J. W. (1986). *The relation of social perspective stages to Kegan's stages of ego development* (Unpublished doctoral dissertation). University of Toledo, OH.

Drago-Severson, E. (2004a). *Becoming adult learners: Principles and practices for effective development.* New York, NY: Teachers College Press.

Drago-Severson, E. (2004b). *Helping teachers learn: Principal leadership for adult growth and development.* Thousand Oaks, CA: Corwin.

Drago-Severson, E. (2009). *Leading adult learning: Supporting adult development in our schools.* Thousand Oaks, CA: Corwin and The National Staff Development Council.

Drago-Severson, E. (2012). *Helping educators grow: Strategies and practices for supporting leadership development.* Cambridge, MA: Harvard Education Press.

Drago-Severson, E., & Blum-DeStefano, J. (2011, May). Leading and learning together (part 2): Promising practices for principals supporting adult development. *Instructional Leader, 24*(3), 9–12. Texas Elementary Principals and Supervisors Association. Austin, Texas.

Goodman, R. (1983). *A developmental and systems analysis of marital and family communication in clinic and non-clinic families* (Unpublished doctoral dissertation). Harvard University, Cambridge, MA.

Greenwald, G. M. (1991). *Environmental attitudes: A structural developmental model* (Unpublished doctoral dissertation). University of Massachusetts, Amherst.

Heifetz, R. (1994). *Leadership without easy answers.* Cambridge, MA: Harvard University Press.

Kegan, R. (1982). *The evolving self: Problems and process in human development.* Cambridge, MA: Harvard University.

Kegan, R. (1994). *In over our heads: The mental demands of modern life.* Cambridge, MA: Harvard University.

Kegan, R. (2000). What "form" transforms? A constructive-developmental approach to transformative learning. In J. Mezirow & Associates (Eds.), *Learning as transformation: Critical perspectives on a theory in progress* (pp. 35–70). San Francisco, CA: Jossey-Bass.

Kegan, R., Broderick, M., Helsing, D., Popp, N., & Portnow, K. (2001). *Toward a "new pluralism" in the ABE/ESOL classroom: Teaching to multiple "cultures of mind"* (NCSALL Monograph #19). Boston, MA: World Education.

Kegan, R., & Lahey, L. L. (2001). *How the way we talk can change the way we work.* San Francisco, CA: Jossey-Bass.

Kegan, R., & Lahey, L. L. (2009). *Immunity to change: How to overcome it and unlock the potential in yourself and your organization.* Boston, MA: Harvard Business School Press.

Knefelkamp, L. L., & David-Lang, T. (2000, Spring/Summer). Encountering diversity on campus and in the classroom: Advancing intellectual and ethical development. *Diversity Digest*, p. 10.

Kohlberg, L. (1969). Stage and sequence: The cognitive-developmental approach to socialization. In R. A. Goslin (Ed.), *Handbook of socialization theory and research* (pp. 347–480). Chicago, IL: Rand-McNally.

Kohlberg, L. (1984). *The psychology of moral development.* San Francisco, CA: Harper & Row.

Lahey, L. (1986). *Males' and females' construction of conflicts in work and love.* (Unpublished doctoral dissertation). Harvard Graduate School of Education, Cambridge, MA.

Lahey, L., Souvaine, E., Kegan, R., Goodman, R., & Felix, S. (1988). *A guide to the subject-object interview: Its administration and interpretation* (Unpublished manuscript).

Levine, S. L. (1989). *Promoting adult development in schools: The promise of professional development.* Boston, MA: Allyn & Bacon.

McCallum, D. C. (2008). *Exploring the implications of a hidden diversity in group relations conference learning: A developmental perspective* (Unpublished doctoral dissertation). Teachers College, Columbia University, NY.

Nicolaides, A. I. (2008). *Learning their way through ambiguity: Explorations of how nine developmentally mature adults make sense of ambiguity* (Unpublished doctoral dissertation). Teachers College, Columbia University, NY.

Perry, W. G., Jr. (1970). *Forms of intellectual and ethical development in the college years.* New York, NY: Holt, Rinehart & Winston.

Piaget, J. (1952). *The origins of intelligence in children.* New York, NY: International Universities Press.

Piaget, J. (1963). *The origins of intelligence.* New York, NY: Norton.

Piaget, J. (1965). *The moral judgment of the child* (M. Gabain, Trans.). New York, NY: Free Press. (Original work published 1932)

Wagner, T., Kegan, R., Lahey, L., Lemons, R. W., Garnier, J., Helsing, D., . . . & Rasmussen, H. T. (2006). *Change leadership: A practical guide to transforming our schools.* San Francisco, CA: Jossey-Bass.

Winnicott, D. (1965). *The maturation processes and the facilitating environment.* New York, NY: International Universities Press.

Chapter 4

Argyris, C. (1982). *Reasoning, learning, and action: Individual and organizational.* San Francisco, CA: Jossey-Bass.

Argyris, C., & Schön, D. A. (1974). *Theory in practice: Increasing professional effectiveness.* San Francisco, CA: Jossey-Bass.

Drago-Severson, E. (2004). *Helping teachers learn: Principal leadership for adult growth and development.* Thousand Oaks, CA: Corwin.

Drago-Severson, E. (2009). *Leading adult learning: Supporting adult development in our schools.* Thousand Oaks, CA: Corwin and The National Staff Development Council.

Drago-Severson, E. (2012). *Helping educators grow: Strategies and practices for supporting leadership development.* Cambridge, MA: Harvard Education Press.

Drago-Severson, E., Asghar, A., Blum-DeStefano, J., & Roloff Welch, J. (2011). Conceptual changes in aspiring school leaders: Lessons from a university classroom. *Journal of Research on Leadership Education, 6*(4), 83–132.

Gardner, H. (2006). *Changing minds: The art and science of changing our own and other people's minds.* Boston, MA: Harvard Business School Press.

Guskey, T. R. (1999). *Evaluating professional development.* Thousand Oaks, CA: Corwin.

Heifetz, R. (1994). *Leadership without easy answers.* Cambridge, MA: Harvard University Press.

Kaser, L., & Halbert, J. (2009). *Leadership mindsets: Innovation and learning in the transformation of schools.* New York, NY: Routledge.

Kegan, R. (1982). *The evolving self: Problems and process in human development.* Cambridge, MA: Harvard University Press.

Kegan, R. (1994). *In over our heads: The mental demands of modern life.* Cambridge, MA: Harvard University Press.

Kegan, R. (2000). What "form" transforms? A constructive-developmental approach to transformative learning. In J. Mezirow & Associates (Eds.), *Learning as transformation: Critical perspectives on a theory in progress* (pp. 35–70). San Francisco, CA: Jossey-Bass.

Kegan, R., & Lahey, L. L. (2001). *How the way we talk can change the way we work.* San Francisco, CA: Jossey-Bass.

Moller, G., & Pankake, A. (2006). *Lead with me: A principal's guide to teacher leadership.* Larchmont, NY: Eye On Education.

Senge, P. M., Kleiner, A., Roberts, C., Ross, R. B., & Smith, B. J. (1994). *The fifth discipline fieldbook: Strategies and tools for building a learning organization.* New York, NY: Doubleday.

Wagner, T. (2007). Leading for change: Five "habits of mind" that count. *Education Week, 26*(45), 29, 32.

Wagner, T., Kegan, R., Lahey, L., Lemons, R. W., Garnier, J., Helsing, D., . . . & Rasmussen, H. T. (2006). *Change leadership: A practical guide to transforming our schools.* San Francisco, CA: Jossey-Bass.

Chapter 5

Argyris, C. (1990). *Overcoming organizational defenses: Facilitating organizational learning.* Boston, MA: Allyn & Bacon.

Browne-Ferrigno, T. (2007). Developing school leaders: Practitioner growth
    during an advanced leadership development program for principals
    and administrator-trained teachers. *Journal of Research on Leadership
    Education*, 2(3). Retrieved July 8, 2007, from http://www.ucea.org/
    JRLE/vol2_issue3_2007/BrowneFerrignoArticle.pdf
Byrne-Jiménez, M., & Orr, M. (2007). *Developing effective principals through
    collaborative inquiry.* New York, NY: Teachers College Press.
Donaldson, G. A. (2008). *How leaders learn: Cultivating capacities for school
    improvement.* New York, NY: Teachers College Press.
Drago-Severson, E. (2004a). *Becoming adult learners: Principles and practices for
    effective development.* New York, NY: Teachers College Press.
Drago-Severson, E. (2004b). *Helping teachers learn: Principal leadership for adult
    growth and development.* Thousand Oaks, CA: Corwin.
Drago-Severson, E. (2009). *Leading adult learning: Supporting adult development
    in our schools.* Thousand Oaks, CA: Corwin and The National Staff
    Development Council.
Drago-Severson, E. (2012). *Helping educators grow: Strategies and practices for sup-
    porting leadership development.* Cambridge, MA: Harvard Education Press.
Kegan, R. (1982). *The evolving self: Problems and process in human development.*
    Cambridge, MA: Harvard University.
Kegan, R. (2000). What "form" transforms? A constructive-developmental
    approach to transformative learning. In J. Mezirow & Associates
    (Eds.), *Learning as transformation: Critical perspectives on a theory in
    progress* (pp. 35–70). San Francisco, CA: Jossey-Bass.
Senge, P. M., Kleiner, A., Roberts, C., Ross, R. B., & Smith, B. J. (1994). *The fifth
    discipline fieldbook: Strategies and tools for building a learning organization.*
    New York, NY: Doubleday.
Stoll, L., & Seashore-Louis, K. (2007). *Professional learning communities.*
    Columbus, OH: Open University Press.

Chapter 6

Drago-Severson, E. (2004a). *Becoming adult learners: Principles and practices for
    effective development.* New York, NY: Teachers College Press.
Drago-Severson, E. (2004b). *Helping teachers learn: Principal leadership for adult
    growth and development.* Thousand Oaks, CA: Corwin.
Drago-Severson, E. (2009). *Leading adult learning: Supporting adult development
    in our schools.* Thousand Oaks, CA: Corwin and The National Staff
    Development Council.
Drago-Severson, E. (2012). *Helping educators grow: Strategies and practices for sup-
    porting leadership development.* Cambridge, MA: Harvard Education Press.

Chapter 7

Ackerman, R. H., & Maslin-Ostrowski, P. (2004). The wounded leader and
    emotional learning in the schoolhouse. *School Leadership & Management*,
    24(3), 309–326.

Barth, R. (1980). *Improving schools from within: Teachers, parents, and principals can make the difference.* San Francisco, CA: Jossey-Bass.

Barth, R. S. (1990). *Improving schools from within.* San Francisco, CA: Jossey-Bass.

Bennett, C. (1991). The teacher as decision maker program: An alternative for career-change preservice teachers. *Journal of Teacher Education, 42*(2), 119–130.

Donaldson, G. A. (2008). *How leaders learn: Cultivating capacities for school improvement.* New York, NY: Teachers College Press.

Drago-Severson, E. (2004a). *Becoming adult learners: Principles and practices for effective development.* New York, NY: Teachers College Press.

Drago-Severson, E. (2004b). *Helping teachers learn: Principal leadership for adult growth and development.* Thousand Oaks, CA: Corwin.

Drago-Severson, E. (2009). *Leading adult learning: Supporting adult development in our schools.* Thousand Oaks, CA: Corwin and The National Staff Development Council.

Drago-Severson, E. (2012). *Helping educators grow: Strategies and practices for supporting leadership development.* Cambridge, MA: Harvard Education Press.

Dunn, R. S., & Dunn, K. J. (1979). Learning styles/teaching styles: Should they . . . can they . . . be matched? *Educational Leadership, 36*(4), 38–44.

Erikson, E. H. (1968). *Identity: Youth and crisis.* New York, NY: Norton & Co.

Erikson, E. H. (1980). *Identity and the life cycle.* New York, NY: W. W. Norton & Co.

Evans, R. (1996). *The human side of school change: Reform, resistance, and the real-life problems of innovation.* San Francisco, CA: Jossey-Bass.

Guskey, T. R. (2000). *Evaluating professional development* (2nd ed.). Thousand Oaks, CA: Corwin.

Kegan, R. (1994). *In over our heads: The mental demands of modern life.* Cambridge, MA: Harvard University Press.

Kegan, R. (2000). What "form" transforms? A constructive-developmental approach to transformative learning. In J. Mezirow & Associates (Eds.), *Learning as transformation: Critical perspectives on a theory in progress* (pp. 35–70). San Francisco, CA: Jossey-Bass.

Mezirow, J. (2000). Learning to think like an adult: Core concepts of transformation theory. In J. Mezirow & Associates (Eds.), *Learning as transformation: Critical perspectives on a theory in progress* (pp. 3–33). San Francisco, CA: Jossey-Bass.

Tyack, D., & Cuban, L. (1995). *Tinkering toward utopia: A century of public school reform.* Cambridge, MA: Harvard University Press.

Weinstein, C. S. (1989). Teacher education students' preconceptions of teaching. *Journal of Teacher Education, 40*(2), 53–60.

Chapter 8

Daloz, L. A. (1986). *Effective teaching and mentoring: Realizing the transformational power of adult learning experiences.* San Francisco, CA: Jossey-Bass.

Donaldson, G. A. (2008). *How leaders learn: Cultivating capacities for school improvement.* New York, NY: Teachers College Press.

Drago-Severson, E. (2004). *Helping teachers learn: Principal leadership for adult growth and development.* Thousand Oaks, CA: Corwin.

Drago-Severson, E. (2009). *Leading adult learning: Supporting adult development in our schools.* Thousand Oaks, CA: Corwin and The National Staff Development Council.

Drago-Severson, E. (2012). *Helping educators grow: Strategies and practices for supporting leadership development.* Cambridge, MA: Harvard Education Press.

Guskey, T. R. (1999, April). *New perspectives on evaluating professional development.* Paper presented at the annual meeting of the American Educational Research Association, Montreal, Canada. ERIC Document Reproduction Service No. ED430024.

Guskey, T. R. (2000). *Evaluating professional development* (2nd ed.). Thousand Oaks, CA: Corwin.

Heifetz, R. (1994). *Leadership without easy answers.* Cambridge, MA: Harvard University Press.

Kegan, R. (1982). *The evolving self: Problems and process in human development.* Cambridge, MA: Harvard University.

Kegan, R. (1994). *In over our heads: The mental demands of modern life.* Cambridge, MA: Harvard University.

Kegan, R. (2000). What "form" transforms? A constructive-developmental approach to transformative learning. In J. Mezirow & Associates (Eds.), *Learning as transformation: Critical perspectives on a theory in progress* (pp. 35–70). San Francisco, CA: Jossey-Bass.

Kegan, R., & Lahey, L. L. (2009). *Immunity to change: How to overcome it and unlock the potential in yourself and your organization.* Boston, MA: Harvard Business School Press.

Lugg, C. A., & Shoho, A. R. (2006). Dare public school administrators build a new social order? Social justice and the possibly perilous politics of educational leadership. *Journal of Educational Administration, 44*(3), 208–223.

Murnane, R., & Willett, J. (2010). *Methods matter: Improving causal inference in educational and social science research.* New York, NY: Oxford University Press.

Wagner, T., Kegan, R., Lahey, L., Lemons, R. W., Garnier, J., Helsing, D., . . . & Rasmussen, H. T. (2006). *Change leadership: A practical guide to transforming our schools.* San Francisco, CA: Jossey-Bass.

Resource A. Research Appendix

Coffey, A., & Atkinson, P. (1996). *Making sense of qualitative data: Complementary research strategies.* Thousand Oaks, CA: Sage.

Drago-Severson, E. (2004). *Helping teachers learn: Principal leadership for adult growth and development.* Thousand Oaks, CA: Corwin.

Drago-Severson, E. (2009). *Leading adult learning: Supporting adult development in our schools.* Thousand Oaks, CA: Corwin and The National Staff Development Council.

Drago-Severson, E. (2012). *Helping educators grow: Strategies and practices for leadership development.* Cambridge, MA: Harvard Education Press.

Geertz, C. (1974). From the native's point of view: On the nature of anthropological understanding. *Bulletin of the American Academy of Arts and Sciences, 28,* 221–237.

Maxwell, J. (2005). *Qualitative research design: An interactive approach* (2nd ed.). London, UK: Sage.

Maxwell, J. A., & Miller, B. (1998). *Categorization and contextualization as components of qualitative data analysis* (Unpublished manuscript).

Miles, M. B., & Huberman, A. M. (1994). *An expanded sourcebook: Qualitative data analysis* (2nd ed.). Thousand Oaks, CA: Sage.

Seidman, I. (1998). *Interviewing as qualitative research.* New York, NY: Teachers College Press.

Seidman, I. (2006). *Interviewing as qualitative research: A guide for researchers in education and the social sciences* (3rd ed.). New York, NY: Teachers College Press.

Strauss, A., & Corbin, J. (1998). *Basics of qualitative research: Techniques and procedures for developing grounded theory.* Thousand Oaks, CA: Sage.

Resource B. Leadership for Transformational Learning (LTL) Course Topics

Drago-Severson, E. (2003). *Course syllabus.* Cambridge, MA: Harvard Graduate School of Education.

Drago-Severson, E. (2004). *Course syllabus.* Cambridge, MA: Harvard Graduate School of Education.

Drago-Severson, E. (2005). *Course syllabus.* Cambridge, MA: Harvard Graduate School of Education.

Drago-Severson, E., Asghar, A., Blum-DeStefano, J., & Roloff Welch, J. (2011). Conceptual changes in aspiring school leaders: Lessons from a university classroom. *Journal of Research on Leadership Education, 6*(4), 83–132.

Resource C. Leadership for Transformational Learning (LTL) Citations for Course Readings

Drago-Severson, E. (2003). *Course syllabus.* Cambridge, MA: Harvard Graduate School of Education.

Drago-Severson, E. (2004). *Course syllabus.* Cambridge, MA: Harvard Graduate School of Education.

Drago-Severson, E. (2005). *Course syllabus.* Cambridge, MA: Harvard Graduate School of Education.

Drago-Severson, E., Asghar, A., Blum-DeStefano, J., & Roloff Welch, J. (2011). Conceptual changes in aspiring school leaders: Lessons from a university classroom. *Journal of Research on Leadership Education, 6*(4), 83–132.

Glossary

Argyris, C. (1990). *Overcoming organizational defenses: Facilitating organizational learning*. Boston, MA: Allyn & Bacon.

Drago-Severson, E. (2004a). *Becoming adult learners: Principles and practices for effective development*. New York, NY: Teachers College Press.

Drago-Severson, E. (2004b). *Helping teachers learn: Principal leadership for adult growth and development*. Thousand Oaks, CA: Corwin.

Drago-Severson, E. (2009). *Leading adult learning: Supporting adult development in our schools*. Thousand Oaks, CA: Corwin and The National Staff Development Council.

Drago-Severson, E. (2012). *Helping educators grow: Strategies and practices for supporting leadership development*. Cambridge, MA: Harvard Education Press.

Heifetz, R. A. (1994). *Leadership without easy answers*. Cambridge, MA: Harvard University Press.

Kegan, R. (1982). *The evolving self: Problems and process in human development*. Cambridge, MA: Harvard University Press.

Kegan, R. (1994). *In over our heads: The mental demands of modern life*. Cambridge, MA: Harvard University Press.

Kegan, R. (2000). What "form" transforms? A constructive-developmental approach to transformative learning. In J. Mezirow & Associates (Eds.), *Learning as transformation: Critical perspectives on a theory in progress* (pp. 35–70). San Francisco, CA: Jossey-Bass.

Index

CORWIN

A SAGE Company

The Corwin logo—a raven striding across an open book—represents the union of courage and learning. Corwin is committed to improving education for all learners by publishing books and other professional development resources for those serving the field of PreK–12 education. By providing practical, hands-on materials, Corwin continues to carry out the promise of its motto: **"Helping Educators Do Their Work Better."**